D.L. Moody:
Turning Points toward Text-Driven Preaching

Mark H. Ballard

Volume 1

D.L. MOODY:
Turning Points toward Text-Driven Preaching

MARK H. BALLARD

ACADEMIC THEOLOGICAL STUDIES

D.L. Moody
Turning Points towards Text-Driven Preaching
Copyright © 2022 by Mark H. Ballard

Published by Northeastern Baptist Press
      Post Office Box 4600
      Bennington, VT 05201

All rights reserved. No part of this book may be reproduced in any form without prior permission from Northeastern Baptist Press, except as provided for by USA copyright law.

Scripture taken from the New King James Version®.
Copyright © 1982 by Thomas Nelson. Used by permission.
All rights reserved.

Cover design by Leason Stiles & Jared August

Hardcover ISBN: 978-1-953331-14-4

This monograph is dedicated to Cindy,
my faithful wife and partner in all adventures,
to Benjamin, the true son of my right hand,
and to my Lord and Savior, Jesus,
without whom I would have nothing
to preach and nothing to write.

Contents

Series Introduction — i

Foreword — iii

Preface — viii

Chapter One
    Introduction — 1

Chapter Two
    Turning Points in the Life of Dwight Lyman Moody — 17

Chapter Three
    Methodology for Classifying D.L. Moody's Sermons — 49

Chapter Four
    An Examination of Moody's Early Sermons — 83

Chapter Five
    An Examination of Moody's Middle Sermons — 111

Chapter Six
    An Examination of Moody's Late Sermons — 117

Chapter Seven
    Conclusion — 249

Bibliography — 265

Series Introduction

Northeastern Baptist Press publishes Christian books that inform, inspire, and encourage people to follow Jesus Christ. Realizing the need for an academic series that is tethered to the Baptist Faith and Message 2000, NEBP has developed the Academic Theological Studies (ATS) series.

The ATS series is comprised of doctoral dissertations as well as academic monographs that are carefully selected based on solid recommendations and rigorous peer review. Each study makes a unique and distinct contribution to the broader field of theology. Although all books in this series are specialized, they are not written for specialists. The ATS series provides the church at large with quality resources that have significant implications for practical issues. Toward this end, we publish within the fields of biblical studies, systematic and historical theology, Christian counseling, education, and pastoral ministry.

We foresee the ATS series growing into a significant collection of academic studies that provide the church with an accessible, yet academically rigorous avenue for theological inquiry.

Jared M. August
Ralph H. Slater
Series Editors

Foreword
By Paige Patterson

About 3 AM this morning I awakened with a stunning thought. Before sleeping, I had been awake late reading my copy of Dr. Mark H. Ballard's superb assessment of the movement toward text-driven preaching in the preaching of Evangelist D.L. Moody. The thought arresting me was that Dr. Ballard is young enough to assess my sermons, which are much too widely available. Then a comforting thought seemed to be ferried to me on angel's wings. The Lord seemed to say, "I know D.L. Moody, and I know Patterson. And Patterson, you are no Moody!"

Safe from such analysis, I now recall that I received from my father as a fifteen-year-old boy a copy of *Bush Aglow*, Richard Ellsworth Day's biography of Moody. With relish I read the book and followed with other biographies about this evangelist. Subsequently I visited the venues of Moody's ministry from England to Northfield to Chicago and thanked God for the way in which He used this humble evangelist. About the only consistent criticisms of Moody were that his preaching majored on stories and illustrations while being limited in Bible exposition. Imagine my delight to discover that Mark Ballard had embarked on strategic research and penned this book, which you now cradle in your hand. *D.L. Moody: Turning Points Toward Text-Driven Sermons* is about the influential preaching of Dwight Moody, perhaps the evangelist who blazed the trail more than anyone else for the coming of Billy Graham. And this is a book by a college president and evangelist who knows more about Moody than

D.L. MOODY:
TURNING POINTS TOWARD TEXT-DRIVEN PREACHING

most alive today. Mark Ballard serves today in Bennington, Vermont, at Northeastern Baptist College, not far from Northfield, Massachusetts, where Moody lovingly and devotedly labored.

Dwight Moody's life was punctuated by dramatic moments, which God in turn used to mold the evangelist not only in his life events but also in his methodology for preaching. The meeting of the young evangelist with Henry Moorhouse was a pivotal development in a long-lasting development of Moody into what today would be termed a text-driven preacher. Ballard chronicles all of these life-changing events and tied them to a slow revolution that transpired in the preaching of this matchless evangelist.

The approach that Ballard has chosen is greatly aided by the relative thesaurus of Moody sermons preserved from the crusades and Bible conferences. Twenty-two early sermons are selected from 1867 to 1869. Twenty sermons are chosen from the Boston campaign of 1875 to 1892. Finally, Ballard examines the Northfield sermons, from which he has selected twenty-eight of the messages of the mature Moody. With an eye to the impact made on the evangelist from years of studying the Bible, the author demonstrates the increase of exposition of Scripture in Moody's preaching.

Why should an average congregant care about the technicalities of sermon preparation? The answer to this query is that expositional or text-driven preaching never develops from common sources. Preachers do not wake up in one morning saying that they have determined to embark on a new trajectory in preaching and thereby embrace a text-driven, text-conscious method. Neither do congregations typically demand that the pastor begin a series of expositions on Romans or some other Bible book.

A pastor or evangelist embraces a text-driven approach for one reason only. A realization has dawned in his mind and heart that God had something to say! And if it be the case that God has actually spoken, then by definition, what God has to say about anything is more crucial to life and to eternity than anything any human could think or utter. The preacher loves his congregation, and he profoundly desires that they grasp what God thinks. Not being sufficiently presumptuous to assume that he knows what God has said, the preacher begins the intricate examination of God's Word with the intent of assisting his listeners in fathoming the Word of the Lord and flourishing in the keeping of that which God has vouchsafed to His people.

More determinative than the preacher's love for his assembled people is his love for God. The passing of years never dimmed Moody's memory or the permanent effects of his conversion under the guiding hand of Edward Kimball. Neither could he deny the miracle of God in London or the sobering realizations that developed from the great Chicago Fire. All of this enhanced Moody's love for and devotion to Christ so that his love for Christ deafened all other interests that might have appealed to some preachers. To secure the focus on Christ as revealed in the Bible increasingly became the consuming fire in Moody's soul.

And that is why Mark Ballard has penned this book. "The love of Christ constrains us," notes 2 Corinthians 5:14. More often than not the preacher whose love for Christ is like the depths of the Marianna Trench will also love his Lord's words. And the exposition of God's Word will become the most critical aspect of the preacher's life and ministry. Ballard has recounted in this monograph the amazing story of what transpired with Dwight Moody. Read this volume and rejoice!

Preface

Chapter One serves as the intrduction to this monograph. The chapter begins with the research question: how did Dwight Lyman Moody's preaching change over the course of his preaching tenure? This monograph argues that the content of Moody's sermons changed over time, moving toward a text-driven model. This chapter also presents the delimitations of the study, the state of the current research, and the importance of the study not only to Moody observers, but also to the fields of Church History, Applied Theology, and Homiletics.

Chapter Two presents the life of D. L. Moody in a fashion that demonstrates a life of continual growth. Fourteen turning points in Moody's life will be described. This will set his life within a context of growth. His constant drive to grow in all areas of life demonstrates a heart and mind ready and willing to grow in his homiletical ability.

Chapter Three describes the methodology used to evaluate Moody's sermons. The chapter surveys various homiletics textbooks. Four sermon categories are chosen and described. These categories include expositional, textual, biographical, and topical sermons. A sermon rubric is presented that includes the descriptions of each category followed by the criteria used to evaluate Moody's sermons.

Chapter Four begins the examination of Moody's sermons. Twenty-two messages are examined from the early years of Moody's public speaking. Though sermons from this era are difficult to find, twenty-two messages and

D.L. MOODY:
TURNING POINTS TOWARD TEXT-DRIVEN PREACHING

sermon summaries were discovered and evaluated. By comparing the messages to the sermon rubric one gains a sense of the biblical content of his preaching during this era. The findings confirm the testimony of Moody's contemporaries.

Chapter Five examines twenty sermons from Moody's most popular years. From 1873–1875 Moody conducted an evangelistic campaign in England. Though he faced opposition in the early days of the campaign, all England was stirred. Newspapers began to publish his sermons. His popularity grew so much that upon his return to the United States the doors opened for him to preach extended campaigns in the large cities of the nation. One of these campaigns was held in Boston, MA. The newspapers ridiculed him in the early days of the campaign, but just as happened in England, they began to publish his sermons. Twenty of these sermons are evaluated in this chapter and they give a strong testimony to the biblical content of Moody's preaching during the middle years of his life.

Chapter Six evaluates sermons from the final years of Moody's life. The present researcher discovered twenty-eight verbatim sermon reports from the Northfield summer conferences of 1894–1899. Each of these are evaluated to present a strong testimony to the biblical content of Moody's preaching in the final years of his life.

Chapter Seven serves as the conclusion to the monograph. The first section of the chapter will summarize the evaluation of sermons throughout the three stages of Moody's preaching ministry. From these findings, the monograph will draw conclusions about the growth of his sermon content. The findings will reveal the level of growth toward text-driven preaching reached by the evangelist. The next section will consider implications of the findings in understanding the life and ministry of Moody. Additionally, implications will be considered that effect the discipline of homiletics. Implications for the general fields of Applied Theology and Church History will also be discussed. The final section offers suggestions for further research into the life and work of D. L. Moody.

A debt of gratitude that can never be repaid goes to Paige Patterson and Daniel Akin, who have encouraged me, challenged me, and mentored me in various ways over the last thirty years.

Charles and Pauline Hogue deserve special recognition. They have loved, encouraged, and prayed for their son-in-law. I must also thank Benjamin Enoch

Preface

Zhijiang Ballard, the true son of my right hand. Your laugh, smile, and hugs encourage me more than you will ever know.

Words cannot express the gratitude felt and owed to Cindy Sue Ballard. My best friend on earth, my partner through so many adventures, and a faithful, loyal, and loving wife. I thank the Lord for you, and I thank you for sticking with me through thick and thin, for all these years of life, ministry, and education. If it were not for your encouragement, this preacher would likely have never even attended college, much less complete all the educational pursuits since those early days. Thank you!

My greatest thank you is reserved for God the Father, Jesus the Son, and the Holy Spirit, without whom there would be no reason to preach, to teach, or to write.

Chapter One

Introduction

The purpose of this monograph is to answer the research question: how did Dwight Lyman Moody's preaching change over the course of his preaching tenure? This monograph will argue that the content of Moody's sermons changed over time, moving toward a text-driven model.[1]

While many who study the life of Moody acknowledge the fact that he and Charles H. Spurgeon were two of the most significant preachers of the nineteenth century, they would also question Moody's preaching ability in the context of the biblical content of his sermons. Moody's son, William, reported that Dr. Cuyler of Brooklyn said, "Of one thing I feel sure, and that is, if another book of the Acts of Christ's faithful Apostles were to be written, probably the largest space in the record of the nineteenth century would be given to the soul-saving work of Charles H. Spurgeon and Dwight L. Moody."[2] Yet Paul Moody acknowledged that homiletic students would be amazed that his dad's sermons moved people so greatly.[3] More recent biographers affirm the findings of the evangelist's sons William and Paul. They acknowledge the reality that

---

1. The term "Text-Driven" is taken from a homiletics book, Daniel L. Akin, David Allen, and Ned L. Matthews, eds., *Text-Driven Preaching* (Nashville: B&H Academic, 2010).

2. William R. Moody, *The Life of Dwight L. Moody* (New York: Fleming H. Revell Company, 1900), 258.

3. Paul D. Moody, *My Father, An Intimate Portrait of Dwight Moody* (Boston: Little, Brown and Company, 1938), 111.

D.L. MOODY:
TURNING POINTS TOWARD TEXT-DRIVEN PREACHING

God used Moody in a great way but question the biblical content of the preacher's sermons.[4]

Despite the assumptions of previous Moody biographers, there has yet to be a thorough examination of the content of Moody's sermons. This monograph argues that examining Moody's sermons clearly shows that Moody grew toward a text-driven model throughout his life. There were at least two major turning points in Moody's life that indicate his desire to move toward preaching text-driven messages.[5] Through an examination of early, middle, and late sermons, this monograph will show his growth toward fulfilling his desire.

Delimitations

When one begins research into the life of Dwight Lyman Moody, he or she quickly recognizes the vast influence of the man. One could examine Moody's influence in publishing, education, leadership, public worship, church growth, evangelistic meetings, among other spheres of Western Christianity. Beyond these areas Moody strongly influenced the Young Men's Christian Association (YMCA), the American Sunday School movement, and the temperance movement. In addition, he exhibited influence in the areas of business and philanthropy. While there is a plethora of information written about Moody, the examination of Moody's preaching remains an area few have considered.

---

4. Wilbur M. Smith, *The Best of D. L. Moody* (Chicago: Moody Press, 1971), 16. Smith indicated, "Sometimes two-thirds of an entire sermon would consist only of a series of illustrations." Lyle W. Dorsett, *A Passion For Souls, The Life of D. L. Moody* (Chicago: Moody Publishers, 1997), 184–185. Citing evidence from A. T. Pierson, Lyle Dorsett suggested that Moody's sermons were full of illustrations that prepared the heart for the Gospel. These few examples illustrate the fact that both early and recent biographers recognize God's work through Moody, while questioning the biblical content of his sermons. This suggests that the evangelist's sermons were likely not text-driven.

5. Chapter Two of the dissertation will provide a biographical sketch of Moody around fourteen distinct turning points in his life. Two of those turning points relate specifically to changes in his preaching. First, he began to include more biblical content, albeit in sermons that were basically topical. Second, he began calling for expositional preaching.

Introduction

In order to study Moody's preaching, one must have a grasp of homiletical theory. Within the field of homiletics there is a variety of theories one could pursue. However, this monograph set its boundaries by considering homiletical theory from within a conservative evangelical perspective. In chapter three the monograph will survey the field of evangelical homiletics and narrow the focus to four sermon types that will guide the examination of Moody's sermons.

State of Research

Numerous biographies have been written about Moody. His son William published the official authorized biography within a year of Moody's death.[6] When Paul Moody published his work about his dad in 1938, he stated, "There are some fifty-six or more biographies and none of them have completely captured him."[7] Since that time additional biographies, academic papers, thesis, and monographs have been written.[8] John Pollock's biography published in 1963 has often been quoted.[9] In 1997 Lyle Dorsett presented a biography that many look to as a more contemporary standard biography.[10] Kevin Belmonte added only a few new insights in his popular biography published in 2014.[11] However, as Lyle Dorsett comments, "Most authors (both popularizers and scholars) have emphasized Moody's evangelistic efforts and knitted in his other enterprises as

---

6. William R. Moody, *The Life of D. L. Moody*.
7. Paul Moody, *Father*, Preface.
8. Research into works about D. L. Moody began with Wilbur Smith's annotated bibliography, where he attempted to detail every mention of Moody in print. The work is thorough and considered a standard starting place for Moody researchers. Wilbur M. Smith, Dwight Lyman Moody: An Annotated Bibliography (Chicago: Moody Press, 1948). The researcher also considered several the bibliographies of various biographies, dissertations, and thesis about Moody, his life, and his work. Furthermore, searches were conducted on ATLA, ProQuest, and World Cat in the attempt to be certain all relevant material was considered.
9. Pollock, *Moody*.
10. Dorsett, *Passion*.
11. Kevin Belmonte, *D. L. Moody: A Life* (Chicago: Moody Publishers, 2014).

of secondary importance."[12] Though most biographers say something about his preaching, few have attempted to understand the content of his sermons.

Stanley Gundry authored a dissertation, later edited and presented in book form, which sought to identify Moody's theology.[13] The material included a consideration of Moody's sermons. However, Gundry's text sought to glean theological themes evident in his preaching. Two other academic works considered various aspects of Moody's preaching. One, by Rollin Quimby, attempted to understand Moody's success by considering the historical realities of the day and the rhetorical methods of his preaching.[14] The other, by James Walling, attempted to compare his evangelistic sermons with those of Billy Graham.[15] In this later work, the author endeavored to classify sermons in various ways. One chapter briefly considered whether the sermons were topical, textual, or expositional. However, the writer completed his work without establishing clear criteria for these categories. Walling was more concerned with demonstrating the evangelistic nature of both Moody and Graham rather than a thorough analysis of the biblical content of the sermons. In addition, Walling's sampling of sermons came from one book of sermons preached by Moody in Chicago.

Wilbur Smith notes that Moody preached relatively few sermons, but preached many of them repeatedly. Smith wrote, "He preached from 160 texts, of which 119 were from the New Testament, and in addition, on about 96 different subjects, making a total of perhaps something over 260 different sermons preached during that quarter of a century, some of them sixty or seventy times, on both sides of the Atlantic, and some of them only once."[16] At first glance

---

12. Dorsett, *Passion*, 23.

13. Gundry, *Love Them In*.

14. Rollin Walker Quimby, "Dwight L. Moody: An Examination of the Historical Conditions and Rhetorical Factors which Contributed to His Effectiveness as a Speaker" (PhD diss., University of Michigan, Ann Arbor, MI: University Press, 1951).

15. James D. Walling, "Study of the Evangelistic Preaching of D. L. Moody and Billy Graham based upon their published sermons" (Master's Thesis, Columbia Bible College, Columbia, SC, 1971).

16. Smith, *The Best of D. L. Moody*, 14–15.

then, it may appear that Walling did well to consider forty sermons. However, Moody's own testimony indicates a desire to change the content of his messages on more than one occasion.[17] Therefore, it is necessary to consider the differences in content from the early years, the middle years, and the later years.

This monograph will extend the field of knowledge of Moody studies by being the first to provide specific criteria for classification of the sermons. Classification terms will be clearly defined and a specific examination rubric will be established.[18] Additionally, this study will consider more than seventy sermons from three different time periods of Moody's ministry. Thus, more than forty-three percent of the sermons Moody preached more than once will be considered.

Importance of the Study

Students at evangelical seminaries are familiar with D. L. Moody and recognize the fact that he was greatly used of God. This recognition is confirmed by the fact that more than one hundred and twenty-one years after his death, books and articles continue to consider the impact of his life.[19] While many scholars have considered Moody's influence, few have studied his preaching. This monograph will show that an understanding of his sermons speaks not only to Moody studies but also to at least three additional areas of evangelical concern. The fields of Church History, Applied Theology, and Homiletics will benefit from understanding the movement toward text-driven preaching in the content of Moody's sermons.

---

17. Paul Moody, *Father*, 184–185.

18. The sermon rubric will be established in chapter three of the dissertation. It will include four sermon categories. The rubric will provide a description of each category followed by three primary criteria that will distinguish each category. For instance, while the expositional and textual categories have similarities, the criteria will show a distinction between the two. See n 34 below for sermon choice details.

19. Kevin Belmonte, *D. L. Moody: A Life* (Chicago: Moody Publishers, 2014). This Moody biography was written in 2014, giving further evidence of his continued influence.

D.L. MOODY: TURNING POINTS TOWARD TEXT-DRIVEN PREACHING

Church History

While Church History readily acknowledges the importance of the life and ministry of D. L. Moody, very little has been written about his preaching. Most biographers describe his preaching in a few sentences or a few pages at most.[20] Likewise, Church History surveys tend to mention Moody, but say little to nothing about his preaching content. One such historian noted Moody "spoke with great simplicity and directness.... his own preaching was based on biblical literalism and a few fundamentals of the faith."[21] While this assessment of Moody's preaching clearly contrasts his general content with the more modernist approach of his day, it fails to give the reader a view of the actual biblical content of his sermons.

Another noted church historian, Mark Noll, recognized the popularity and importance of Moody's life and ministry. He states, "During the second half of the nineteenth century no evangelist was better known than Dwight Lyman Moody."[22] Noll devotes three pages to overview Moody's work and then references him several times throughout his book. Concerning Moody's preaching the author notes, "He spoke calmly and plainly ... he did not expound learned theology ... the many stories Moody used in his sermons illustrated his ability to present Protestant conceptions of the gospel in an emotionally powerful form."[23] Noll clearly recognizes the extent of Moody's evangelistic efforts in the nineteenth century but fails to address the content of Moody's sermons beyond his use of illustrations.

---

20. William R. Moody, *The Life of D. L. Moody*, is the only officially authorized biography. Biographers since his time have relied heavily upon his work. Other examples of this pattern can be seen in John Pollock, *Moody The Biography* (Chicago: Moody Press, 1963), Dorsett, Passion, and Belmonte, A Life.

21. Lefferts A. Loetscher, "Variant Orthodoxies" in *American Christianity: An Historical Interpretation with Representative Documents* (New York: Charles Scribner's Sons, 1963), II:321.

22. Mark A. Noll, *A History of Christianity in the United States and Canada* (Grand Rapids: Eerdmans, 1992), 288.

23. Ibid., 289–290.

This monograph will provide church historians with a fresh analysis of the content of Moody's sermons. This analysis will demonstrate that Moody continually grew toward a text-driven model. While in the early days he may not have concerned himself with specific biblical content, over time he moved toward filling his sermons with biblical quotations in a topical fashion. Toward the end of his life, he began calling for expositional preaching. Even during his last campaign, he spoke with a group of preachers indicating that he believed text-driven preaching was the need of the new century.[24] The sermon evaluation rubric adopted in chapter three will demonstrate a difference in an expositional and a textual sermon. However, it will also consider both categories within the broader concept of a text-driven approach. The research of Chapter Six may show that Moody never reached the point of preaching an expositional sermon. It will show that he preached textual sermons in the latter years of his life. Therefore, over time, Moody moved toward a more text-driven model. Gaining a better understanding of the growth in the biblical content of Moody's sermons will help church historians understand Moody and his growing influence throughout his ministry.

Applied Theology

The field of Applied Theology seeks to relate theological belief to practical application in ministry. Many have assumed that D. L. Moody had no system of theology. Stanley Gundry affirms this general assessment of Moody when he writes, "Evangelists in general have not had a reputation for being theologically acute, and if one is speaking of systematics, Moody certainly fits the stereotype. Neither by training nor interest would Moody have been inclined to formulate a systematic statement of his understanding of theology."[25] However, Gundry goes on to demonstrate that Moody had strongly held theological beliefs and that those beliefs impacted his practice.

Much like the stereotypes of his theology, Moody researchers have assumed that Moody spent a lifetime preaching topical sermons with little to no regard for biblical content or context. This monograph will demonstrate that

---

24. William R. Moody, *The Life of D. L. Moody*, 548.
25 Stanley N. Gundry, *Love Them In* (Chicago: Moody Publishers, 1999), 63.

while Moody's sermons lacked biblical content in the early days, this trend changed over time. Gradually, he grew in his use of biblical content with concern for keeping his text in context. Paul Moody wrote of his dad's preaching,

> I have heard learned men deliberately do violence to a text. If my father ever did this it was in ignorance, and such was his honesty that once aware of it he could never do it again. The truth to him was clear enough in the Scripture without need of reading in what was not there or doing violence to what was.[26]

In demonstration of Moody's desire to preach the Word of God accurately, Paul recorded that at a Bible conference, his father interrupted a speaker's exposition. The purpose of the interruption was to confess before the gathered crowd that because of what he just learned, Moody would have to throw out one of his sermons.[27] The evangelist learned to understand a verse within its context and immediately determined to change his preaching method.

This monograph will speak to the discipline of Applied Theology. The study will demonstrate that D. L. Moody's theology of Scripture began to influence his practice. As he grew in his understanding of theology and hermeneutics, that growth was reflected in his preaching. Thus, his hermeneutics and his theology influenced his preaching.

Homiletics

In 1892 Moody invited Henry Weston to speak at the Northfield Conferences. While Weston expounded his text, Moody remarked, "There goes one of my sermons."[28] Upon inquiring about his meaning, Moody explained to Weston in front of the entire conference gathering that he clearly had been preaching the text inaccurately and now that he understood its meaning he could no longer preach one of his sermons. Later in the exposition Moody was heard to say,

---

26 Paul Moody, *Father*, 185–186.
27 Ibid., 184–185.
28 Ibid.

"There goes another."[29] Exposed to what it meant to keep a verse in its context, Moody determined to stop preaching some of his sermons.

By 1892, Moody was famous throughout the United States and Europe. Already recognized as one of the greatest Christian leaders of his day, he was constantly in demand as a speaker. Yet, when he was confronted with the reality that his preaching had not been in context, he immediately confessed his failure to the entire conference. Over the next seven years, he occasionally called for expositional preaching of the Word of God.[30]

Homileticians today can learn from Moody's example. Despite his reputation and popularity, he sought to grow and he exhibited humility. Moody's humility serves as an excellent example. Second, his willingness to grow as a preacher is commendable. Today's homiletician can also seek to humbly grow in his ability to preach the Bible effectively, no matter how long he has been preaching, or what level of popularity he enjoys.

Research Methodology

The methodology of research for this monograph will include five steps. First, to understand D. L. Moody properly and put his preaching within the context of his life, a short biography will be presented. This study will consider over sixty works that have been published about Moody. An interview with his great-grandson will be included in the research material. Materials available through the newly opened Moody Center in Northfield, MA and the Northfield-Mount Hermon Archives provide additional support for the brief biographical sketch of the evangelist's life. The Moody Bible Institute in Chicago provided additional supporting materials.

The second step in the methodology of this monograph will be to consider various ways of classifying sermons. This monograph will primarily draw on homiletic works written by evangelicals. A general classification system will be developed, terms will be clarified, and a sermon rubric will be established. This

---

29 Paul Moody, *Father*, 184–185.
30 See footnote 11.

D.L. MOODY: TURNING POINTS TOWARD TEXT-DRIVEN PREACHING

rubric will then be utilized to evaluate a sampling of Moody's sermons during different time segments in his life. This process will provide an overall sense of growth in the biblical content of his sermons. Sermons will be selected for evaluation from his early years, from his most popular years, and from the final seven years of his life.

In the third step, this researcher will gather and analyze sermons from Moody's early years. The focus will consist of sermons preached prior to his first European Campaign held from 1873–1875. These sermons are the most difficult to assess. While sermons from this early era can be found, they are not as readily available as those preached after his return to the United States in 1875. However, these sermons provide a strong sense of Moody's preaching prior to becoming convinced of the importance of including biblical content in every message. Twenty-two messages and sermon summaries from this era will be analyzed.[31] Unedited sermons will be utilized as much as possible. Additional comments about this era of his preaching ministry will be noted from various eyewitnesses and biographers.

The fourth step will be to gather and analyze sermons from 1875–1892. A plethora of materials are available from these years. Moody's son Paul noted that, "newspapers of the day ... often reported him verbatim, much to his embarrassment."[32] Paul also noted that if one wanted to get a real sense of his dad's preaching, these verbatim reports "give the clearest impression."[33] Many of these sermons have been collected and published in book form. Some of the books were

---

31. As noted below, sermons following Moody's return from the campaign in England are plenteous. However, sermons prior to this trip are rare. He did not make extensive notes, and the one's he made were destroyed upon his death. The later sermons were preserved because newspapers would take down verbatim records of the sermons and print them the following day. These were later edited and published. Despite the challenges, twenty-two short messages and sermon summaries from the years 1867-1869 were discovered. While these messages do not provide as much material as the verbatim reports of Moody's sermons preached after the British campaign, they do offer some of his exact words and summaries of the messages. Coupled with the testimony of one of Moody's contemporaries, the evidence for the level of biblical content in Moody's early sermons becomes clear.

32. Paul Moody, *Father*, 111.

33. Ibid.

heavily edited, while others were only lightly edited. Many times, actual newspaper reports of entire sermons can be found. The researcher will gather twenty sermons from this era and evaluate them using the established rubric.[34]

The fifth step will be to gather and analyze twenty sermons preached from 1892–1899. While the sermons preached during this period are not as readily available as those from his most popular years, they can be found. These sermons

---

34. Wilbur Smith stands as one of the most recognized authorities on Moody materials, having published an annotated bibliography of all things Moody. Wilbur M. Smith, *An Annotated Bibliography of D. L. Moody* (Chicago: Moody Press, 1948). Smith also published a book of sixteen sermons. In the introduction to this work Smith wrote, "He preached from 160 texts, of which 119 were from the New Testament, and in addition, on about 96 different subjects, making a total of perhaps something over 260 different sermons." Wilbur M. Smith, *The Best of D. L. Moody* (Chicago: Moody Press, 1971), 14–15. Smith went on to indicate that Moody preached many of these repeatedly. When one looks at the printed volumes of Moody's sermons, it becomes obvious that many of the books have reprinted the same sermons repeatedly, sometimes under different titles. Another complication is that many of the books edited the sermons heavily. As noted elsewhere in this monograph, Paul Moody argued that the best way to get to the actual sermon was to read the verbatim newspaper accounts, or the books with little editing. This greatly limits the possible number of sermons to choose from today. The present researcher has gathered and read around 100 sermons that were taken down verbatim and printed in the newspapers, in conference proceedings, and only slightly edited volumes. The majority of these were preached between 1875–1882, which were Moody's most popular years. Twenty-five to thirty of these sermons were preached in his later years, 1894–1899. This researcher evaluated seventy sermons. This means that seventy percent of Moody's extant unedited, and lightly edited sermons have been chosen, read, and evaluated for this monograph. Twenty sermons from Moody's middle years give a strong sample of his sermon content at this stage of his ministry. Chapter Five will demonstrate such a consistency that the addition of more sermons would not change the findings. While there are fewer sermons to choose from in the latter years, twenty sermons were chosen from this era as well. These sermons demonstrate growth in the biblical content of his preaching. Once again, including more sermons would not add to the point of this monograph. Also noted elsewhere in this chapter, the fact remains that sermons prior to Moody's British campaign are very difficult to find. Despite this challenge, twenty-two early sermons and sermon summaries were discovered. In the end, this monograph will evaluate twenty-two early sermons and sermon summaries as well as forty-eight of the extant edited or lightly edited sermons from the middle and late years.

are important to understanding Moody's growth toward text-driven preaching. As noted earlier, in 1892 he confessed to Weston, in front of the entire conference, that he had previously failed to preach texts within their context.[35] After this event he began calling for men to take their Bible and preach from it.[36] He specifically called for expositional preaching on several occasions.[37] By examining sermons from the last seven years of his life, the researcher will discover just how close Moody came to preach expositional sermons in his later years. He certainly grew towards text-driven content, and he clearly began calling for exposition. The analysis of these sermons will reveal just how far he moved toward his own stated goal.

Upon completing the five steps outlined above, the researcher will summarize the findings, draw conclusions, consider implications, and suggest areas where further research is needed in the final chapter of the monograph. This monograph will provide academic insight into the sermon content of D. L. Moody in ways previously unexamined. The researcher believes relevant implications will be clear not only to Moody researchers but also to the disciplines of Church History, Applied Theology, and particularly to the field of Homiletics.

---

35. Paul Moody, *Father*, 184–185.

36. William R. Moody, *The Life of D. L. Moody*, 548.

37. Ibid. One night following a service during his final campaign Moody gathered some of the preachers in the room. As he leaned upon the piano he told them, "Well, I am not a prophet, but I have a guess to make that I think will prove a true prophecy. You hear so much nowadays about the preacher of the twentieth century. Do you know what sort of a man he will be? He will be the sort of preacher who opens his Bible and preaches out of that. Oh, I am sick and tired of this essay preaching! I'm nauseated with this 'silver-tongued orator' preaching! I like to hear a preacher, and not windmills."

Introduction

Summary of Chapters Two Through Seven

Chapter Two

Chapter Two will present the life of D. L. Moody in a fashion that demonstrates a life of continual growth. The researcher discovered fourteen distinct turning points in Moody's life. The biographical sketch will set the context of the evangelist's life. In addition, a sense of his constant drive to grow in all areas of his life demonstrates a heart and mind ready and willing to constantly grow in his homiletical ability.

Chapter Three

Chapter Three will describe the methodology that will be used in examination of Moody's sermons and provide a general description of the sermons to be evaluated. Utilizing various homiletic textbooks, the chapter will give specific definitions for four different classifications of sermons. On one end of the spectrum the rubric will provide a description and criteria for the category of expositional sermons. The second category in the rubric will be textual sermons. The third category that will be presented in the rubric is biographical sermons. The fourth category will be topical sermons. The rubric that will guide the examination of the sermons will be presented in this chapter. The later portion of the chapter will provide a description of the sermons chosen for evaluation.

Chapter Four

Chapter Four will begin the examination of Moody's sermons. Twenty-two messages will be examined from Moody's early years of public speaking. Sermons preached prior to 1873 are difficult to find. The primary reason for this difficulty rests in the growth of Moody's popularity during his campaign carried out in England from 1873–1875. Prior to this trip, Moody constantly grew in popularity but not to the point that his sermons were being collected. Even though sermons from this era are not readily available, twenty-two messages and sermon summaries were discovered from the years 1867—1869. These messages were recorded in a newspaper published by the Congregational churches of Chicago. Moody's sermons were short in the early days. Often, they were five or ten minutes in length. In some cases, the reports of these early sermons are only summaries. Yet, the material provides a sense of the biblical content of his messages, which is confirmed by the testimony of his contemporaries. The chapter will conclude with a summary of findings from the evaluation of Moody's early sermons.

Chapter Five

Chapter Five will examine twenty sermons from Moody's most popular years. When Moody arrived in England in 1873, it appeared his campaign was destined for failure. Yet, the preacher persevered. Before the campaign came to its completion, Moody had become one of the most popular preachers on two continents. Upon his return to the United States, newspaper reporters followed him nearly everywhere he went. They created verbatim transcripts of his sermons and printed them in local newspapers the next day. Many of these sermons were later collected by Moody's family, friends, and staff members. These collections were adapted into book form and published. Some of the sermons were edited heavily and some only slightly. Thus, sermons preached between 1875 and 1892 are readily available.

Twenty sermons will be selected from this era for evaluation. These sermons will come from the newspaper verbatim reports and from books that contain these reports with slight editing. Dwight Moody's son Paul indicated these sermons provide the best picture of his dad's preaching.[38] A summary of findings from the middle preaching years will bring the chapter to its conclusion.

Chapter Six

Using the rubric established in Chapter Three, this chapter will examine twenty-eight sermons from the final seven years of Moody's life. A significant moment

---

38. Paul Moody, *Father*, 111.

came in the preaching of Moody in 1892. During one of his Bible conferences held that year, he confessed his previous failure to preach verses within their textual and historical context.[39] Following this event, the preacher began calling for expositional preaching right up until his last campaign in November of 1899.[40] The present researcher discovered twenty-eight verbatim sermon reports from the Northfield summer conferences of 1894–1899. Each of these are evaluated to present a strong testimony to the biblical content of Moody's preaching in the final years of his life. A summary of findings will bring this chapter to a close.

Chapter Seven

Chapter Seven will serve to conclude the monograph. The first section of the chapter will summarize the evaluation of sermons throughout the three stages of Moody's preaching ministry. From these findings, the monograph will draw conclusions about the growth of his sermon content. The findings will reveal the level of growth toward text-driven preaching reached by the evangelist. The next section of the conclusion will consider implications of the findings in understanding Moody as well as implications for the discipline of Homiletics. Implications for the general fields of Applied Theology and Church History will also be considered. The final section of the concluding chapter will offer suggestions for further research into the life and work of D. L. Moody.

Conclusion

This chapter began by establishing the research question and the thesis of this monograph. Delimitations were then established for the study. The chapter considered the state of the current research and demonstrated the importance of this study. The research method employed was then presented, followed by a summary of Chapters Two through Seven. The monograph will now consider the key turning points in Moody's life.

---

39. Paul Moody, *Father*, 184–185.
40. William R. Moody, *The Life of D. L. Moody*, 548.

Chapter Two

Turning Points
in the Life of
Dwight Lyman Moody

Introduction

Describing the life of D. L. Moody in a single chapter presents at least two major challenges. First, very few men in church history have accomplished so much in diverse areas of Christian work and also touched so many lives in such a short time. Indeed, he continues to impact lives one hundred and twenty-one years after his death. Moody's great-grandson, David S. Powell, notes Moody's continuing influence in the foreword to a 2014 work honoring his grandfather: "I have met and come in contact with people from all over the United States and several foreign countries. I am continually amazed at how these people from different religions, nationality, age, gender, economic and geographical backgrounds still love and respect Dwight L. Moody."[1] Reducing such a man to a brief biography seems impossible.

A second challenge in presenting a brief biographical sketch of Moody relates to the plethora of information already written about the famed evangelist. During his childhood, this author became interested in learning about Moody after having read Faith Coxe Bailey's biography of the preacher.[2] Interest was renewed and expanded in 1999 when the author visited Moody's birthplace

---

1. Kevin Belmonte, *D. L. Moody: A Life* (Chicago: Moody Publishers, 2014), 11.
2. Faith Coxe Bailey, *D. L. Moody: The Greatest Evangelist of the Nineteenth Century* (Chicago: Moody Publishers, 1937).

D.L. MOODY:
TURNING POINTS TOWARD TEXT-DRIVEN PREACHING

and burial site for the first time. This visit was made just a few months prior to the 100th anniversary of the evangelist's death. Since that time, this writer has discovered, collected, and read more than sixty books, master's theses, and doctoral dissertation about Moody. In addition, numerous collections of the preacher's sermons have been read, which often have some biographical or anecdotal information from family, friends, or collectors.

One would think that little could be added to the biographies written by Moody's own children. Most researchers would consider William R. Moody's book on his dad the authoritative biography. Moody's son Paul, though he acknowledged the work of William as the most complete and authoritative, put his hand to present his view of his dad as well. In the preface to his book published in 1938 Paul wrote, "There are some fifty-six or more biographies and none of them have completely captured him.... Every biography is but partial. God alone knows all."[3]

Kevin Belmonte found plenty of material to present a fresh biography in 2014.[4] However, this researcher has moved in yet another direction. With the plethora of Moody material available, very little has been written about his preaching. Most biographers, historians, and researchers limit their comments to a few sentences, a paragraph, or maybe a couple of pages. Therefore, this author's research has focused more on the preaching of Moody than previous studies. Before our research and findings on such a specific topic may be presented, it is necessary to attempt the difficult task of writing a short biographical sketch that offers some unique feature to the many volumes dedicated to Moody's life.

Moody faced several pivotal moments in his life that were indeed defining moments. These moments were also turning points in his life. If he reacted to the circumstances presented in one way, his life would go in one direction. If he responded in another way, his life would move along an altogether different path. This author has identified fourteen distinct turning points in Moody's life beginning with his birth and ending with his death. Therefore, the following pages present a view of the life of D. L. Moody considering those turning

---

3. Paul D. Moody, *My Father: An Intimate Portrait of Dwight Moody* (Boston: Little, Brown and Company, 1938), viii.

4. Belmonte, *Moody: A Life*.

points. As Paul Moody indicated in his preface, this list certainly is not exhaustive and "God alone knows all.... I am only telling what he seemed like to me."[5] This chapter now considers the turning points, beginning with Moody's birth.

New Life in a Small Village

D. L. Moody was born on February 5, 1837, in Northfield, Massachusetts, located a short distance from New Hampshire and a few miles from the Green Mountains of Vermont. He was the sixth son born to Edwin and Betsy Moody. Edwin's family could trace their New England roots to the 1630's, as could Betsy Holton. Several generations of Moody's ancestors on both sides of the family lived in the Connecticut River Valley.[6]

Following in the tradition of his own dad, Edwin worked as a brick and stone mason. Despite his hard work, Edwin struggled to take care of his family. The homestead was purchased with the help of a mortgage, and he constantly piled on debt to keep the family going.[7] Edwin made just enough money to stay ahead of his creditors.

Betsy seemed to take it all in stride, despite her more comfortable upbringing. She worked hard to make a home for Dwight and his siblings. From all accounts Betsy and Edwin had a happy marriage. Some reports indicate Edwin may have been given to drinking, and he certainly had a reputation of being carefree in his approach to life. Yet, their family continued to grow: "By planting time in 1841, thirteen years after their wedding, there were seven children and Betsy was pregnant again."[8] Betsy's hard work and tender care served to provide a sense of security for her family.

---

5. Paul Moody, *Father*, xiii.

6. Lyle W. Dorsett, *A Passion for Souls: The Life of D. L. Moody* (Chicago: Moody Press, 1997), 28.

7. Dorsett, *A Passion for Souls*, 28–29.

8. Ibid.

Moody's Father Dies

Edwin Moody died unexpectedly on May 28, 1841. Betsy was home with the younger children. Four-year-old Dwight and his older siblings were studying at the local schoolhouse. Edwin was busy with his latest construction job. Sometime before lunch however, Edwin felt a sharp pain in his side. As the pain continued, he went home to rest. The pain increased in the early afternoon until Edwin fell on his knees beside his bed and died suddenly.[9] Death took the sole breadwinner of the family. The forty-one-year-old left his pregnant wife and seven children to face the creditors alone.

Moody learned the news of his dad's passing while sitting in the Northfield schoolhouse. A neighbor stuck his head in an open window. After asking if any of Edwin's children were in the building, he told them the tragic news.[10] We do not know the impact the words had on four-year-old Dwight. Very little is written about the actual events of the day, or of Edwin's funeral. Belmonte noted, "Little Dwight retained no memory of his father's funeral."[11]

Moody did recall for his entire life the difficult days of financial struggle for his family brought on by his dad's death. This fact is reflected in William's biography of his dad. William's entire recounting of his grandfather's death focused on the fact that he died leaving his widow and children "with practically no means of support."[12] The reality of financial hardship greatly influenced Moody's childhood and early adult years.

Nearly all Moody's biographers note that the family would have lost their home, were it not for Massachusetts law protecting a widow from foreclosure. Though the creditors could not evict the family, they did take what they could. William reported, "The creditors took everything which they could secure, to the very kindling wood in the shed, and left the widow with her seven children

---

9. Belmonte, *Moody: A Life*, 20.
10. Ibid.
11. Ibid.
12. William R. Moody, *The Life of Dwight L. Moody* (New York: Fleming H. Revell Company, 1900), 20.

in utmost straits."[13] The poverty was so severe that the family was left without a means of heating the home. It is commonly reported that Betsy would have the children stay in their beds to keep warm until it was time to send them to school.[14] The lack of heat was not the only problem.

The situation became even more difficult when, shortly after her husband's death, Betsy gave birth to twins, leaving a total of ten mouths to feed. Betsy's brother Cyrus and a local minister, who was new in town, began to watch out for the family and help where they could. With this help, along with Betsy's insistence, and her constant reminder to trust the Lord, the family stayed together.[15] Though they stayed together, the path proved difficult on everyone in the family.

There are at least two ways this turning point in Moody's life influenced him for years to come. First, the young boy figured out quickly that he did not like being poor. Moody wanted to grow up, head to the city, and get rich. This desire became a driving force in his young adult years. His primary goal in life was to work hard, live sparingly, and save money until he had $100,000 in the bank.[16] This goal drove Moody's life for several years, even after his conversion to Christ.

The second impact on Moody lasted until the day of his own death. While he lived sparingly himself, he was generous towards others, particularly to those who were in need. On several trips to visit the birthplace and grave site of the famed evangelist, this researcher had the privilege to talking with several of the curators of the Moody Museum. On one such occasion, the curator was discussing Moody's life. The question was asked, "What do you personally believe to be the most significant accomplishment of D. L. Moody?" The curator did not hesitate, stating,

> He did much for this community and the world, but as far as I am concerned the greatest thing about Moody is that he rose from such poverty and never forgot people who were worse off than himself. He had millions

---

13. William R. Moody, *The Life of D. l. Moody*, 20.
14. Belmonte, *Moody: A Life*, 21.
15. William R. Moody, *The Life of D. l. Moody*, 21–22.
16. Dorsett, *Passion*, 45, 53.

of dollars run through his hands, but he never kept the money for himself. He used it to help others.[17]

The curator's sentiments may not be considered "the greatest thing about Moody" by his biographers, but they all note his generous spirit in general and his care for the poor specifically.[18] Without a doubt, the loss of his dad was a major turning point in Moody's life.

Moody Leaves Home

Moody was no stranger to work. His son William mentions the fact that at eight years old he and his twelve year-old brother, "secured employment in the cutting of broom corn."[19] Moody and his siblings continued to work throughout his childhood and teen years. Yet, he always had his sights set on something greater. He wanted to be in business, to make money, and to leave the life of poverty behind.

Samuel Holton, brother to Moody's mother Betsy, lived in Boston and owned a shoe store. On one occasion while visiting in Betsy's home, Moody mentioned to his uncle Samuel that he would like to work for him in his shoe store. His uncle seemed to simply ignore his statement but later consulted with Moody's older brother George. George discouraged the idea.[20] About six months later, "While cutting and hauling logs on the mountainside with his brother Edwin … he exclaimed, in his characteristically abrupt manner, 'I'm tired of this! I'm not going to stay around here any longer. I'm going to the city.'"[21] Moody left Northfield.

---

17. This particular quotation came from the primary curator of the Moody Birthplace and Museum in October, 2001. Her name has long since been lost by this writer and to his knowledge, there is no way to contact her today.

18. Belmonte notes an example of Moody's generosity particular in regards to educating the poor in his work *D. L. Moody: A Life,* 141.

19. William R. Moody, *The Life of D. L. Moody*, 22.

20. John Pollock, *Moody: The Biography* (Chicago: Moody Press, 1983), 21.

21. William R. Moody, *The Life of D. L. Moody*, 35.

Moody headed for Boston on foot. On the way, he encountered his older brother George. When George inquired about where he was going, how he was going to get there, and so forth, he realized there was no stopping his little brother. Thus, he gave Moody five dollars, which he used for travel so that he did not have to walk.[22] Upon arriving in the city, he had no money and no place to stay. Moody was certain his uncle Samuel would be excited to offer him a position in his shoe store. He made his way to his uncle's main shop and announced his arrival.

Moody misjudged his uncle's response. Samuel inquired as to how the young man expected to make a living in the big city. Moody was unwilling to appear in need and desired to show his independence. He simply suggested that he would find a job.[23] Moody's pride would not allow him to ask his uncle for help.

The best outcome of his visit to the shoe store was that another uncle, Lemuel Holton, offered for Moody to live in his house while looking for work. After a few long days of searching for a job, the young man was discouraged. He suggested to his uncle Lemuel that that he would walk to New York City and look for work there. Lemuel discouraged such a move and counseled Moody to humble himself, return to his uncle Samuel, and ask for a job.

Taking Lemuel's advice, Moody returned to his uncle Samuel's shop and humbly asked for a job. His uncle expressed concern. He said Moody would have to do whatever he was asked to do. He would also have to attend his church and its Sunday School. Moody quickly agreed to these and other conditions set by his Uncle Samuel. Years later, after Moody had become famous, his uncle Samuel was in great need and asked Moody for help. Pollock records Moody's answer, "You gave me work & good advice & I look back to that hour as the turning point in my life & I feel as if I owe you a debt I can never pay so the money I send you is not a loan but a part payment of what I owe you."[24] Moody received the gracious generosity of two of his uncles in his early days in Boston. Later, he had opportunity to demonstrate grace and generosity in return.

---

22. William R. Moody, *The Life of D. L. Moody*, 35–36.
23. Dorsett, *Passion*, 42–43.
24. Pollock, *Moody*, 22.

D.L. MOODY: TURNING POINTS TOWARD TEXT-DRIVEN PREACHING

Upon reading Moody's comments to his uncle Samuel, one cannot help but realize that his move to Boston was a major turning point in his life. What exactly was the "turning point" to which Moody referred? The immediate and most obvious answer is that the young man was in great need. He was in the city with no money and no job. His uncle gave him an opportunity to work, first in the stockroom, and later as a salesman. Moody began to make money, live sparingly, and save towards his goal of having $100,000 in the bank. He did well as a shoe salesman, and this opportunity set him on his way to reaching his goal.

A closer look at Moody's words, however, reveals an even greater turning point. Notice his words again, "I look back on that hour as the turning point in my life & I feel I owe you a debt I can never pay."[25] While Samuel Holton gave Moody a job, the great likelihood is that he also made quite a bit of money because of Moody. The debt he refers to must not be financial.

Indeed, the greatest debt Moody felt towards his uncle was the fact that he insisted the young man attend church and Sunday School. Edward Kimball became Moody's teacher. For about a year, Kimball watched him come to class each week and the young man seemed to be learning. However, Kimball's burden for Moody's salvation grew to a climax on April 21, 1855. He set out to Samuel Holton's shoe shop to speak to Moody about surrendering his life to Jesus. Passing the store, for fear of embarrassing the young man in front of his co-workers, the burden grew even stronger. Thus, he turned back, went straight in, and asked to see Moody.

Moody was in the back of the store wrapping and shelving shoes. Kimball approached him. He put his hands on the young man's shoulders and shared the gospel with him. That day brought the greatest turning point in Moody's life and he was converted. He turned from sin and self, and turned to Jesus in faith. As Belmonte notes, "Moody could not have known it, but years later, his conversion would be considered so seminal an event in the religious history of America that the city of Boston honored it with a bronze memorial plaque."[26] One hundred and sixty-seven years later, the shoe store is long gone. However, on Court Street the bronze plaque can still be read. Belmonte records the exact wording of the plaque as follows:

    25. Pollock, *Moody*, 22.
    26. Belmonte, *Moody: A Life*, 42.

> D. L. MOODY
> CHRISTIAN EVANGELIST,
> FRIEND OF MAN,
> FOUNDER OF THE NORTHFIELD SCHOOLS,
> WAS CONVERTED TO GOD
> IN A SHOE STORE ON
> THIS SITE
> APRIL 21ST, 1855[27]

Moody Moves to Chicago

Moody enjoyed success in the shoe business. He did a good job for his uncle Samuel. He managed his money well. He reached for the goal of personal wealth so that he could avoid a return to the poverty he had known from the time of his dad's death. Despite his success, the young man had a greater vision. He wanted more than his working in his uncle's store could offer.

Hearing about the booming city of Chicago, Moody began to set his mind on heading west to make his fortune. William notes,

> For some months he had fretted under the conservative methods of the business house in which he was engaged, and had longed to enter a larger sphere of activity, and when a crisis finally came in his relationship with his employer, and there seemed little opportunity for advancement, he decided to go to Chicago.[28]

He and his uncle struggled to continue to work together. Moody wanted more financial reward. He was ready to move on to bigger opportunities. He was certain the time was right, and so he headed west to make his mark on the business world.

---

27. Belmonte, *Moody: A Life*, 42.
28. William R. Moody, *The Life of D. L. Moody*, 46.

D.L. MOODY:
TURNING POINTS TOWARD TEXT-DRIVEN PREACHING

Arriving in Chicago in the fall of 1856, Moody found a new position within two days. The position offered him opportunities for advancement, which he soon experienced through increasing responsibility and income.[29] In a time when people regularly worked for a dollar a day, Moody steadily made significant money, lived sparingly, and saved his funds, moving him toward his goal of having $100,000 in the bank.[30] Moody's plans grew as he continued to strive toward his objective.

The young man not only found success as a salesman but he also began to think of additional ways to increase his income. Pollock notes, "Within a year he was showing the signs of a future millionaire, putting his savings into land, which he would sell at a profit, making loans at high rates, and thinking up this scheme and that to increase his income and capital."[31] Summing up his new-found success, William quotes a letter Moody wrote to his brother George: "I can make more money here in a week than I could in Boston in a month."[32] There is no question that the move to Chicago was a turning point in Moody's ability to earn money. However, there was another growing concern inside the young man.

Ever since Edward Kimball led Moody to Jesus, the young man had a desire for others to come to faith in Christ. When he arrived in Chicago, the burden for others continued to grow. He knew that most of the unchurched in Chicago would not go to church of their own volition. They needed someone to go and seek them out. Belmonte reports, "He would go to where they were, just as Edward Kimball had sought him out in the shoe store back in Boston. In this, he had a model that meant everything to him. He would follow it in Chicago."[33] Follow it he did. He spent nearly all his free time serving the Lord by bringing others to Sunday School, to church, and most importantly, to a personal relationship with Jesus.

Moody's Sunday School work grew significantly and rapidly. He turned a saloon into a Sunday School class. Before long the classes out grew the saloon,

---

29. William R. Moody, *The Life of D. L. Moody*, 47.
30. Dorsett, *Passion*, 52.
31. Pollock, *Moody*, 34.
32. William R. Moody, *The Life of D. L. Moddy*, 50.
33. Belmonte, *Moody: A Life*, 49.

and he moved the school into North Market Hall in the fall of 1859. Moody had over 300 students in regular attendance. During this time, Emma Revell began to volunteer to help Moody in his Sunday School.[34] In Emma, the young man found his life mate. Paul reported that they first met when Emma was twelve, and they became engaged when she was seventeen. Then in 1862, they were married after a two-year engagement.[35]

There is no doubt that the move west proved to be another significant turning point in Moody's life. First, it was a turning point in financial growth. Second, it was a turning point in increased service for the Lord, Finally, it was the turning point that led him to his wife and life-long friend and partner. His new-found life in Chicago was both rewarding and fulfilling, but it also led to another major turning point in Moody's life.

A Vision Lost, A Vision Gained

William reports that by 1860 his dad had saved $7,000 toward his goal. In a single year, he made $5,000 above his regular salary.[36] He was well on his way to fulfilling his ambition to live a wealthy life. He could provide well for Emma.[37] Few men under the age of twenty-five could have boasted such success in his day. Yet, there was something that threatened to derail him from his vision.

Since his arrival in Chicago, Moody had not only been successful at business, but also his Sunday School work continually increased. He felt a growing burden for reaching the unchurched, and he was bringing them in. Dorsett reports that by the end of 1860, the North Market Hall School reached 1,500

---

34. Dorsett, *Passion*, 68.
35. Paul Moody, *Father*, 54.
36. William R. Moody, *The Life of D. L. Moody*, 63.
37. In describing Moody's ability to take care of Emma at the time of his marriage proposal, Belmonte reports that he was a highly successful young businessman with money in the bank that in today's dollars would be $150,000 saved with an annual salary of $200,000 in modern currency. For more on this account, see Belmonte, *Moody: A Life*, 78.

D.L. MOODY:
TURNING POINTS TOWARD TEXT-DRIVEN PREACHING

in regular attendance.[38] His Sunday School success even caught the attention of President-elect Abraham Lincoln, who stopped by for a visit on his way to Washington DC to assume his new duties.[39] The more Moody's Sunday School work grew, the more time Moody wanted to spend serving the Lord.

William makes it clear that Moody did not let his Sunday School work interfere with his business duties. Nor did he let his business duties interfere with serving the Lord.[40] Yet inside the young man, a war began to rage. Moody often was heard to say, "The greatest struggle I ever had in my life was when I gave up business."[41] With both his business responsibilities increasing, and his Sunday School work growing rapidly, Moody knew one day he would have to make some difficult decisions.

Moody's son William recounts his Dad's own version of how he exchanged his vision of being a wealthy businessman for being a full-time servant of the Lord. In just over two pages William describes that while his Sunday School continually grew, there was one class of young girls who exhibited no desire to be saved. Their teacher was dying. Under the doctor's orders, he needed to move to extend his life. The teacher's greater concern, however, was that he had not been able to lead even one of his students to Christ. Over the next ten days the teacher and Moody went to the house of each girl. The teacher shared Jesus with each of his students. One by one, they trusted Christ.[42] The Lord was working not only to save these girls but also to solidify Moody's direction.

The night before the teacher left Chicago, the last girl trusted Jesus. That night Moody called all the girls together to have a prayer meeting with their beloved teacher. Consider Moody's own account of that prayer meeting: "There God kindled a fire in my soul that has never gone out. The height of my ambition had been to be a successful merchant and if I had known that meeting

---

38. Dorsett, *Passion*, 73.
39. Ibid., 74.
40. William R. Moody, *The Life of D. L. Moody*, 62.
41. Ibid.
42. Ibid., 63–66.

was going to take that ambition out of me, I might not have gone. But how many times I have thanked God for that meeting!"[43] Moody's vision of having $100,000 in the bank was gone and had been replaced with a vision to be used by God to lead people to Jesus. From that day forward, he would serve his Lord full time for the rest of his life.

Moody Visits England

Having left business, Moody set himself to serving the Lord full time. The nation was ravaged by the Civil War, and it had its impact on Moody. Lyle Dorsett dedicated an entire chapter to the years 1861–1865. The chapter describes Moody's involvement in the conflict, as well as, the war's effects upon his life and ministry.[44] For the scope of this chapter, the author will refrain from speaking of Moody's war service, other than to say that he continually sought to lead soldiers to Christ. Indeed, he nearly wore himself out and even risked conflict to get the gospel to men on both sides of the battlefield.[45]

With the help of Emma and their friend John Farwell, the mission Sunday School continued to operate. When the absence of Moody slowed the growth, Emma would redouble her efforts and work hard to keep the school growing. As the war years ended, the work in Chicago increased. The Sunday School grew so much that it was decided a new church must be started, and Moody assumed the pastorate. Soon thereafter, the Chicago YMCA asked Moody to serve as the president, which he agreed to do. He served in this capacity from 1865 – 1870.[46]

The grueling schedule took its toll on both Moody and his wife Emma. Moody knew he needed some time away from Chicago and thought a trip to England would provide rest. According to William, his dad longed to meet George

---

43. William R. Moody, *The Life of D. L. Moody*, 65.
44. Dorsett, *Passion*, 79–117.
45. Ibid., 87–98.
46. Ibid., 122–124.

D.L. MOODY:
TURNING POINTS TOWARD TEXT-DRIVEN PREACHING

Muller and Charles Haddon Spurgeon.[47] Pollock notes, "Nothing would have come of Moody's hankerings for England, had not asthma so pained Emma during the early winter of 1866 – 1867 that the doctor advised a sea voyage."[48] With Emma's mother agreeing to watch their daughter, Dwight and Emma boarded a ship and travelled to England.

While in England, Moody wanted to hear Spurgeon preach. At his first attempt, he was told that he could not get into the church to hear Spurgeon because he had no ticket. However, somehow he was able to secure a spot. Though he did not meet Spurgeon on this first visit to the Metropolitan Tabernacle, he did hear Spurgeon preach several times. Pollock notes that upon hearing Spurgeon, Moody "longed to preach like that, and to see singing led like that."[49] Eventually the two preachers did meet and became great friends.

During Moody's visit to meet George Mueller, Dorsett reported that he "assumed the role of student ... he soaked up stories about how God had led him and his wife, met their needs, and touched the lives of children."[50] Dorsett also adds concerning Moody and Mueller's interaction that, "Among the many things Moody received from his visit with Mueller was an introduction to the fairly young sect of evangelical Christianity called the Plymouth Brethren."[51] Henry Varley, a man about Moody's age, was among the Plymouth Brethren that Moody interacted with in England. Varley opened the door for Moody to preach in several places. However, the most significant impact Varley had on Moody, and quite possibly the most significant moment of the entire trip, came in the words Varley spoke at a Bible study Moody attended. William records the words and his dad's reaction. Varley states, "The world has yet to see what God will do with and for and through and in and by the man who is fully and whol-

---

47. William R. Moody, *The Life of D. L. Moody*, 131.
48. Pollock, *Moody*, 81–82.
49. Ibid., 83.
50. Dorsett, *Passion*, 135.
51. Ibid.

ly consecrated to Him."⁵² Only eternity will tell the extent of the impact these words had on Moody and on two continents. However, his immediate response was recorded by William:

> He said, a man ... he did not say a great man, nor a learned man, nor a rich man, nor a wise man, nor an eloquent man, nor a smart man, but simply a man. I am a man, and it lies with the man himself whether he will or will not make that entire and full consecration. I will try my utmost to be that man.⁵³

Thus, Moody returned from his first trip across the sea, with a new resolve to live totally yielded to his Lord.

Moody Meets Moorhouse

Moody's interactions with the Plymouth Brethren while in England brought about another important encounter. Within a short time, this encounter proved to be another major turning point in his life. He was introduced to a young man referred to as "the Boy preacher."⁵⁴ Once a pickpocket, Henry Moorhouse turned to faith in Jesus and became a preacher. When Moody first met Moorhouse, he was unimpressed. Dorsett describes Moody's attitude toward Henry: "He scarcely took Henry seriously.... He was short, with a boyish-looking face. He did not appear to be a day older than seventeen.... Moody was certain he could not preach."⁵⁵ Henry Moorhouse was happy to meet D. L. Moody and had no idea of the evangelist's thoughts towards him. So, he offered to travel back to the Unites States with

---

52. William R. Moody, *The Life of D. L. Moody*, 134.
53. Ibid.
54. Henry Moorhouse is often referred to by the nickname "Harry." Some biographers use only the name "Henry" while others like Pollock and Belmonte prefer "Harry." Dorsett's introduction to the boy preacher presents his name as "Henry 'Harry' Moorhouse" and then in the following discussions most often refers to him as "Harry" or simply as "Moorhouse." This author chose to stick with his given name.
55. Dorsett, *Passion*, 137.

D.L. MOODY:
TURNING POINTS TOWARD TEXT-DRIVEN PREACHING

Moody and preach in Chicago. Moody did not offer specific information about when he was returning home and thought the issue closed.

Upon settling back into life in Chicago, Moody received a letter from Moorhouse stating he was in the United States and would be happy to come preach for Moody in Chicago. Pollock describes the letter as an "unexpected irritant."[56] William gives his dad's recollection of his response to the letter: "Well, I sat down and wrote a very cold letter: 'If you come West, call on me.' I thought that would be the last I should hear of him."[57] Henry Moorhouse did not seem to take offense and did not let the letter discourage him. Before long, Moody received another letter offering to come to Chicago and preach. William indicates that Moody wrote a second letter in which he stated, "If you happen to come West, drop in on me."[58] Henry sent a third letter stating he would be in Chicago the following Thursday.

Moody had to be away on Thursday and Friday. He met with some of the leaders of the Chicago church and suggested they let Moorhouse preach on Thursday. If he was no good, the leaders were to simply have a prayer meeting on Friday. Concerned that the boy may negatively impact attendance they were reluctant to allow him to preach, but Moody insisted for a reason which he did not seem to understand himself.[59] The leaders agreed and planned to have the young man preach Thursday evening. If he was good, they would have him preach Friday as well. Then they would decide whether to announce him for the weekend or to leave it open for Moody to preach upon his return.

Returning to Chicago, Moody was anxious to find out what happened. He inquired of Emma. She explained that she and the whole congregation liked Henry. He preached both services on John 3:16. William quotes her as saying, "He tells the worst of sinners that God loves them."[60] Moody was not pleased with this idea. He was used to telling sinners they needed to repent because God's judgment was coming. However, Emma insisted that he needed to hear the kid from Ireland for himself. In the next service, Henry once again preached

---

56. Pollock, *Moody*, 87.
57. William R. Moody, *The Life of D. L. Moody*, 137.
58. Ibid.
59. Dorsett, *Passion*, 138.
60. William R. Moody, *The Life of D. L. Moody*, 137.

from John 3:16, and Moody was moved to a deeper understanding of the love of God. Henry Moorhouse continued to preach every day for seven days, and each time he took John 3:16 as his text and boldly proclaimed the love of God.

Henry's visit to Chicago was another major turning point in Moody's life. Indeed, Dorsett argues that, "Nothing prior to this time, except his conversion, had such a profound impact on his soul."[61] His life and ministry were impacted in three major ways. First, he never understood how much God loved mankind until hearing this week of sermons given by Moorhouse. This understanding changed the direction of Moody's preaching forever. He began to preach the profound love of God.

Second, Moody was impressed at the depth of scriptural knowledge Moorhouse exhibited. Dorsett notes that "Moorhouse told Moody that he needed to become a better student of the English Bible."[62] Moody took on the attitude of a student and asked Henry to teach him how to study the Bible.

Moorhouse encouraged Moody to get a concordance and taught him how to trace out a word to see everything the Bible says about the topic at hand. Dorsett correctly notes that Mueller had encouraged Moody to study the Bible a book at a time, which is better.[63] However, the fact remains that after his time with Moorhouse, Moody began doing topical studies of the verses from which he would preach. Indeed, this transition is evident in the increase of the use of multiple passages of Scripture in his sermons.[64]

Belmonte noted a third adjustment D. L. Moody made in his ministry practice because of Henry Moorhouse's first visit to Chicago. After Moody requested Moorhouse teach him how to study the Bible, "They invited friends to his Chicago home for the first of the 'Bible Readings' that would become famous as a part of his ministry."[65] Through these readings, Moody taught thousands of believers to do topical studies of various scriptural themes.

---

61. Dorsett, *Passion*, 139.
62. Ibid., 140.
63. Ibid.
64. This will be demonstrated in chapters four and five.
65. Belmonte, *Moody: A Life*, 96 (ed. note: topical studies v. book studies is still discussed).

D.L. MOODY: TURNING POINTS TOWARD TEXT-DRIVEN PREACHING

Moody and the Chicago Fire

Moody's friends sought to encourage him and help meet the needs of his family. Dorsett described a particular gift when he wrote, "On January 1, 1868 Emma and Dwight were given the keys to a new house, fully furnished, on State Street, about three blocks from where they were living."[66] Their friend John Farwell built the house for them. Other friends contributed the furniture. All this was done as a statement of gratitude for Moody. Shortly after moving into their new home, on January 7, a fire broke out in downtown. The fire destroyed Farwell Hall and several other buildings. Moody immediately committed himself to the task of raising money to rebuild. The challenges of fund-raising along with numerous other regular tasks and all the travel wore on the evangelist.

The trial by fire faced in January of 1868 was only a foreshadowing of the trial that was to come on October 8, 1871, the night of the Great Chicago Fire. William describes how this event became another turning point in his dad's life:

> On the fifth Sunday night, October 8th, he preached to the largest congregation that he had ever addressed in that city, having taken for his text, "What then shall I do with Jesus which is called Christ?" After preaching—or talking as he did not call it preaching then—with all his power of entreaty, presenting Christ as a Savior and Redeemer, he said: "I wish you would take this text home with you and turn it over in your minds during the week, and next Sabbath we will come to Calvary and the cross, and we will decide what to do with Jesus of Nazareth." "What a Mistake!" he said, in relating the story to a large audience on Chicago on the twenty-second anniversary of the great fire in that city in 1871: "I have never dared to give an audience a week to think of their salvation since. If they were lost they might rise up in judgment against me…. I have never seen that congregation since. I have hard work to keep back the tears today(sic)…. I want to tell you of one lesson I learned that night, which I

---

66. Dorsett, *Passion*, 145.

have never forgotten, and that is, when I preach, to press Christ upon the people then and there, and try to bring them to a decision on the spot."[67]

After the Chicago Fire, Moody determined to never preach again without asking his hearers to make a decision for Christ.

Moody Is Overwhelmed by God

Even before the Chicago Fire, Moody was growing weary in his busy schedule. He exerted all the strength he could muster to do the Lord's work, but the load was heavy: "Signs appeared showing that Dwight Moody was on a guilt-ridden and work-laden pathway toward emotional and spiritual collapse."[68] During this time, two ladies became heavily burdened for the evangelist. Sarah Cooke and Mrs. W. R. Hawxhurst began to attend all of Moody's meetings and pray for him. After each meeting, they would tell him what they did. He was becoming rather annoyed with them. Dorsett reports that after one of the meetings, the ladies told him they were praying for him. Moody responded, "Why are you praying for me? Why don't you pray for the unsaved?"[69] They were undaunted by his response and continued to pray for him to "get the power."[70] Eventually, Moody met with them for prayer and asked them to explain what they meant by "get the power." They taught him their view of the Holy Spirit and said he needed to be filled with the Spirit. They prayed for him, then he prayed, asking the Lord to fill him with the Spirit.[71] Moody left the prayer meeting unchanged.

Following the Chicago Fire, Moody's schedule only intensified. Many of Chicago's buildings used for religious purposes had been destroyed, including the building in which Moody held services. He immediately set his hand to raising money for the rebuilding efforts. Within a couple of months, he was able to put up a temporary tabernacle in which to hold meetings. Then Moody headed

---

67. William R. Moody, *The Life of D. L. Moody*, 144–145.
68. Dorsett, *Passion*, 148.
69. R.A. Torrey, *Why God Used D. L. Moody* (Kindle Edition), Location 285.
70. Ibid.
71. Dorsett, *Passion*, 151.

D.L. MOODY:
TURNING POINTS TOWARD TEXT-DRIVEN PREACHING

east to raise funds to rebuild numerous religious buildings throughout the city. While he was experiencing a good measure of success in the fundraising efforts, his heart was not in the work. He was walking up and down the streets of New York City, when something amazing happened. Consider R. A. Torrey's explanation of the event:

> He was walking up Wall Street in New York; (Mr. Moody very seldom told this and I almost hesitate to tell it) and in the midst of the bustle and hurry of that city his prayer was answered; the power of God fell upon him as he walked up the street and he had to hurry off to the house of a friend and ask that he might have a room by himself, and in that room he stayed alone for hours; and the Holy Ghost came upon him, filling his soul with such joy that at last he had to ask God to withhold His hand, lest he die on the spot from very joy. He went out from that place with the power of the Holy Ghost upon him, and when he got to London ... the power of God wrought through him mightily.[72]

From this time, Moody began to speak more and more of the Holy Spirit and the need for preachers to have his power to be effective. Quoting Moody's sermon, "Glad Tidings," Gundry writes, "The only work that is going to stand for eternity is the work done by the Holy Ghost, and not by any one of us. We may be used as his instruments, but the work that will stand to eternity is that done by the Holy Ghost.... If He does not do it they won't be converted."[73] Moody learned to rely on the power of the Spirit, rather than his own strength. From this point forward, Moody's effectiveness grew significantly.

Moody seems to have used the phrases, "baptism of the Holy Spirit" and "filling of the Holy Spirit" interchangeably. This usage has caused much confusion as to exactly what the evangelist believed by his use of the two phrases. George and Donald Sweeting argue, "In saying D. L. Moody believed in a 'baptism of the Holy Spirit,' it is important to make several clarifications.... Moody did not link this empowering with speaking in tongues.... Moody did not link

---

72. Torrey, *Why*, Location 291.

73. Stanley Gundry, *Love Them In: The Proclamation Theology of D. L. Moody* (Chicago: Moody, 1976), 82.

this empowering with a belief in entire sanctification.... Moody did not limit this empowering to a second blessing alone."[74] A careful study of Moody's life reveals that George and Donald Sweeting are correct in their argument. There is no record that he ever suggested that he was involved in "speaking in tongues" personally. There is no evidence that he believed in "sinless perfection." Rather than a "second blessing," Moody constantly referred to the fact that he, and every other preacher, needs a fresh filling of the Spirit for each act of service.

Yet, the fact remains that this event proved to be another major turning point in Moody's life and ministry. While he had experienced some measure of success prior to this event, his preaching had a new and fresh power. In addition, he learned to let the Spirit work through him, rather than trying to work for the Lord in his own strength. All this came just before he made his second trip to England.

Moody's British Campaign

Moody and his family boarded a ship bound for England in June of 1873. His first trip had been designed for rest, relaxation, and personal study. However, the evangelist embarked on this trip with the intent of joining Reverend Pennefather of the Established Church in London and Mr. Cuthbert Bainbridge of the Wesleyan Church in Newcastle in "gospel work."[75] In addition, William

---

74. George and Donald Sweeting, *Lessons from the Life of Moody* (Chicago: Moody Press, 1989), 94–95.

75. W. H. Daniels, *Moody: His Words, Works, and Workers* (New York: Nelson & Phillips, 1877), 41. A few significant points should be noted about this work. First, it is an unauthorized biography. Moody desired that none be written prior to his death and then he wanted his son William to write the official biography prior to the publication of any other such volumes. Second, the first sixty-four pages present a brief biographical sketch, while the balance of the book presents some of his more famous character sermons, an outline of Moody's doctrine as Daniels understood it, a presentation of Moody's co-laborers, and a recounting of his work with the temperance movement. While unauthorized, having an original copy of this work is a treasure for Moody researchers. It demonstrates how some viewed him at the height of his evangelistic ministry.

D.L. MOODY: TURNING POINTS TOWARD TEXT-DRIVEN PREACHING

notes that Moody had a third invitation from Henry Bewley of Dublin.[76] Upon Moody's arrival in England, he was dismayed to find out about the deaths of all three of these men who issued the invitation to come overseas.

While it appeared the door closed, Moody was not one to be easily distracted. Nevertheless, the trial was great. They now had no invitation to be there. The men who had invited them also had pledged to raise money for their support while serving in England. Therefore, upon learning about their deaths, there appeared no means of visible support. The Moodys went to London to stay with Emma's relatives. The Sankeys, who had come along to lead music and provide general support to the campaign, went to stay with Henry Moorhouse.[77] While it appeared the trip was a waste, Moody was confident God would do something to turn things around.

Moody had a friend in York by the name of Bennett, and he thought that a door might be slightly opening for them to begin their work in that city. However, Bennett was uncertain that the time was right. He sent Moody a cable suggesting it would take at least a month to break through the spiritual coldness and prepare for Moody's arrival. He then asked that Moody give him a date to plan for the beginning of the campaign. Moody cabled back indicating he would arrive in York that night. He then sent for Sankey, and they went to see if the door would open wider.[78] William, who went along on this trip, reported that in the beginning Moody and Sankey were looked upon with suspicion and received little support. Further, the congregations were small.[79] But over time, the situation began to change.

Daniels described Moody's own take on the early days in England: "We have not done much in York and Sunderland ... because the ministers opposed us; but we are going to stay in Newcastle till we make an impression and live down the prejudices of good people who do not understand us."[80] Moody was determined that despite all the challenges, they were not going to give up.

---

76. William R. Moody, *The Life of D. L. Moody*, 154.
77. Dorsett, *Passion*, 177.
78. William R. Moody, *The Life of D. L. Moody*, 156.
79. Ibid., 157.
80. Daniels, *Moody*, 42.

Moody's faith was rewarded. Concerning the work in Newcastle, Daniels reports, "Before the close of these remarkable services the outpouring of the Spirit of God upon the entire population of the place proved that the Lord honored the faith of his servant."[81] The Spirit had breathed on a dying ember, and a spiritual fire was started that turned into a blaze which swept across the British Isles.

Though William Penne's father died before Moody's arrival, he had before his death predicted the coming revival led by Moody. Dorsett's account notes: "He predicted that the United Kingdom was a parched land waiting to be ignited. He also prophesied that Mr. Dwight L. Moody was the man who would set the fire."[82] The fire spread across the United Kingdom from Newcastle to numerous cities including: Edinburgh, Glasgow, Belfast, Dublin, Manchester, Birmingham, Liverpool, and London.

Moody's first British campaign lasted from June 1873 to July 1875. In just over two years, England experienced a fresh working of the Holy Spirit, and revival fires were ablaze. Belmonte offers a description of the campaign: "It is said to have reached its zenith in the final five months, between March 9, and July 21, 1875, when Moody addressed, in total, 'over 2 ½ million people at four venues: the Agricultural Hall, Islington; the Royal Opera House, Haymarket; Camberwell Green and Bow Common.'"[83] Preaching to 2.5 million people in just under five months, without the aid of radio, television, or the Internet, is a remarkable accomplishment.[84] Even more remarkable was the impact the entire British campaign had not only on that continent but also in America.

The first British campaign served as a turning point not only for the United Kingdom but also for the United States. While preaching across the Atlantic, newspapers in America began carrying reports of the revival fires spreading across the British Isles. Hearing of Moody's work in England caused several

---

81. Daniels, *Moody*, 42.
82. Dorsett, *Passion*, 179.
83. Belmonte, *Moody: A Life*, 108.
84. It should be noted that the 2.5 million attendees refer to the total number of attendees and does not distinguish between first time attenders and those who attended the services repeatedly. However, to preach to such crowds without the aid of modern technology remains a significant accomplishment.

cities in the United States to desire Moody to come preach for them. Belmonte notes, "America's cities would welcome Moody's revival work, largely due to all that had unfolded during his extraordinary mission work just concluded in Great Britain."[85] So upon his return to his homeland, Moody began preparing to preach in America's great cities, noting, "Water runs downhill, and the highest hills in America are the great cities. If we can stir them we shall stir the whole country."[86] Invitations from several cities began pouring in, asking the evangelist to come and preach.

Impacting a Nation

William notes that upon Moody's return to the United States, several cities formed committees across denominational lines for organizing series of meetings and inviting his dad to come preach. In some cases, the invitations came to Moody's hand while he was still in the United Kingdom.[37] After a short visit to Northfield, Moody accepted the invitation to lead a campaign in Brooklyn, and it began in October 1875. The number of people who attended required careful planning for holding services, including the use of The Brooklyn Tabernacle, a converted ice rink, and for holding overflow meetings in various places with the help of local clergy. The campaign lasted four weeks.

From Brooklyn, Moody headed for "The City of Brotherly Love" to share the love of Jesus. Belmonte notes, "The first gospel meeting was held on November 21 in a freight depot.... [T]his depot could accommodate seating for 12,000 people, but attendance increased so rapidly that more meetings had to be rescheduled for other venues to meet the demand."[88] Attendees to the Philadelphia campaign included President Ulysses S. Grant, James A. Garfield (a future president), several members of Congress, and other government officials. The services lasted for nine weeks going right through the Christmas season and continuing until January 20, 1876.

---

85. Belmonte, *Moody: A Life*, 124.
86. William R. Moody, *The Life of D. L. Moody*, 263.
87. Ibid., 254.
88. Belmonte, *Moody: A Life*, 127.

After a short rest back in Northfield, Moody began his New York City campaign on February 7, and it lasted until April 19, 1876. For ten weeks, the evangelist and his team held worship services, Bible readings, and meetings for both men and women. Pollock notes that the campaign "... had been prepared as carefully as the one in Philadelphia. At the end, it could be said that Moody's 'position today, whether at home or abroad, is unrivaled.'"[89] Wherever Moody went, people crowded in to hear him.

In his biography, Pollock titled his twenty-first chapter, "All America Stirred."[90] The chapter title sums up the influence that Dwight Lyman Moody had on this nation after his return from England. Leaving New York, Moody headed west. His son William chronicles his return to Chicago and then back to Boston. Pollock describes a continuously busy schedule of traveling to Georgia, Nashville, St. Louis, Kansas, Nebraska, and Iowa referring to this time as "a sort of whistle-stop tour that laid a trail of illuminated lives across the Middle West."[91] From the fall of 1875 through 1876, Moody's influence upon his own nation took on a new level of impact that certainly must be described as a major turning point in his life and ministry.

Moody Extends his Ministry Through Education

Nearly all of Moody's biographers recount a funny story that occurred during the evangelist's few weeks of rest in Northfield, taken shortly after his return from England. He arrived in Northfield on August 16, 1875 to spend a few weeks relaxing and visiting his mother. Some of her chickens left her small farm and made their way into a neighbor's corn field. The neighbor, Elisha Alexander, was not pleased and began to protest loudly. Not wanting to deal with the hassle, and certainly not wanting his mother to have to put up with the continual problem, Moody offered to purchase the cornfield.

---

89. Pollock, *Moody*, 204.
90. Ibid., 201–211.
91. Ibid., 210.

D.L. MOODY:
TURNING POINTS TOWARD TEXT-DRIVEN PREACHING

Alexander was more than willing to accommodate Moody by selling the field, but there was a catch. Moody would have to purchase the entire farm from the neighbor. While Moody had long ago given up business and saving money for such things, the Lord had already provided the money to make the purchase possible. Edward Studd had recently given Moody more than enough to handle the purchase, despite Moody's repeated insistence against the gift. What may seem like an impulsive act of purchasing a farm over his mother's chickens would prove to be the provision for the next phase of Moody's ministry.

Upon visits to his home in Northfield, Moody would think through his strategy for the future. According to Dorsett, there are five observations which should be understood about his developing strategy.[92] First, Moody continued to believe that to reach the most people, an urban emphasis was necessary. Second, Moody recognized for a work to be truly effective in the long-term, it required personal, one-on-one instruction, as used in his "inquiry room." This meant the evangelist needed more laborers. Dorsett indicates that these first two observations led Moody to his third focus. He needed to train workers who understood poverty themselves. The fourth observation points to the fact that Moody believed he must train and send out "an army of missionaries to go to the uttermost parts of the earth."[93] Dorsett believes the fifth observation arose from Moody's sentimentality over his own poverty. He wanted to help poor children, particularly those from rural New England.[94] These five observations prepared the way for Moody to focus on education.

Moody's newly acquired farm provided the place for the strategy to begin implementation. In the fall of 1878, Moody began purchasing properties that adjoined his farm, with a plan to begin a new school for poor girls. These girls would have no opportunity for education without his intervention. The following spring, construction on the first building began. Knowing the building would not be ready in time to begin school in the fall of 1879, Moody altered his own home in order for studies to begin in November.

---

92. Dorsett, *Passion*, 264–266.
93. Ibid., 266.
94. Ibid.

While he anticipated eight girls the first year, twenty-five showed up. Classes were held in his dining room until the initial building was completed.[95] The evangelist determined not only to provide these girls with an education but also to raise up young ladies who would spend a lifetime serving the Lord.

The same month (November 1879) classes began at the "Northfield Seminary for Girls," Moody purchased one hundred and seventy-five acres to provide a boys' school nearby. With the help of Hiram Camp from Connecticut, an additional 100 acres was purchased to make certain the boys' school would have plenty of property. Preparations began, and the boys' school received its first students on May 4, 1881. The school was named, "Mount Hermon School for Boys."[96] The evangelist, with little formal education of his own, was now the founder of two schools.

Moody's training of laborers continued to expand. On September 26, 1889, "The Bible Institute for Home and Foreign Missions" formally began in Chicago. R. A. Torrey was brought on board to serve as the "superintendent" of the institute. The institute included instruction in Bible study, doctrine, practical ministry, and music. Mornings were spent in the classroom, while evenings were spent doing "practical work among the unconverted."[97] Moody wanted the students to not only gain a strong Biblical foundation and practical ministry skills, but also to gain real life experience in leading people to faith in Jesus.

In addition, Moody started "The Northfield Bible Training School." This school provided training for women who had little education but wanted to serve the Lord. This fourth school began official operations in October 1890.[98] It first met in the Moody's home. Eventually, the ladies moved to the Northfield Hotel. Dorsett notes this to be one of Moody's most successful educational ventures.[99]

While D. L. Moody continued to hold evangelistic campaigns across the United States and England, his later ministry focused on raising up laborers. He trained them to take the gospel to the ends of the earth. Moody had purchased

---

95. William R. Moody, *The Life of D. L. Moody*, 320–321.
96. Ibid., 327.
97. Ibid., 343.
98. Dorsett, *Passion,* 300–301.
99. Ibid.

a small farm to avoid conflict with a neighbor over his mother's chickens. This event would prove to be another major turning point in Moody's life.[100] From this event, Moody became an educational leader of four schools.

The Conference Leader Changed

During a campaign in Cleveland, Ohio, Moody sat listening to H. B. Hartzler speak on the importance of prayer. Dorsett describes the event:

> While Hartzler was speaking, Moody sat attentively in the front row with head bowed.... 'He lifted his head, flashed a glance ... as though struck with a bolt'.... After the meeting Moody rushed up to Hartzler, grabbed him by the arm, and pulled him into the pastor's study. With his usual abruptness he said, 'I want you to come to Northfield next summer. Will you? I want to have a meeting to wait on God. I want you.[101]

With this conversation, the Northfield Summer Conferences were born. Countless lives would be changed through these conferences.

The first conference, held in 1880, was only the beginning. Summer after summer throughout Moody's life and for many years beyond, people from all over the nation and even from the United Kingdom would gather at Northfield for several weeks of conferences. Many were called to ministry at the summer conferences held in Northfield, Massachusetts.

The conferences proved to be a source of refreshment, encouragement, instruction, and a call to reach the world for Jesus. This was true not only for the conference attendees but also for the conference leader himself. It is commonly reported that Moody would gather the conference speakers for private discussion and personal learning.[102] In addition to the private discussions, Moody

---

100. Dorsett, *Passion,* 298–301.
101. Ibid., 346.
102. Not only is this fact mentioned in numerous biographies but also this is a regular part of the presentation one receives about the life of Moody when visiting the Moody Birthplace and Museum. On numerous visits to the Museum with various

learned from the actual conference presentations as well. Moody's son Paul notes, "It was father's frequent custom, after introducing a speaker, to carry a chair down off the platform and sit at the speaker's feet."[103] Such occasions demonstrate Moody's teachable spirit and his own willingness to change when convinced God's Word demanded it.

As will be demonstrated in later chapters, Dwight Moody knew nothing of biblical exposition until the later years of his life and ministry. Yet, he was always willing to learn and to grow. In his earliest days, Moody would speak on biblical concepts without sensing a need to quote Scripture. Thus, through the direction of men like George Mueller and Henry Moorhouse, Moody began to study the Bible himself and included more and more Scripture in his sermons.

In the later years of his life, Moody prevailed upon Dr. Henry Weston, the President of Crozier Theological Seminary, to speak at the Northfield conferences. Weston was known as "an expositor" of the Word. Paul recounts the first time Weston spoke at one of the Northfield Conferences. After introducing the speaker, Moody characteristically carried his chair off the platform and sat at Weston's feet. Shortly after he began his exposition of the text, Weston heard Moody speak out, "There goes one of my sermons."[104] Upon inquiring about his meaning, Moody explained to Weston, in front of the entire conference gathering, that he clearly had been preaching the text wrong. Now that he understood its meaning, he could no longer preach one of his sermons. Later in the exposition Moody again was heard to say, "There goes another."[105] Moody was ready to abandon a popular sermon so that he could accurately preach the Word of God.

Commenting on this event, Paul further notes his dad's desire to proclaim the truth of Scripture accurately: "I have heard learned men deliberately do violence to a text. If my father ever did this it was in ignorance, and such was his honesty that once aware of it he could never do it again. The truth to him was

---

groups, this writer has listened to Mr. Peter Weis, the Northfield/Mount Hermon Archivist, and at least three different curators of the Museum discuss this reality as part of the tour.

103. Paul Moody, *Father*, 185.
104. Ibid.
105. Ibid.

clear enough in the Scripture without need of reading in what was not there or doing violence to what was."[106] Moody desired to preach the Bible accurately and was willing to change his method to do so.

Reading of this event several years ago sent this writer on the journey of analyzing Moody's sermons. The purpose of the analysis was to determine his growth from speaking about biblical concepts, to quoting Scripture, to relying on the Bible as the primary source of his content. Through an analysis of his sermons the following pages will demonstrate the extent to which Moody changed. Time may have prevented him from moving to regular exposition himself. Only a careful analysis of his sermons will show the extent to which Moody adjusted his preaching following this event. This analysis will be the subject of chapters four, five, and six.

Coronation Day

While the conferences filled Moody's summer schedule, he continued holding preaching campaigns throughout the winter months. Moody spent November and December of 1898 holding meetings in several towns in Colorado including: Denver, Greeley, Pueblo, Florence, Canyon City, and Leadville. He spent Christmas in Colorado City.[107] The dawn of 1899 found the evangelist holding meetings in Arizona and California before returning east to speak at Yale.

Following his time at Yale, he returned to Northfield for the 20th anniversary of the start of his educational ventures and to preside over the summer conferences. In November 1899 Moody headed west again, beginning with a campaign in Kansas City.[108] The evangelist did not realize that this preaching engagement would be his last.

---

106. Paul Moody, *Father*, 185–186.
107. Belmonte, *Moody: Life,* 235.
108. One night following a service during this campaign, Moody gathered some of the preachers in the room. As he leaned upon the piano he told them, "Well, I am not a prophet, but I have a guess to make that I think will prove a true prophecy. You hear so much nowadays about the preacher of the twentieth century. Do you know what sort of a man he will be? He will be the sort of preacher who opens his Bible and preachers

From the outset of his arrival in Kansas City, Moody's health began to deteriorate. Dorsett reports, "Moody's keen sense of humor in Kansas City masked a serious ailment. The family later learned that he had suffered heart pain all summer and fall, but he told absolutely no one lest they worry."[109] C. C. Case, the musician for the Kansas City campaign, later indicates, "I could see that he was all the time growing weaker, and the last two days he had to be taken to the hall in a carriage."[110] After preaching on November 16, 1899, a local doctor insisted that Moody notify his family of his health challenges and return home for a time of rest and healing.[111] Moody boarded a train and returned to Northfield.

In the early days of his return to Northfield, it was hoped that with rest his health would be restored, even if it meant he would have to slow down. As the days passed, his condition only worsened. By the time December 22 arrived, everyone knew the end was near.

Most of Moody's waking hours were restless until about six o'clock in the evening. After some sleep, he spoke suddenly, "Earth recedes; Heaven opens before me."[112] Later he spoke again, "This is my triumph; this is my coronation day! I have been looking forward to it for years."[113] Seeming to gain some strength, he later got out of bed and made his way across the room to sit in a chair. Soon his weakening condition led him back to the bed. Writing from an eyewitness account, William reports, "In a few moments more another sinking turn came, and from it he awoke in the presence of Him whom he loved and served so long and devotedly."[114] Moody's time on this earth ended.

Yet, this moment in time was not the end of Dwight Lyman Moody's life. Rather, it was another turning point. Moody himself once declared, "Some day

---

out of that. Oh, I am sick and tired of this essay preaching! I'm nauseated with this 'silver-tongued orator' preaching! I like to hear preachers, and not windmills." See William R. Moody, *The Life of D. L. Moody*, 548.

109. Dorsett, *Passion*, 378.
110. Ibid., 379.
111. Ibid., 380.
112. Ibid., 380.
113. William R. Moody, *The Life of D. L. Moody*, 554.
114. Ibid.

you will read in the papers that D. L. Moody, of East Northfield, is dead.... Don't you believe a word of it! At that moment I shall be more alive than I am now."[115] For the believer, death is but a door to an eternity with God the Father. It is indeed the final turning point in the life of every believer.

Conclusion

Few men have impacted the world with the intensity and longevity of Dwight Lyman Moody. He was born into a humble home in a small Massachusetts village. With the death of his dad, he lived a difficult life of poverty. From that poverty, he arose to face the world as a strong, successful businessman. Like the Apostle Paul, the things that were gain to him, he counted loss for the sake of serving Jesus. Leaving business and a life of comfort behind, he served the Lord, influencing two continents directly. He influenced the world through his schools and his publications. Indeed, Moody continues to influence lives one hundred and twenty-one years after his death.

Having reviewed Moody's life as a life of growth, one must now consider the growth in the content of his sermons. To complete this task adequately, one must have a grid through which to analyze the sermons. Developing a specific sermon rubric will enable the researcher to evaluate Moody's sermons consistently. Development of this rubric serves as the focus of Chapter Three.

---

115. William R. Moody, *The Life of D. L. Moody*, 554–555.

Chapter Three

Methodology For Classifying D. L. Moody's Sermons

As noted in Chapter One, Charles H. Spurgeon and D. L. Moody served as two of the most influential Christian leaders in the latter half of the nineteenth century. While Spurgeon and Moody had much in common, they were different in many ways. Spurgeon served primarily as a pastor, while Moody served primarily as a traveling evangelist. Spurgeon wrote extensively, while Moody preached and gave talks. After Moody's first British campaign, reporters would take down verbatim reports of his orations and publish them in local newspapers. These verbatim reports allowed others to publish his sermons and talks. Spurgeon was known for his excellent speaking abilities, while Moody was often criticized for his lack of oratory skill.[1] Both men were greatly used by God, yet when it came to preaching ability, many homileticians would argue that Spurgeon held the high ground. Still, Moody was used by God to impact millions with the gospel of Jesus Christ.

---

1. Moody's lack of homiletical skill is documented by many. One example can be found in Henry Drummond. Drummond wrote, "As a public speaker up to this time Mr. Moody was the reverse of celebrated. When he first attempted to speak, in Boston, he was promptly told to hold his tongue, and further efforts in Chicago were not less discouraging." Henry Drummond, *Dwight L. Moody: Impressions and Facts* (Whitefish, MIT: Kessinger Publishing's Legacy Reprints, 1900), 64. Another example is found in the writing of A. T. Rowe. He states, "In Mr. Moody's preaching he violated most of the rules of homiletics and many of the rules of English." A. T. Rowe, *D. L. Moody The Soul-Winner* (Anderson, IN: Gospel Trumpet Company, 1927), 87.

D.L. MOODY:
TURNING POINTS TOWARD TEXT-DRIVEN PREACHING

Considering the extensive criticism Moody's preaching received, the question must be asked, "Why would a homiletician examine Moody's sermons today?" In a collection of Moody material, author Harry J. Albus quotes C. I. Scofield's assessment of Moody's preaching:

> As a preacher D. L. Moody was much criticized from the standpoint of academic homiletics. Nor would any think of defending his preaching method on that ground. But the fact that for thirty-five continuous years, in centers of culture and active practical thought in the English-speaking world, this self-taught preacher drew the greatest audiences which have faced any modern speaker on any theme-this fact, one would say, should suggest to teachers of homiletics that possibly they might learn something from him.[2]

Indeed, there is no question that God used Moody's preaching to bring countless individuals to faith in Jesus. Further, many have been motivated by his preaching and his life to forego earthly pursuits and give themselves fully to serving the Lord. As Scofield notes, homileticians would do well to consider his preaching.

Much has been written about Moody, but very little has been written about his preaching. With more than 60 biographies and monographs available today, one would expect to find a plethora of information on Moody's preaching. Biographers tend to give only a few paragraphs, or at best a few pages to his preaching. However, most biographers do at least mention his preaching and this information compels further study.

Before considering how Moody's sermons themselves can be analyzed, part one of this chapter will briefly consider what can be learned from previous writings about him. First, attention will be given to material from some of the more recent biographies. Information from the early biographers serves as

---

2. Harry J. Albus, *A Treasury of Dwight L. Moody* (Grand Rapids: Eerdmans, 1949), 39. While this sentiment is attributed to Scofield in several places, including William R. Moody's biography of his father, this researcher has yet to find the original source that definitively demonstrates whether this assessment was written or spoken by Scofield.

the next source of material. While there have been a handful of dissertation and theses written about D. L. Moody, only two examine his preaching. These scholarly works will also be considered.

Ultimately, to really understand the preaching of Moody, his sermons themselves must be examined. Therefore, the primary focus of this chapter will be to establish a rubric by which the sermons will be considered. To accomplish this task, part two of this chapter will examine various classifications offered by evangelical homileticians. Part three will set forth the proposed description and criteria of four sermon types. A specific rubric will be built using the descriptions and criteria. This rubric will serve as the guide for examining Moody's sermons in Chapters Four through Six. Part four of this chapter will provide a brief description of the sermons that will be evaluated in the following chapters.

Moody's Preaching According to Other Researchers

Recent Biographers

Several works available should be classified as relatively recent, the oldest being written in 1963, and the latest written in 2014. Biographies seek to describe the entirety of a man or woman rather than simply one aspect. Such a description is true of the many biographies of D. L. Moody. However, no biography of the preacher could help but speak to the unique nature and impact of his sermons.

Summary of Findings

Many of the biographers' comments are of a general nature and have only a little bearing on the subject at hand. This type of information can be represented by the comments from James Findlay Jr. He writes about the early days of Moody's speaking in relationship to the children's Sunday School movement: "The evangelist evidently had the knack of speaking quite effectively to a mixed

D.L. MOODY:
TURNING POINTS TOWARD TEXT-DRIVEN PREACHING

audience of children and grown-ups."[3] He continues by discussing how adults began coming to hear Moody while he spoke to the children.

Another biographer, Burnham Carter, gives a historical account of the Northfield and Mount Hermon schools. He writes, "He was not an orator. He did not write his sermons, and when he attempted to do so later for book publication, they did not read well. The words needed the man: they had to be illuminated by his faith and warmed by his love."[4] Carter's brief comment about Moody's preaching fits well with most biographers' accounts.

At times, the information discovered leaves one wondering how to take the claim. For instance, John Pollock quotes "a learned theological professor," saying, "It is perfectly astounding to me that a man with so little training should have come to understand the public so well. He cannot read the Greek Testament; indeed he has difficulty with parts of it in the English version, but he excels any man I ever heard in making his hearers see the point of the text of Scripture."[5] Two problems occur with this statement.

First, Pollock fails to identify the "learned theological professor." Second, the quotation does not allow the reader to understand the professor's assessment of Moody's preaching. Pollock certainly was amazed at Moody's ability to understand human nature and to make "his hearers see the point of the text of Scripture." However, without additional context readers do not know what the professor means by "point of the text." This comment could indicate the professor believes Moody preached the main exegetical idea of a passage in an understanding way. The note could also mean simply that Moody made a point from the text and applied it to the lives of his listeners. Pollock leaves the researcher unsure about the meaning of his quotation.

Findlay makes a similar statement that may also be taken as evidence for an exegetical component to Moody's sermons. He writes, "When reading Scripture the evangelist spoke slowly, as though repeating a difficult matter to a small child. Frequently particular passages evoked digressions for exposition and

---

3. James F. Findlay Jr., *Dwight L. Moody, American Evangelist, 1837–1899* (Chicago: The University of Chicago Press, 1969), 111.

4. Burnham Carter, *So Much to Learn* (Northfield, MA: Northfield Mount Hermon School, 1976), 17–18.

5. John Pollock, *Moody* (Chicago: Moody Press, 1983), 215.

explanation."[6] This quotation could be taken as evidence that Moody indeed involved himself in "exposition" of Scripture. On the next page, however, Findlay makes a statement that causes one to question his meaning of "exposition." Concerning Moody, he states, "His success lay primarily in his ability to tell a story, to recite a piquant anecdote, to inject pathos and humor into the biblical accounts he used repeatedly in his sermons."[7] This tension in Findlay's analysis will be briefly discussed in the section below.

In 1971, Wilbur Smith committed to the task of editing sixteen of Moody's sermons for publication. In the introduction to the book, he makes several comments about the evangelist's approach to preaching. Smith argues Moody's sermons focus on two primary objectives: the salvation of the lost and the engagement of believers in the Lord's work. He further indicates Moody had a unique ability to use illustrations—an ability greater than any other preacher of his day. Speaking of this fact Smith writes, "Sometimes two-thirds of an entire sermon would consist only of a series of illustrations."[8] Such a comment leads the exegetical preacher to be suspect of the driving force behind the content of Moody's sermons. Smith's comment raises the question whether Moody placed too much focus on illustration and not enough on explanation.

Two years before the 100th anniversary of Moody's death, Lyle Dorsett wrote an updated biography from an evangelical perspective. Citing evidence from A. T. Pierson and an unnamed lady who heard Moody preach on several occasions, he describes the evangelist's sermons as riddled with stories and anecdotes that prepared the heart to receive the truth of the gospel.[9] The emphasis again is on telling illustrative stories. Though this information alone does not compel one to abandon hope of finding an exegetical basis for Moody's sermons, taken with the previous statements from Smith, it certainly seems to indicate a weakness in exegetical and expositional content.

---

6. Findlay Jr., *American Evangelist*, 222.

7. Ibid., 223.

8. Wilbur M. Smith, *The Best of D. L. Moody* (Chicago: Moody Press, 1971), 16.

9. Lyle W. Dorsett, *A Passion for Souls, The Life of D. L. Moody* (Chicago: Moody Publishers, 1997), 184–185.

D.L. MOODY:
TURNING POINTS TOWARD TEXT-DRIVEN PREACHING

As noted in Chapter Two, Dorsett indicates a shift in the driving force of Moody's sermons that began shortly after returning from his first trip to England. Henry Moorhouse came to visit Moody in Chicago. Though believing the young man to be incapable of doing a good job, Moody gave him an opportunity to preach. After Moorhouse preached for seven nights, the evangelist changed his view and began a life-long friendship with the young preacher. Dorsett claims Moorhouse influenced Moody in two ways. First, he compelled Moody to consider the love of God and emphasize it more than he ever had before. Second, he spoke to Moody about his preaching by compelling the evangelist to spend more time studying and proclaiming the Bible itself rather than his own opinions.[10] The change in Moody's preaching after Moorhouse's visit is readily acknowledged by most biographers.

Analysis

Burnham Carter's account certainly does not purpose to examine the preaching of the evangelist. He focuses on explaining the founding and development of Moody's Massachusetts schools. There is no evangelical concern in Carter's presentation. By 1976, the school no longer had an evangelical emphasis. Despite this reality, Carter could not discuss Moody without making some reference to his preaching. Carter also had to acknowledge that preaching was Moody's primary concern. Due to this emphasis, Carter had to make at least a brief statement about the style of Moody's sermons. However, this statement does not help this researcher determine much about the content of Moody's sermons.

Findlay approached Moody from the perspective of a historian. This approach may account for the fact that he presents statements which can be taken as indicators of both an expositional and a non-expositional approach. His lack of evangelical purpose may suggest an understanding of the word "exposition" different from the understanding of an evangelical homiletician. Indeed, Findlay

---

10. Dorsett, *A Passion For Souls, The Life of D. L. Moody*, 140.

may see Moody's stories and applications as sufficient explanation of the term "exposition." This perspective may be all he intended by the use of the term.

Smith and Dorsett support a clear evangelical perspective. Both men indicate a lack of hermeneutical concern in Moody's sermons. Both are grateful for Moody's life and work and would not attempt to cast doubt about the man's usefulness in God's economy. However, both men also take an honest look at the preacher they admire. Dorsett certainly attempts to indicate a change in Moody's approach with a greater emphasis on the text of Scripture itself as time progressed. Neither man intended their works to be a full analysis of Moody's sermons. Their statements should be considered, but leave this researcher wanting more.

Early Biographers

Having gained a sense of the recent biographers' view of Moody's preaching, attention now turns to writers closer to Moody's day. Indeed, many of the following authors knew him well and heard him preach first hand. These men enjoyed the benefit of analyzing his sermons while he spoke. They also had the opportunity to talk with him and get his perspective on his preaching. Students of Moody are greatly indebted to these works.

Summary of Findings

Henry Drummond, a good friend of Moody, produced a biography published the year following Moody's death. He made several statements about Moody's sermons, all of which are very complimentary. According to Drummond, "He knew only two books, the Bible and Human Nature."[11] Drummond found it difficult to answer why Moody's sermons were so effective. The most crucial ingredient he found was Moody's strong conviction. A second characteristic Drummond believed important was the "pointed" nature of every word.

---

11. Henry Drummond, *Dwight L. Moody* (New York: McClure, Phillips & Co, 1900), 66.

D.L. MOODY:
TURNING POINTS TOWARD TEXT-DRIVEN PREACHING

A final consideration was Moody's unparalleled persuasiveness.[12] Drummond recognized that God used Moody greatly but considered the method of delivery the reason for his effectiveness. He failed to give evidence that would suggest the sermons were text-driven.

In this same vein, Charles Erdman claims "the supreme quality of his delivery was his earnestness ... always moved by intense moral passion."[13] Another key to Moody's effectiveness according to Erdman was his love for people. Erdman states, "Moody made men feel that he loved them, and he did love them."[14] Like Drummond, Erdman had great respect for Moody but found his effectiveness in his passion more than in his content.

The first authorized biography of D. L. Moody originated from the hand of his oldest son, William. William rushed to get the book published in 1900, attempting to fulfill his dad's desire. He later revised the original work, and published anew in 1930. William described his dad's early speaking method at his "Bible Reading" sessions:

> He would call upon someone in the audience to read a certain text. This would give him time to collect his thoughts, and he would then say a few words or relate an anecdote to light up the text. When he found himself running dry, he would call for another text to be read, and on this he would offer a few comments in a similar fashion.[15]

William's assessment of the early years indicates that Moody spoke whatever came to mind in the moment, rather than presenting instruction based upon careful exegesis.

Speaking of his later years, Moody's younger son Paul indicated his father spent much time in preparation for preaching. Describing times when the family would be on vacation, Paul notes even then his dad "... rose early and retreated to his upstairs study, where he worked for a time. His work usually consisted

---

12. Drummond, *Dwight L. Moody*, 68–69.
13. Charles R. Erdman, *D. L. Moody, His Message For Today* (New York: Fleming H. Revell Co, 1928), 99.
14. Ibid., 100.
15. William R. Moody, *Life of D. L. Moody*, 438.

in the days when I knew him of preparing new sermons, writing outlines and reading what related to what he was preparing his notes about."[16] In contrast to William, Paul (who was much younger) watched his dad spend significant time in study during his later years.

In a biography of Moody, J. Wilbur Chapman gives an extensive quotation from Moody concerning his preaching and studying the Bible. He quotes Moody as saying,

> [I]t is not the man now that makes a fine oration in the pulpit so much as it is a man that expounds the Word of God that we need.... The churches are not now hunting after a man that will make a grand oration, so much as they are for a man that will unfold to them the Word of God.[17]

There are two key words in this quotation. The word "expounds" and the word "unfold" could convey a concern for text-driven preaching. However, on the same page Chapman points out that Moody encouraged his listeners to "Take the Bible topically."[18] As an example Moody said, "Suppose you spend three or four months reading all you can find about love; after that you will be full of love."[19] Chapman's contribution leaves one wondering if Moody's use of the terms "expounds" and "unfold" convey a text-driven model.

When considering the content of Moody's sermons, Erdman makes several additional comments of significance. He argues that Moody's knowledge of the Bible developed slowly. In the early days, Moody's attempts at teaching the Bible were filled with personal anecdotes and stories he heard from others. He did not focus on explaining the Scripture itself. Erdman speaks of Moorhouse's influence on Moody as well. He quotes Moorhouse as telling Moody, "You are sailing on the wrong track. If you will change your course, and learn to preach

---

16. Paul Moody, *My Father* (Boston: Little, Brown and Company, 1938), 38–39.

17. J. Wilbur Chapman, *The Life & Work of Dwight Lyman Moody* (Philadelphia: American Bible House, 1900), 1–10, http://biblebelievers.com/moody/25.html (accessed October 29, 2008).

18. Ibid.

19. Ibid.

D.L. MOODY:
TURNING POINTS TOWARD TEXT-DRIVEN PREACHING

God's words instead of your own, He will make you a great power for good."[20] Moorhouse certainly influenced Moody to begin formulating his sermons from texts of Scripture.

At this point in Moody's life, Moorhouse's influence seems to have led him to a more topical approach of study and presentation. Erdman notes the evangelist's method of study:

> As to the secret of his sermon-making he said: 'I have no secret; I study more by subjects than I do by texts. If when I am reading, I meet a good thing on any of these subjects, I slip it in the right envelope and let it lie there. I always carry a notebook, and if I hear anything in a sermon that will throw light on that subject, I put it down. Perhaps I let it lie for a year or more. When I want a sermon I take everything that has been accumulating. Between what I find there and the results of my own study I have material enough. Then, I am all the time going over my sermons, taking out a little here and adding a little there. In that way they never get very old.[21]

From the time of Moorhouse's instruction, it appears that Moody began spending more time in study and preparation. That preparation was guided by the study of topics. He collected all he could find on a topic and then reviewed the material before preaching a text.

Holding the Fort is a collection of Moody's sermons gathered by M. Laird Simons. Simons wrote an introduction to the work. In that introduction, he cites Moody's perspective on study:

> I think I have the key to the study of the Bible: take it up topically. Take love for instance, and spend a month in studying what the Bible says about love, from Genesis to Revelation.... Spend six months studying Genesis; it is the key to the whole book;... Read the same chapter over and over again, and don't leave it until you have understood it.[22]

---

20. Erdman, *D. L. Moody: His Message*, 40–42.
21. Ibid.
22. M. Laird Simons, ed., *Holding the Fort* (Cincinnati: United States Book and Bible Company, 1879), xxii.

Simons' quotation fails to offer much help in understanding Moody's primary method of studying the Bible in preparation for preaching. The first part of the quotation seems to indicate a thematic approach on Moody's part. However, the final statement may indicate that Moody understood the importance of studying a verse within the textual context. In the end, one must look elsewhere to discover Moody's typical practice at this stage of his ministry.

Analysis

Drummond's statements provide a strong assessment of the effectiveness of Moody's preaching from one of his contemporaries. However, his comments say more about the delivery than about the content of Moody's sermons. Erdman's early statements fall into this same category. Although they are thought-provoking, they do not really help with the question of this monograph.

William Moody's biography cannot be ignored by anyone who desires to understand William Moody's father. Despite their disagreements, William's younger brother Paul described William's work as, "The one authoritative biography... and the one to which future students of his life must turn for accurate information.... My brother struggled hard to make it as objective as possible."[23] Most biographers rely heavily on Williams's work. He is often quoted by others who attempt to describe Moody's life, whether in a full biography or in a brief assessment. William's presentation of his dad continues to be the most authoritative biography.

William does not embellish his dad's early speaking. He simply describes the pattern Moody followed. The pattern appears to be one of extemporaneous speech that relates to the various verses read. Moody's instruction came from the immediate impressions of the speaker, rather than from concentrated study. This assessment indicates Moody's preaching was very practical in orientation but lacking in exegetical content.

Paul Moody does not claim to be writing a formal biography or a historical account of his dad's life. Rather, he shares stories and impressions from his own relationship with his dad. His comments must be understood with this caveat

---

23. Simmons ed., *Holding The Fort*, 206.

D.L. MOODY:
TURNING POINTS TOWARD TEXT-DRIVEN PREACHING

recognized. In addition, it must be realized that he intentionally moved away from a conservative evangelical perspective on Scripture and other doctrinal issues. Therefore, he would most likely be more inclined to accept preaching that emphasized "what the verse means to me," rather than simply "what does the verse mean."

Paul's recollections demonstrate that by the time he began to take notice, his dad was concerned with studying the Bible and being prepared for preaching. His story of the visit by Dr. Weston indicates a lack of hermeneutical accuracy in Moody's early and middle years. However, his story also demonstrates that when Moody was convinced of the correct interpretation of a passage, he adjusted his own thinking. He was even willing to jettison earlier sermon content based on a clearer understanding of a text of Scripture.

Chapman's quotations of Moody concerning "the need of the hour," demonstrate a desire for biblical preaching. Moody's statement about needing preachers who will "unfold" the Scripture before the people, leads one to assume an exegetical concern. Yet, in light of his statements about a topical approach, the question remains as to the meaning of "unfold." It is possible that Moody simply meant that verses should be studied by cross referencing words without regard to context, then illustrated and applied to everyday life when preaching.

Erdman's later comments support the claim of growth in Moody. His assessment indicates that early on the preacher was not too concerned about explaining a biblical text. As time progressed, however, Moody became more and more committed to the accuracy of both his interpretation and his presentation. Yet, even after these developments, it appears Moody was more inclined to follow a thematic approach. The description from Moody's own mouth seems to indicate that a topical approach primarily drove the content of his preaching.

Simons' evaluation of Moody provides somewhat contradictory information. He quotes Moody directly, indicating that he believes a topical approach is best. Once again, this evaluation would lend itself to having a more thematic instead of an exegetical concern. Still one is left with uncertainty because Moody also encouraged the reader to continue in a single chapter of Scripture until he or she fully understood it. This statement could argue for a contextual emphasis that could overrule the thematic concerns, learned simply by using a concordance to follow every mention of a particular topic. In the end, Simons fails to resolve the issue at hand.

What has been demonstrated thus far can be summarized in five statements: 1) Moody's unique preaching impacted the lives of millions of people in his own day and beyond. 2) His sermons were marked by the power of God and the persuasion of men. 3) There seems to be a development from the early days of simply talking about biblical truths to being concerned with sharing the Bible itself. 4) His messages began to take on a topical format without losing their illustrative nature. 5) Moody may have had a greater concern for hermeneutical accuracy in his later years. While the various biographers' information has been somewhat helpful, more information is needed. Focus will now shift to consider what can be learned from a dissertation and a thesis that assess Moody.

A Dissertation and A Thesis

There are two works that should be noted in the context of this study. The first is a Master's Thesis presented to the University of Michigan by Richard Curtis in 1954. While the material is well written and considers Moody's sermons, the primary focus of the thesis is a comparison of words used by D. L. Moody and words used by Billy Graham.[24] The work contributes to understanding Moody's word choice in his preaching, but does not assess the biblical content of his sermons. Rollin W. Quimby presented a PhD dissertation to the University of Michigan in 1951. Quimby's approach centered on finding reasons for Moody's success in the historical context of his day, along with an examination of the rhetorical factors evidenced in Moody's sermons. He states his purpose on the first page of the dissertation: "This investigation is an attempt to discover the historical and rhetorical factors which contributed to Moody's greatness as an evangelistic speaker."[25] Following a brief introduction, the author dedicates ten chapters to present his findings, followed by four appendixes and an extensive

---

24. Richard Curtis, "The Pulpit Speaking of Dwight L. Moody" (MA thesis, Michigan: University Microfilms, 1954).

25. Rollin Walker Quimby, "Dwight L. Moody: An Examination of the Historical Conditions and Rhetorical Factors which Contributed to His Effectiveness as a Speaker" (PhD diss., University of Michigan, Ann Arbor, MI: University Press, 1951), 1.

bibliography.[26] While any scholarly researcher of Moody will want to read this work, it too fails to address the issues of concern to the present writer. Attention must shift to Moody's sermons themselves.

In order to understand the development of Moody's preaching in relationship to the text of Scripture, a thorough examination of his sermons is essential. A sampling of sermons from his speaking prior to Henry Moorhouse's Chicago visit must first be considered. Sermons preached during the revivals of the 1870s also require an analysis. Finally, sermons preached by the evangelist during the last eight years of his life must be studied. In order to give a consistent and fair examination of the content of each sermon, a pre-determined description and criteria of various sermon types will be established. Part two of this chapter moves in that direction, with a consideration of various approaches used by evangelical preachers to classify sermons.

Various Approaches to Classifying Sermons

Preaching itself has been under attack for many decades in the American context. In fact, Fred Craddock argued that preaching has always been on the defensive. He states, "These are not new sounds; to a large extent, the pulpit has from the first century received poor reviews."[27] The attacks of the last fifty years have, in reality, led to "… a resurgence of interest in preaching, in all segments of the church. An avalanche of books, periodicals, seminars, and other programs testify to a hunger for information and assistance in strengthening the ministry of the pulpit."[28] With the plethora of perspectives on the preaching

---

26. Ibid. Quimby effectively argued that while Moody may have never been trained in the principles of rhetoric, he exhibited rhetorical skills in his preaching. He spoke of the importance of pathos, ethos, and logos. Moody certainly demonstrated skill in pathos and ethos, even if it simply came to him naturally. While Quimby recognizes the historical conditions of his day contributed to Moody's success, he demonstrates that it is a misunderstanding to assume Moody did not possess good rhetorical skills.

27. Fred B. Craddock, *As One Without Authority* (Nashville: Abingdon Press, 1979), 1.

28. Michael Duduit, ed., *Handbook of Contemporary Preaching: A Wealth of*

task available in print today, one inevitably finds various ways of responding to the attacks on preaching. Some desire to reduce its presence in the church, while others call for a reinvigoration of historical models of preaching.[29] In between these two positions, one will find various approaches to enhance the sermon's position in the church today.

This writer approaches the topic of preaching from a conservative evangelical perspective. The Bible is the Word of God. It is inspired (God-breathed), infallible, and inerrant. The Bible is the final authority for all matters of faith and practice. Though it is not a strictly historical book nor a book of science, where it speaks to these topics, it speaks truthfully and accurately. God cannot lie. While he used men with their unique personalities, styles, and emphasis in the writing of his Word, he superintended the process by his Spirit. Thus, he ensured the accuracy of the human authors' writings.

In light of the doctrinal stance of this writer described in the previous paragraph, this paper will consider classifications and definitions of various types of sermons from recognized conservative evangelical works. A consideration of the various methods and classifications that lie beyond the above-described presuppositions are beyond the scope of this monograph. We will now consider ways sermons are classified in a few of the leading evangelical works on the subject at hand.

Power in the Pulpit

Power in the Pulpit, written by Jerry Vines and Jim Shaddix, is based upon two earlier works on preaching authored by Vines. A revised edition appeared in 2017 from the same authors, though Shaddix added significant material and additional organization to the earlier works.[30] The focus of this monograph

---

Counsel for Creative and Effective Proclamation (Nashville: Broadman Press, 1992), 9.

29. For a discussion of the various positions on dealing with the attacks on preaching today see David W. Henderson, *Culture Shift* (Grand Rapids: Baker Books, 1998).

30. In June of 2017, Vines and Shaddix released a newly revised edition of *Power in the Pulpit*. In the revised edition, the authors chose to focus all the attention on expository preaching. They gave a shorter and more precise definition on page 31 and then unpacked that definition over the next ten pages. The new approach de-emphasizes

D.L. MOODY:
TURNING POINTS TOWARD TEXT-DRIVEN PREACHING

is the preparation and delivery of expository sermons. However, in the first chapter, the authors not only define expository sermons but they also provide a snapshot definition of seven other sermon types under the heading, "Traditional Sermon Models."

Vines and Shaddix define the "Expository Sermon" as "A discourse that expounds a passage of Scripture, organizes it around a central theme and main divisions which issue forth from the given text, and then decisively applies its message to the listeners."[31] The remaining portion of the book focuses on helping the reader understand how to prepare both the preacher and the sermon. It also demonstrates how to present the sermon thus prepared. Before moving further into the purpose of the book, the authors identify and describe the following types of "traditional sermons."

Power in the Pulpit describes one type of "traditional sermon," the "Topical Sermon," as follows: "The topical sermon is built around some particular subject . . . Usually the preacher gathers what the Bible teaches about one particular topic, organizes those passages into a logical presentation, and then delivers a topical sermon."[32] In this description, the topic may or may not come from a specific text of Scripture, but it is filled with scriptural content. This type of sermon contains both reading and/or quotation of various verses from the Bible, but the verses are arranged according to the preacher's purpose.

Vines and Shaddix also provide an explanation of the "Textual Sermon": "A textual sermon is one based on one or two verses from the Bible. The main theme and major divisions of the sermon come from the text itself. This sermon seeks

---

the divisions of the sermon being based on the divisions of the text. The new approach also emphasizes the intent of the Holy Spirit in a *Sensus Plenior* fashion, arguing for a Christocentric approach to every sermon. The present writer chose to utilize the 1999 edition of the book, believing the multiple definitions provided in that edition were more helpful to the purpose of this chapter. However, the reader is encouraged to carefully examine the definition and explanation provided in the new edition. It provides much helpful information. Jerry Vines and Jim Shaddix, *Power in the Pulpit: How to Prepare and Deliver Expository Sermons,* (rev. ed., Chicago: Moody Press, 2017), 31–41.

31. Jerry Vines and Jim Shaddix, *Power in the Pulpit: How to Prepare And Delivery Expository Sermons* (Chicago: Moody Press, 1999), 29.

32. Ibid.

to expound what the text itself actually says."[33] The main distinction that Vines and Shaddix make between expository sermons and textual sermons comes in the size of the passage preached. According to the authors, exposition typically focuses on a paragraph, while a textual sermon focuses on one or two verses. While both types are viewed as somewhat "text-driven," the typical exposition keeps the verse(s) in context and relies more on the emphasis of the author.

A third type of "traditional sermon" discussed by Vines and Shaddix is the "Narrative Sermon." The authors distinguish between the traditional understanding of narrative preaching versus the contemporary usage of the concept. Traditionally, the concept referred to sermons preached from narrative passages of Scripture. The emphasis was on the genre of the passage preached: "However, some homileticians have defined it by sermonic form instead of literary genre. Thus, contemporary narrative sermons frequently encompass those messages that, from the outset to conclusion, bind the entire message to a single plot as theme."[34] According to their classification, the concept of narrative may either refer to the genre of the passage or the sermonic form of the message.

A fourth type of "traditional sermon" is the "Biographical Sermon." The emphasis here is on presenting the life of a biblical character: "The facts about that particular character form the basis for a message with contemporary application."[35] Chuck Swindoll has been particularly noted for presenting this type of sermon over the last twenty years. D. L. Moody enjoyed preaching on biblical characters as well. In the coming chapters, we will consider sermons Moody preached on Jacob, Joshua, Peter, and Moses, just to name a few. In addition, he preached a sermon on Daniel many times over.

A "Dramatic Monologue Sermon" is a fifth "traditional sermon" type. In this approach to the message the preacher "… acts out the message of the character, often dressing himself in the authentic biblical attire."[36] This method tends to engage the attention of the hearers by engaging not only their ears but also their sight and their imagination. Done well, this method can be both very engaging and very biblical in content.

---

33. Vines and Jim Shaddix, *Power in the Pulpit*, 29.
34. Ibid., 21.
35. Ibid., 30.
36. Ibid., 30.

A sixth "traditional sermon" type is the "Theological Sermon." It is similar to a topical sermon, but one that is doctrinal in nature. The reason the authors present it as a separate category is that they believe that in this method, the sermons "usually rely more on references to general theological concepts in Scripture than on specific texts themselves."[37] This writer sees very little distinction between this type of sermon and a topical sermon that is doctrinal.

The seventh sermon type is the "Ethical Sermon." It is defined as a discourse that "... is based upon a specific Bible motif that teaches the believer an ethical lesson. The purpose is to build Bible morality into the members of the congregation."[38] This type of sermon should be placed under the broader category of being topical in nature. It is a specific type of topical sermon, but it still follows a topic. The distinction to be made is that the topic is an ethical one rather than a theological, or practical ministry topic.

Handbook of Contemporary Preaching

The *Handbook of Contemporary Preaching* is edited by Michael Duduit. The book's purpose is summarized on the first page of its introduction: "This Handbook reflects the need to provide, in a single volume, an accessible overview of the contemporary preaching scene."[39] The book is divided into nine sections. Part One examines the roots of preaching in the late twentieth century. Part Two describes the most prominent preaching methods of the day. The process of sermon preparation serves as the focus of Part Three. Insights into preaching the various genres of Scripture provide the subject matter of Part Four. The actual proclamation of the sermon serves as the subject of Part Five. Part Six considers how preaching interacts with the other areas of ministry. All people have needs, and the role of preaching in meeting those needs provides content to Part Seven. Part Eight consists of three final chapters that address issues of special consideration in the late twentieth century. An extensive bibliography fills the pages of the ninth and final part of the book.

---

37. Vines and Jim Shaddix, *Power in the Pulpit*, 30.
38. Ibid.
39. Duduit, ed., *Handbook of Contemporary Preaching*, 9.

Part Two presents information pertinent to the subject at hand. Chapter Five, written by Paul Borden, discusses "Expository Preaching." An examination of "Textual Preaching" provides the content of Chapter Six, presented by Al Fasol. Francis C. Rossow considers "Topical Preaching" in the seventh chapter. Chapter Eight, written by Timothy George, focuses the reader's attention on the topic of "Doctrinal Preaching." Calvin Miller presents a discussion of "Narrative Preaching" in Chapter Nine. The final chapter of this section, written by Bryan Chapell, considers "alternative models" of preaching.

In his chapter on expository preaching, Borden determined to describe exposition in a series of characteristics rather than supply the reader with a definition. His characteristics are as follows: 1) "A clear statement of the primary biblical idea that is legitimately derived from a passage or passages."[40] 2) "The structure of the sermon must be consistent with the structure of the text or texts."[41] 3) "The sermon must be relevant to listeners."[42] 4) "The idea, outline, applications, illustrations, and assertions must fit with each other as well as with the context and intent of the biblical text."[43] Borden's characteristics can easily be reconciled with the definition offered by Vines and Shaddix above. In fact, the two approaches offer a great description of expository preaching. Combining the definition of Vines and Shaddix with the description of Borden provide a well-rounded understanding of what an expository sermon entails.

Al Fasol presents a short chapter on the concept of textual preaching. He begins his chapter by suggesting that this type of preaching has fallen on hard times. Some reject it altogether. Others give it a nod but eclipse the method by emphasizing expository preaching instead. He then presents a quick survey of the field, describing how a handful of evangelical preachers have described textual preaching. He concludes, "The concept of textual preaching is still with us. However, Brown, Greidanus, Thompson, and others have pointed the way to a better understanding of preaching by assessing its biblical authority and its biblical purpose rather than by describing preaching by just its form alone."[44] In

---

40. Duduit, ed., *Handbook of Contemporary Preaching*, 63.
41. Ibid., 64.
42. Ibid.
43. Ibid.
44. Ibid., 82.

the end, Fasol fails to add anything to the basic definition presented above by Vines and Shaddix.

Concerning topical preaching, Francis C. Rossow states,

> I call a sermon 'topical' when the preacher is free to choose a text from the Bible rather than preach on the pericope assigned by the lectionary; when the preacher has an idea and then searches for a biblical text (or texts) treating that idea; even when the preacher writes on an assigned text but feels free to develop the sermon without rigid adherence to the structure of the text and without the compulsion to deal fully with every verse, phrase, or word in that text.[45]

Many evangelicals do not follow the lectionary. This definition would most certainly declare all sermons outside the lectionary assigned passages as topical. The result of this definition is that any sermon not based on the lectionary must be viewed as topical. This reduction is obviously problematic to the many evangelicals who attempt to preach expositional sermons, but who do not utilize the lectionary.

The primary key, however, to understanding Rossow's definition resides in the statement that the preacher "… feels free to develop the sermon without rigid adherence to the structure of the text and without the compulsion to deal fully with every verse, phrase, or word in that text."[46] The consistent element is that the topical sermon does not follow the structure of the passage under consideration. While this definition is not as clear as Vines and Shaddix, one can find similarities between the two definitions.

In Chapter Eight, Timothy George attempts to reject the strong distinction often made between doctrinal preaching and expository preaching. He states, "Every doctrinal sermon must be contextually rooted in sound exegesis; and every expository or biblical sermon should place a given passage in the widest theological framework possible."[47] He presents a model of exposition that has a heavy doctrinal element to it. George's approach to doctrinal preaching is

---

45. Duduit, ed., *Handbook of Contemporary Preaching*, 85.
46. Ibid.
47. Ibid., 96.

clearly different from the description Vines and Shaddix offer for either their topical doctrine approach or their theological category. Rather, George suggests that doctrinal preaching should be rooted in exposition.

Calvin Miller discusses Narrative Preaching in Chapter Nine: "The narrative sermon, rather than containing stories, is a story, which from the outset to conclusion, binds the entire sermon to a single plot as theme."[48] Though not mentioned by Vines and Shaddix, their summary definition of narrative preaching was heavily influenced by Miller's chapter in the *Handbook of Contemporary Preaching*. While Vines and Shaddix present two types of narrative preaching, Miller's definition is virtually identical.

The final chapter on the topic of sermon types in the *Handbook of Contemporary Preaching*, is written by Bryan Chapell and considers "alternative models" of presentation. A careful reading of the chapter demonstrates that the emphasis is less on what drives the content of the sermon, as in the previous models considered, and more on the presentation of the content. Indeed, Chapell suggests, "Best friends never seem to change. Proportions may vary and appearances may mature; but, deep down, best friends stay the same. The same is true of preaching . . . . The sermons that communicate well demonstrate unity, organization, truth-establishment, creativity, and application."[49] Chapell continues by distinguishing between various types of "three-phase models," "two-phase models," and "single-phase models."[50] In the final section of the chapter, the author examines the communication model often found in radio and television preachers. He compares and contrasts this model with the typical "informational model" of church preaching.[51] These various models do not offer new information for consideration in this chapter. They are simply new ways to present topical, expositional, or textual sermons.

---

48. Duduit, ed., *Handbook of Contemporary Preaching*, 103.
49. Ibid., 117.
50. Ibid., 117–126.
51. Ibid., 126–130.

Biblical Preaching

Many evangelical preachers today would consider *Biblical Preaching* by Haddon Robinson one of the standard textbooks on expository preaching. Robinson's contribution to the topic has influenced many preachers and academic scholars in the field. While Robinson's purpose was similar to that of Vines and Shaddix, he chose not to provide a definition of any of the other types of sermons. Instead, his entire focus is on the concept of exposition.

Robinson acknowledged the difficulty in defining preaching. He states, "Preaching is a living process involving God, the preacher, and the congregation, and no definition can pretend to capture that dynamic."[52] However, the author realizes the need for a working definition and presents this offering:

> Expository preaching is the communication of a biblical concept, derived from and transmitted through a historical, grammatical, and literary study of a passage in its context, which the Holy Spirit first applies to the personality and experience of the preacher, then through him to his hearers.[53]

While Robinson's definition does not contradict that of Vines and Shaddix, it is not as precise. For instance, his definition says nothing specifically about the structure and divisions of the sermon. Robinson may assume that an expository sermon is based on the structure and divisions of the text, but he does not state this explicitly. Therefore, the present writer would prefer the definition offered by Vines and Shaddix. Indeed, Robinson's definition provides very little room to distinguish textual and expositional preaching.

---

52. Haddon Robinson, *Biblical Preaching: The Development and Delivery of Expository Messages* (Grand Rapids: Baker Book House, 1994), 19.

53. Robinson, *Biblical Preaching*, 21.

Engaging Exposition

In 2011, Daniel L. Akin, Bill Curtis, and Stephen Rummage presented a thorough monograph titled, *Engaging Exposition*.[54] In the first section of this work, Curtis offers ten chapters on discovering the meaning of the text. Akin moves from discovery to development in the second section of the book. Rummage guides the reader through preparing for delivery of the sermon in the final ten chapters.

In the introduction Akin states, "If we were limited to 10 words or less, we would define faithful, expository preaching as, '*Christ centered, text driven, Spirit led preaching that transforms lives.*'"[55] He then expands on the definition:

> Expository preaching is text driven preaching that honors the truth of Scripture as it was given by the Holy Spirit. Its goal is to discover the God-inspired meaning through historical-grammatical-theological investigation and interpretation. By means of engaging and compelling proclamation, the preacher explains, illustrates and applies the meaning of the biblical text in submission to and in the power of the Holy Spirit, preaching Christ for a verdict of changed lives.[56]

In this full definition, the authors provide a thorough description of expository preaching, which is fleshed out in the thirty chapters that follow.

While Vines and Shaddix expand Robinson's definition, the definition offered in *Engaging Exposition* presents even more detail. The three definitions do not contradict one another, but each one offers a unique feature. In the end, *Engaging Exposition* and *Power in the Pulpit* agree that the main issue at hand is, in fact, presenting a message that is true to the meaning of the passage within its context. This writer finds things he likes about both definitions. Akin's definition emphasizes both grammatical-historical interpretation and a strong

---

54. Daniel L. Akin, Bill Curtis, and Stephen Rummage, *Engaging Exposition* (Nashville: B&H Academic, 2011), 2.

55. Ibid.

56. Akin, Curtis, and Rummage, *Engaging Exposition*, 2.

reliance on the work of the Holy Spirit. Vines and Shaddix include a statement about the divisions of the sermon. They indicate that the sermon divisions should follow the divisions of the text itself. This writer believes that following the author's divisions in the text strengthens a sermon and causes the message to be truly text-driven.

Summary

Having surveyed a handful of evangelical writers' approach to the classification of sermons, we must determine what types of categories we will use as a guide in examining the preaching of Dwight Lyman Moody. Four categories described above will form the basis of our consideration. These categories guide the development of a sermon rubric that will be used in analyzing Moody's sermons.

It should be noted that from the list above, this author chose to consider Topical Sermons, Biographical Sermons, Textual Sermons, and Expositional Sermons. As noted previously, theological and ethical sermons can be understood as sub-categories of topical messages. While Moody's sermons were filled with stories, this researcher has never found one that would come close to being considered a "narrative sermon" in the modern sense of the word. Therefore, this category will not be part of his consideration. Dramatic monologues can be viewed as a sub-category of biographical sermons; therefore, they will not be treated as a separate category. In the final section of this chapter, attention will be given to the author's description of each category and the specific criteria that will be used to guide the examination of Moody's messages.

Criteria for Analyzing Moody's Sermons

Part one of this chapter establishes the need to develop criteria by which this author will examine Moody's sermons in chapters Four through Six. Part two surveys various classifications found in some of the standard conservative evangelical texts on preaching. Attention now turns to establishing the categories, the descriptions, and the specific criteria that will guide the examination of Moody's sermons in chapters Four through Six.

The Categories

Moody's sermons will first be examined to determine if they can be classified as Expository Sermons. While many homileticians assume the evangelist would not even know what an exposition looks like, this writer demonstrated earlier that Moody began to advocate for a more biblical approach to preaching in the last eight years of his life. Therefore, while it is almost certain that his early sermons could not be categorized as expository, Chapter Six will seek to demonstrate whether his practice changed to match an expositional model in the final eight years of his life.

Recognizing that Moody may have never fully understood exposition in the way many conservative evangelicals do today, the next logical step is to see if we could categorize his later sermons as Textual. If a sermon fails to reach the criteria for exposition, the researcher will consider the sermon in light of the criteria established for textual preaching. If the sermon fails to reach these criteria, we will examine it in light of the other sermon categories.

The next type of sermon criteria that will be applied to Moody's preaching is that of a Biographical Sermon. Though this type of sermon was discussed in the previous section, this writer will establish three specific tests to determine if Moody's sermons were biographical in nature. Moody certainly liked to speak of Bible characters. In fact, he often spoke of Daniel. Yet it remains to be seen if these oral presentations, in fact, rose to the level of being able to classify them as a biographical sermon.

The fourth sermon type that will be used to examine Moody's sermons is the category of a Topical Sermon. This monograph will treat this term in a general fashion. For instance, the topic may be based on a single word. It may be a theological topic. The concern may be a topic of an ethical nature. Another possibility is that the preacher desires to address a practical topic such as relationships, stress, time management, etc. All of these types of sermons will be treated under the broader category of topical sermons. The specific description and criteria for this category will be set forth below.

D.L. MOODY: TURNING POINTS TOWARD TEXT-DRIVEN PREACHING

The Descriptions and Criteria

Attention must now focus on establishing the specific descriptions and criteria by which to examine the preaching of Dwight Lyman Moody. This study will reduce the consideration to a brief description of each type of message, followed by three criteria that will be used to categorize Moody's messages. Some homileticians may want to add additional criteria for one category or another. However, for the purposes of considering Moody's sermons, the following descriptions, along with the three criteria statements for each sermon type, will be our guide.

Expository Sermon

Description:

As indicated by its name, an expository sermon exposes the meaning of a passage of Scripture within its context. The preacher is primarily concerned with the intent of the author as he wrote to his original recipients. Because a paragraph is the basic unit of thought, an expositional sermon is usually based on a paragraph. The grammatical structure of the paragraph, as well as the larger context of the chapter, section, and book guides the sermon. The divisions of the sermon are based on the grammatical divisions of the structure of the paragraph. Each paragraph has one main theme, which informs the main theme of the sermon. If the author developed that theme by the use of two main points, then the sermon has two main points; if by three then three, four then four. In other words, the sermon is based not only on the words of the text but also on the author's intent and the divisions of the text under consideration. The text is then applied to the preacher and his listeners in the power of the Holy Spirit.

Criteria:

1. To be an expository sermon, the message must be based on the author's intended meaning of the text within its grammatical, historical context.

2. To be an expository sermon, the theme of the message must be based on the theme of the paragraph as presented by the biblical author.
3. To be an expository sermon, the sermon divisions must be based on the divisions of the paragraph as presented by the author.

Textual Sermon

Description:

A textual sermon is a sermon that is based upon a specific text of Scripture but does not necessarily take its structure or divisions from the passage. Textual messages usually take one of two different formats: 1) Often a textual message is based on a single verse of Scripture, and the divisions of the sermon are clearly observable in the verse chosen. However, the context of the paragraph and/or chapter is often ignored, or at least not emphasized. In addition, the grammatical structure of the passage does not impact the content of the sermon. Or, 2) Another form of a textual sermon is often referred to as "a running commentary." In this approach an entire paragraph or chapter is read. The preacher then walks back through the text verse by verse, making comments and application. However, the actual structure and divisions of the paragraph are not emphasized. In either case, the divisions and emphasis of the sermon are based on what the preacher chooses to emphasize from the text, rather than on what the author emphasized. Application is made to the preacher and his listeners in the power of the Holy Spirit.

Criteria:
1. If the sermon is based on one verse of Scripture with the divisions clearly identifiable in the text but without those divisions being defined by the structure of the paragraph in which the verse is found, it will be considered a textual sermon.
2. If the sermon presents a running commentary of a paragraph of Scripture without regard to the grammatical structure and

divisions of the paragraph, it will be considered a textual sermon.
3. If the sermon is clearly based on content from the text but the divisions are based on the preacher's choice, rather than on the author's divisions, it will be considered a textual sermon.

Biographical Sermon

Description:

As its name implies, a biographical sermon focuses on the life of a single character. It may have a single passage as a starting point, but it usually considers several passages that demonstrate specific characteristics the preacher wants to highlight from the life of the character chosen. The sermon may examine a series of texts within a single book, or it may trace the characteristics of the person through several books of the Bible. Typically, application in this type of sermon flows from positive and/or negative characteristics exhibited by the person under consideration. The preacher again relies on the power of the Holy Spirit.

Criteria:
1. If the sermon is based on the life of a person in the Bible, it may be considered a biographical sermon.
2. If the divisions of the sermon are based upon specific characteristics of the biblical person, whether positive or negative characteristics, it may be a biographical sermon.
3. If the sermon seeks to apply specific characteristics of a Bible person to the lives of the preacher's listeners, it may be a biographical sermon.

Topical Sermon

Description:

As the name indicates, this type of sermon is based on a specific topic of concern. The topic may come from a text of Scripture, or it may come from outside Scripture. Normally, the preacher takes his topic of choice and studies various Bible verses that reference the topic. The preacher synthesizes the material and formulates a message he wants to convey about the topic under consideration. He chooses a focal verse, reads it, and moves into his topic. The divisions of the sermon reflect the preacher's choice of emphasis, and various Bible verses are used to show support for each major point.

Criteria:
1. If the sermon is based on a topic rather than a text, it may be considered a topical sermon.
2. If the sermon is based on a single word or concept from a verse or series of verses, without regard to the meaning of the verse within its context, it will be considered a topical sermon.
3. If the divisions of the sermon clearly arise from the speaker's choice, and Bible verses are simply used as support, it will be considered a topical sermon.

Establishing the Sermon Rubric

One final step is necessary to make a consistent analysis of Moody's sermons. Analyzing seventy sermons by the same preacher is a significant task. This task becomes even more complicated when the researcher has great respect for the preacher of the sermons under analysis. It would be easy for a researcher to fall into subjectivity. Therefore, a sermon rubric, based on the descriptions and criteria above, will enable the researcher to complete his analysis of the sermons more accurately and consistently. The rubric can be viewed on the following page.

D.L. MOODY:
TURNING POINTS TOWARD TEXT-DRIVEN PREACHING

Sermon Type	Expository Sermon	Textual Sermon	Biographical Sermon	Topical Sermon
Summary Description	The sermon seeks to explain the meaning of its text within its context, prioritizing the author's intended meaning, and then applies the text to himself and his listeners, in the power of the Spirit.	The sermon is based on a passage of Scripture, either a single verse, or a running commentary of an extended group of verses, but the divisions and structure of the text do not guide the divisions of the sermon.	The sermon is based on the life of a Bible character. The sermon utilizes passages that demonstrate the specific characteristics the preacher wants to emphasize. Application is based on those characteristics.	The sermon is based on a specific topic of concern. The sermon utilizes verses from the Bible that emphasize the points he desires to make concerning the topic.
Criteria One	The sermon is based on a specific text and on the author's intended meaning of that text.	The sermon is based on a single verse, but ignores the structure and divisions of the paragraph.	The sermon is based on the life of a Bible character.	The sermon is based on a topic rather than a text of Scripture.
Criteria Two	The theme of the sermon is based on the theme of the text being preached.	The sermon is a running commentary of a text without regard to the divisions of the paragraph.	The divisions of the sermon are based on various characteristics of the Bible character under consideration.	The sermon is based on a single word or concept from a text, without regard to the context.
Criteria Three	The divisions of the sermon are based on the divisions of the text being preached.	The sermon is based on a text of Scripture, but the divisions of the sermon are based on the preacher's choice rather than the author's grammatical structure.	The sermon seeks to apply specific characteristics of the Bible character to himself and his listeners.	The divisions of the sermon arise from the speaker's choice; verses of Scripture may be used to support the preacher's points.
Results				

A Brief Description of the Sermons to Be Examined

To understand if there is growth in the biblical content of D. L. Moody's sermons, sermons were chosen for evaluation from three distinct time periods. The focus of Moody's sermon content will be demonstrated to have changed at least twice. Therefore, it is important to start with a study of his early preaching. The researcher sought to gather sermons preached prior to his first British campaign that began in 1873. Due to a lack of extant sermons from this era, only a few were available. To gain a sense of his preaching in the early years, this examination was supplemented with eyewitness testimony and the reports of Moody's biographers.

As previously noted, printed sermons following Moody's return to the US in 1875 are readily available. His popularity caused newspapers to send reporters to his meetings. These reporters would take down his words and present them as verbatim reports in the paper.[57] This researcher examined numerous newspaper reports. These newspapers were preserved in microfilm and later converted to PDF files. They are difficult to read, but it is possible.

In addition, the verbatim newspaper reports were often preserved in book form while Moody was still alive. Some compilers applied extensive editing, while others did their best to preserve his actual words. One collection of sermons with little editing work is *To All Peoples*.[58] This work is a collection of sermons and addresses Moody gave in Boston. The book, along with actual newspaper reports from the Boston campaign, provided twenty sermons for evaluation of Moody's preaching during his most popular years.

The sermons preached following the 1892 summer conferences in Northfield will demonstrate the extent of the growth Moody experienced in his preaching content. Twenty-eight sermons were gathered and evaluated from the last few years of Moody's life. Once again, the researcher also looked to newspaper reports for sermons. These reports proved difficult to read because of preservation difficulties. However, another source of sermons from this

---

57. Paul Moody, *Father*, 111.
58. D. L. Moody, *To All Peoples* (Chicago: L. T. Palmer & Company, 1877).

era was found in the annual editions of *Northfield Echoes*.[59] These works are bound collections of the sermons, speeches, and events of Moody's summer conferences. A few of these sermons were repeat messages from the middle years. For instance, Moody often preached his sermon titled, "Sowing and Reaping" and his sermon on Daniel's life. Yet, twenty-eight sermons were clearly unique to the summer conferences of 1894–1899. Like the newspaper reports, the attempt was made to take down verbatim the words of the speaker. These works provide a great source for evaluating Moody's sermon content in the final years of his life.

Conclusion

The purpose of this chapter has been to demonstrate the need to examine Moody's sermons and to establish the categories, descriptions, and criteria that will be used in that examination. The writer began by demonstrating the vast influence of D. L. Moody in his own day as well as his continuing influence today. While his influence is well documented, very little has been written about his preaching. The little research that has been accomplished concerning the evangelist's preaching has left a big hole when it comes to a consideration of the content of the sermons.

In order to examine Moody's sermons for content, categories of sermon types were chosen. This chapter sought to discover the most common categories used by conservative evangelical scholars. Utilizing the categories Vines and Shaddix presented in *Power in the Pulpit* as the starting point, part two of this chapter compared the definitions and descriptions offered by other writers.

Part three of this chapter chose four categories to use in examining Moody's messages. Each of the four categories were then described. Following the description, a series of three criteria were presented. Together, the descriptions and criteria statement can be used to study Moody's preaching. A one-page rubric was established to aid in the examination of Moody's sermons.

---

59. D. L. Moody, Northfield Echoes Volume 3 (Northfield, MA, 1898).

Part four described the sermons chosen for evaluation in chapters four through six. Chapter Four will look at the sermons from the early years of Moody's life as well as eyewitness testimony about Moody's early preaching. Chapter Five will examine sermons from Moody's Boston campaign. Chapter Six will evaluate sermons from the last few years of Moody's life. Considered together, these sermons will demonstrate the growth of biblical content in Moody's sermons.

From what can be determined about Moody's preaching in the biographies, one can deduce that in the early days, he simply gave a religious talk. After his Chicago encounter with Henry Moorhouse, Moody seems to have demonstrated significant concern that his messages be based on Scripture. However, he moved only in a topical direction, with an occasional biographical sermon. In the last eight years of the preacher's life, he made several statements that demonstrate a desire to move towards expository preaching. From the biographies it appears that Moody may have moved from Topical and Biographical preaching toward Textual and Expositional preaching in his later years. In the end, the only way to know if this change in preaching actually happened in the pulpit is to examine sermons preached prior to Moorhouse's visit to Chicago, sermons during the height of his career, and sermons from the last eight years of his life. Now that categories, descriptions, and criteria have been established, the proposed examination is possible. This examination serves as the focus of chapters Four through Six.

Chapter Four

An Examination of Moody's Early Sermons

While Moody became a much sought-after preacher, it is difficult to determine when he began his preaching ministry. Reflecting on the early days Moody said, "If any one were to ask me when I began to preach I couldn't tell him. I began with the children. By and by they brought their parents. Then I noticed that about half the audience were adults."[1] Dorsett confirms Moody's own description of how he moved from being a Sunday School leader to preaching. Dorsett writes,

> By 1864 approximately one thousand children and teens thronged the Illinois Street hall on Sundays, and along with them came nearly three hundred adults. Of the latter group many were parents, but increasingly adults were coming just to hear the Bible taught with such unusual clarity and clear personal application.[2]

As the crowds continued to grow, it was determined that a church was needed for those who attended the mission Sunday School. Dorsett notes, "The Illinois Street Church was formally dedicated December 30, 1864."[3] While Moody declined to be ordained by the Congregational denomination, he as-

---

1. William R. Moody, *The Life of Dwight L. Moody* (Chicago: Revell, 1900), 442.
2. Lyle W. Dorsett, A Passion for Souls (Chicago: Moody Publishers, 1997), 122.
3. Ibid., 123.

D.L. MOODY:
TURNING POINTS TOWARD TEXT-DRIVEN PREACHING

sumed the pastorate and led the church to function as an independent evangelical congregation.

To gain an understanding of Moody's early preaching, one must rely heavily on the testimony of those who heard him speak. The testimony of his effectiveness is readily available. Discovering the content of his early sermons is more difficult. W. H. Daniels helps in this regard. A contemporary of Moody, Daniels published a work about Moody in 1875. Concerning Moody's preaching Daniels writes,

> In the earlier years of Mr. Moody's work for Christ his sermons and addresses, though often founded upon a text of Scripture, were largely made up of personal incidents, arguments drawn from surrounding scenes and circumstances; fervid personal appeals to Christians, inciting them to greater activity; and earnest calls to sinners, urging them at once to repent and believe the Gospel.[4]

Daniels found little or no biblical content in Moody's early sermons. However, he noted a change in Moody's preaching following Henry Moorhouse's visit to Chicago in February of 1868.[5] Regarding the change in Moody's preaching Daniels notes, "Thus, from being merely a point of departure, from which his sermons wandered into highways and byways, the Word of God came to be the entire plane of their projection, and a good part of their solid substance."[6] This testimony suggests that Moody's early sermons were lacking in biblical content but were filled with the Bible following the Moorhouse encounter.

As noted in Chapter One, the best way to get a sense of Moody's preaching in any era of his ministry is through reading verbatim reports of his sermons.

---

4. W. H. Daniels, *Moody and His Work* (Hartford, CT: American Publishing Company, 1875), 174–175.

5. John Pollock, *Moody: The Biography* (Chicago: Moody Press, 1983), 90–91. Pollock notes that Moody first heard Moorhouse preach on February 8, 1868. Moody was so moved he asked Moorhouse to continue preaching all week. By the end of the week, Moorhouse taught Moody how to study the Bible topically and encouraged him to use more Scripture in his preaching.

6. Ibid., 185.

Sermons preached after Moody's British campaign (1873–1875) are readily available. Moody became so popular that the secular newspapers would send reporters to take down his sermons verbatim and publish them the following day. Prior to Moody's British campaign, his sermons were generally not recorded. Moody did not write sermon manuscripts, and the notes he wrote were single words that often only he could understand.[7] The few notes Moody did write are not extant today. These facts create a challenge for one who desires to understand the content of Moody's early sermons.

This researcher spent countless hours seeking early sermons. Initially, the hope was to find at least ten sermons Moody preached prior to hearing Moorhouse preach on February 8, 1868. Eventually, the search was expanded all the way to 1873, attempting to find any sermon Moody preached prior to the British campaign. These sermons would aid in understanding the biblical content of a typical Moody sermon in his early years of preaching and for the first few years after his encounter with Moorhouse. After extensive bibliographic and database searches yielded no fruit, the aid of Moody's great-grandson, David Powell, was sought.[8] The interview with Powell proved enjoyable, and he agreed to search his own private collection for early sermons. Once again, the search yielded no early sermons.

With the aid of Corie Zylstra, archivist at Moody Bible Institute, early messages were finally discovered. From 1867–1917 the Congregational churches in Chicago published a weekly religious newspaper titled, *The Advance*. *The Advance* records twenty-two occasions Moody spoke between the years of 1867–1869. The messages were given at the Chicago's noonday prayer meetings.[9] To this researcher's knowledge, these twenty-two messages are the only

---

7. Paul D. Moody, *My Father* (Boston: Little Brown Company, 1938), 112–113.

8. The present author had the opportunity to participate in the Dedication Ceremonies of the newly established Moody Center in Northfield, MA on May 1, 2017. During the two-day event, David Powell agreed to meet for an interview about Moody. He offered to help in the search for early sermons. The interview revealed no new information, but was certainly an enjoyable day.

9. Chicago's noonday prayer meetings began as part of the Revival of 1857–1858. The leaders of the YMCA who led the prayer meetings, Benjamin Jacobs, John Farwell, and Cyrus Bentley, opened the door for Moody to get involved in the meetings. The meeting included prayer, singing, testimony, and words of exhortation. Moody

D.L. MOODY:
TURNING POINTS TOWARD TEXT-DRIVEN PREACHING

Moody material available from the early years of his preaching ministry. These messages provide a little over a year of material prior to Moorhouse's visit, and an almost two years of material following the visit. The chapter will now seek to understand the context in which these messages were delivered.

The Context of the Early Chicago Sermons

One of the regular columns of *The Advance* reported on Chicago's noonday prayer meetings. While many different preachers were invited to bring a brief message and lead these meetings, Moody did on occasion lead them. *The Advance* published what Moody spoke at these noonday prayer meetings in Chicago twenty-two times between December 1867 and December 1869.

William Moody noted that his dad often spoke only five or ten minutes in the early years.[10] On one occasion Moody was asked, "How long should a sermon be?"[11] He responded, "It is very much better to get a reputation for being brief than to have people say that you preach long sermons. Say what you got to say in just as few words as you can. Then stop when you get through."[12] By Moody's own testimony, he attempted to preach short messages. The testimony of his biographers is that he followed his own advice, particularly in the early years.

The reports in *The Advance* are not very long. Some of the reports are summaries of his already brief messages. However, the accounts often present his actual words on paper. Therefore, even though the accounts given to the following messages are short, some are summaries, and a few are given only in response to other speakers at the prayer meetings, they may indeed give the best view of Moody's early days of preaching.

---

served in any capacity they asked, and as time progressed he was recognized as the city missionary for the YMCA. He was given more opportunities to speak as time progressed. For more on Moody's general involvement with the YMCA see Dorsett, *Passion*, 81–87.

    10. William R. Moody, *The Life of D. L. Moody*, 438.
    11. Ibid., 463.
    12. Ibid.

Description and Evaluation of Twenty-Two Early Chicago Sermons

As noted above *The Advance* published reports from the noonday prayer meetings in Chicago between the years 1867–1869. Twenty-two times they recorded Moody speaking. The focus of this chapter is to gain a sense of the biblical content in Moody's early messages. Therefore, all twenty-two of Moody's reported words will be examined. Below the reader will find the date of the prayer meeting, followed by a brief description of Moody's words. After the content is described, a few words of evaluation will be offered. The evaluation will be guided by the sermon rubric of Chapter Three. Because of the brief nature of the reports contained in *The Advance*, a full evaluation against each sermon type described in the rubric will not be possible. However, enough information will be gained to confirm Daniels' testimony concerning Moody's preaching during this era of his ministry. A summary of the findings will be presented after all messages are evaluated.

Wednesday, November 27, 1867

Description

A man at the prayer meeting repeatedly asked the gathered group to pray for him to be saved from his alcoholism. He claimed to have struggled six years to overcome the problem, but he consistently failed. Moody took the opportunity to speak to the gathered crowd. He says, "Our prayers could not save him. Neither could the prayers of his father. It is not by the prayers of any one that we are saved. Jesus is the Saviour. He is willing to save to the uttermost; but you must quit an idol life and go to work."[13] The reporter indicated that Moody continued with comments that seemed severe. There is no record of any mention of Scripture.

---

13. *The Advance*, December 6, 1876.

Evaluation

The Advance did not provide enough of Moody's words on this occasion to gain a sense of whether he took this opportunity to share a message from Scripture, or simply offered correction to the man during the meeting. Without more information, this message cannot be evaluated in light of the sermon rubric. It should be noted that in the paragraph that was reported he did not mention a Bible verse directly. He did, however, point out that only Jesus can save someone from alcoholism.

Monday, April 13, 1868

Description

Moody began the meeting by talking about faith. He says, "Day after day, we hear the cry for more faith. It comes alike from the lips of ministers and laymen."[14] He then read Hebrews 11:6. Moody went on to describe the growing need for faith. He later says, "Faith has a very clear sight. By its aid Abraham looked forward down through a period of eighteen hundred years and saw the Savior upon the cross."[15] He then says, "It [faith] has a very long arm, for it can reach from earth up to heaven and take the promises out from the hand of God. He is a rewarder of them that diligently seek Him."[16] While Moody quoted a portion of Hebrews 11:6, he did not reference the verse directly.

Moody then told a story about his daughter to illustrate a point he wanted to make. He described her asking for a drink of water, but she kept playing. Moody ignored her, thinking she did not really want the drink. Eventually, she came and grabbed hold of Moody and this time she would not let go of him until he got her some water. He said the same was true of God. Moody believed that too often a Christian asks God for something but does not really care about it.

---

14. *The Advance*, April 23, 1868.
15. Ibid.
16. Ibid.

He suggests that when one gets serious and prays in faith, "leaving everything else," the Father will fulfill the request.[17]

Evaluation

The theme of this short message was faith. Moody began with the need for faith and then read Hebrews 11:6. He described the great need for faith, some benefits of faith, and then illustrated the need for faith. Moody did speak briefly of Christ on the cross, but he did not share the gospel in detail. The focus of his call to faith was for his listeners to believe God would answer one's prayer.

In a short message, as is given on this occasion, it is difficult to see the message as much more than a brief devotional thought. Though he did not begin with Scripture, he did read a verse. Neither the meaning nor the context of the verse was described. One phrase was repeated from the verse, "He is a rewarder of them that diligently seek Him."[18] Most of the words expressed in the message focused on illustration and application. At any rate, the short message cannot be classified as an expository or textual sermon.

The message focused on a single theme. It was presented more as a devotional thought about the need and the rewards of exhibiting faith. In particular, the focus was on praying in faith, which clearly fit the context of a noonday prayer meeting. The brief message was topical in nature.

Monday, September 7, 1868

Description

At the noonday prayer meeting, Moody spoke of answered prayer. He related a story about a previous visit he made to a man named John Allen. Allen was known as the "Wickedest man in New York."[19] Moody did not describe the specific business Allen was in but simply calls it a "hellish business."[20] Moody

---

17. *The Advance*, April 23, 1868.
18. Ibid.
19. *The Advance*, September 17, 1868.
20. Ibid. An Internet search revealed that John Allen owned a bar, dancehall,

indicated that he visited him in his establishment and confronted him on leading young men astray. Moody asked Allen if he allowed his own son to participate in his business. Allen indicated he did not, because he didn't want it to ruin his son. Moody pointed out that he was ruining the sons of other men. Moody says, "I then exhorted him to quit the business and told him I should pray for him until he was converted, and told him to let me know when that occurred."[21] Moody then related that Allen had been converted and was holding prayer meetings in the same room that was once a dancehall.[22] The paper does not record any other words from Moody at this point.

Evaluation

The Advance does not indicate if Moody was preaching a formal message on this occasion, or if he simply offered this story as an encouragement to pray. At any rate, this report does not offer much to evaluate. It does appear that Moody's purpose in telling the story was to encourage those gathered to pray, trusting that God can change the heart of those for whom we care. There is neither any Scripture verse referenced nor was the gospel presented in the brief word Moody spoke. It may be best to consider this a short exhortation to pray in faith, rather than to consider it a full sermon.

---

and prostitution business. https://infamousnewyork.com/2014/05/23/the-wickedest-man-in-new-york-john-allens-dance-hall-304-water-street/ accessed, 082717 2:40pm.

21. *The Advance*, September 17, 1868.

22. While this does not have bearing on the purpose of this chapter it should be noted that further research indicates that indeed John Allen claimed to be converted and held prayer meetings in his former saloon. http://www.rarenewspapers.com/list?page=7&per_page=100&q%5Bcategory_id%5D=107-harpers-weekly&sort=items.id&sort_direction=ASC accessed, 082717, 3:00pm. Allen was later arrested on October 18, 1868. http://www.rarenewspapers.com/view/636920 accessed, 082717 3:03pm.

Tuesday, November 10, 1868

Description

Someone other than Moody led the prayer meeting. However, Moody was given the opportunity to speak. *The Advance* reports as follows:

> Mr. Moody followed, on a subject as diverse as could be imagined, though not untimely: 'I know of three churches in this city that, together, cost their members $35,000 per year. As long as churches cost this much, how can any one say, This is a free gospel? A free gospel! Why, Christianity is getting to be costly. Go up to the members of those churches and ask them to give anything to support a Mission Church, and they can't do it—because their own churches costs them too much. And yet $5,000 will reach more people in a mission church than the $35,000 does, for they have barely a hundred members a piece.'[23]

This report is all that *The Advance* records from Moody on this date. The opening sentence may indicate that he spoke on more than one subject.

Evaluation

The statement about the diversity of Moody's topic could indicate one of two things. It could be that he spoke more than is recorded in the paper and that he spoke on several diverse topics. If this was the case and we had more of the message Moody shared, it may be that he preached a multi-topic sermon without any sense of unity. The diversity comment could also simply mean that Moody's topic was out of sync with the prayer meeting leader's topic. In either case, there is not enough information provided to fully evaluate this message. In what was recorded, Moody did not read Scripture or share the gospel on this occasion.

---

23. *The Advance*, November 19, 1868.

D.L. MOODY:
TURNING POINTS TOWARD TEXT-DRIVEN PREACHING

Wednesday, December 16, 1868

Description

Moody related a story of a sick child from his Mission Sunday School. In the midst of deep trials, the child's faith became convicting to the mother. Moody indicated the child spoke to his mother saying, "Teacher said, mother, that God would take care of us if we would only trust Him. I trust Him. Don't you, Mother?"[24] Moody then related how that the child sang a song of faith. He concludes, "Would that we could all look up with as clear a vision and as bright a faith!" Moody may have related more, but it is not recorded in the paper.

Evaluation

Once again, one has very little to work with from this report. Moody may have said more than is recorded by *The Advance*. However, this is all the researcher has available concerning this event. Moody only related a story. No Bible verse was mentioned or gospel proclaimed. Throughout his life Moody was known for telling stories that touched the heart, and moved people to act. As noted above, Daniels indicates that his early sermons were primarily filled with stories of this sort, along with passionate appeals to be saved or to work for God. In the end, there simply is not enough material available to provide a thorough evaluation of this event.

Monday, December 21, 1868

Description

The Advance's report of the noonday prayer meeting on this day focused on Moody. He began by saying, "When the Lord told Ananias to go and see Saul, he was afraid—just as a good many Christians are now-a-days."[25] Moody

---

24. *The Advance*, December 24, 1868.
25. *The Advance*, December 31, 1868.

then related that when Ananias arrived, he called Saul, "Brother Saul."[26] Moody says, "He took him right in. He didn't keep him on probation. Saul arose and was baptized. And SRAIGHTWAY he preached Christ in the synagogues."[27] From this example, Moody argued that one does not need to study seven years before he or she shares Christ. He suggested that Paul was not yet ready to write letters to the churches, but that he could share Christ. Moody says, "I don't mean to say we shouldn't study any, we should. We should search the Scriptures, and dig away down for the precious truths of the Bible."[28] Moody then discussed the idea that someone must be seminary trained to preach the gospel. He contrasted that position with Paul preaching immediately following his conversion. Moody says, "We ought to preach while we study. If we can't do more, we can 'testify' that Christ is to us the Son of God."[29] With this statement, Moody concluded his remarks.

Evaluation

The present message by Moody seems to be characteristic of the testimony of Daniels noted above. Moody based his thoughts on a biblical event and on a few words from the text of Acts 9. However, he neither made specific reference to the phrases he quoted, nor did he exhibit concern for the context. It appears that he simply used the example of Ananias as support for the point he desired to make. While this short address does not really lend itself to a full examination, there is enough evidence to suggest it was a topical message in accordance with our sermon rubric of Chapter Three. In the portion of the message that was recorded, Moody did not share the gospel.

---

26. *The Advance*, December 31, 1868.
27. Ibid.
28. Ibid.
29. Ibid.

Thursday, December 24, 1868

Description

The entire report of the noonday prayer meeting for this day was once again a record of a short message from Moody. *The Advance* set the context of the message by stating, "The poverty of the excuses made by those that were bidden to the feast, was the subject of the lesson of today."[30] Moody says sarcastically, "It would be a great business man, that would buy a piece of land without seeing it, or a yoke of oxen without proving them."[31] Moody demonstrated that the excuses were ridiculous. He says, "They did not go because they didn't want to. If such excuses were all confined to sinners, it wouldn't be so bad. But we put forth just such miserable apologies."[32] Moody argued that these types of excuses come from the devil. The report in *The Advance* ends without much more information. It is likely that this was a summary of the message for this day and Moody said more than was recorded.

Evaluation

While we have very little to consider with this message, it does seem clear that Moody was not concerned with explaining the parable in its context. He does not focus on the purpose of the parable, but only on the excuses offered by those who refused to attend the feast. It appears Moody used the passage without regard to context, in order to support his topic of concern. Moody did not share the gospel in the portion of his message that was recorded for publication. The portion of the message that is extant today indicates this was likely a topical message.

---

30. *The Advance*, December 31, 1868.
31. Ibid.
32. Ibid.

Wednesday, February 3, 1869

Description

The Advance says that Moody was the chair of the meeting, indicating he was the primary speaker that day.[33] It describes him, "He is blunt, often to the disturbances of people with disordered nerves, but then one can pardon much to obtain the directions of speech and fearlessness of utterance with which our readers are familiar."[34] The paper announced the topic as "Christian Cheerfulness" and then presented Moody's words.

Moody indicated that he would rather have spoken on any other subject because he did not feel cheerful. He says everything seems "cold and dead."[35] Moody says, "But, I read that David when he was left alone in a cave by Israel, thanked the Lord and gave praises unto Him, and when David was caught in the trap that was laid for him, he sang praises unto his God."[36] Moody went on to say, "The reason the world is not converted is because converts fail to retain their first joy. Why, if we kept that, every one would want to be a Christian."[37] This ends *The Advance*'s report of Moody's words on this occasion.

Evaluation

Once again, *The Advance* only gives some of Moody's message, which makes it difficult to assess. However, what is presented follows the pattern of Daniels' testimony above. Moody mentioned two events in David's life. However, he did not explain the events or give us actual words from the Bible. He simply used these events to support his topic. The record does not indicate that Moody proclaimed the gospel on this occasion. From the portion of the message that is extant, it appears to be a topical sermon.

---

33. *The Advance*, December 31, 1868.
34. *The Advance*, February 11, 1869.
35. Ibid.
36. *The Advance*, February 11, 1869.
37. Ibid.

D.L. MOODY:
TURNING POINTS TOWARD TEXT-DRIVEN PREACHING

Wednesday, March 31, 1869

Description

The report of the noonday prayer meeting for this day began with Moody speaking. He alludes to a statement made the day before, "We need less talk and more prayer."[38] Moody says, "I don't know but we have the form of prayer enough, but we don't know how to pray. Often after praying I think I would blush to see that in print."[39] Moody then, indicated that he often found himself praying more to the audience than to the Lord. He used his daughter as an illustration. After his illustration Moody says, "So we must learn to plead."[40] Moody's comments were followed by a reading of Luke 11:1–14 and a time of asking the Lord to teach those gathered to pray.

Evaluation

There is no indication in this report as to whether all of Moody's words were recorded, or if this was only a summary. Like some of the previous reports, this leaves one to wonder if this were a simple testimony, or if Moody delivered the message for the day with this just being the summary. His words are followed with the reading from Luke, but there was no attempt to teach or preach from the passage. Therefore, it seems to be a simple word of exhortation, encouraging those present to ask the Lord to teach them to pray. *The Advance* does not indicate that Moody shared the gospel at this point. As best as can be determined, this is a topical message.

---

38. *The Advance*, April 8, 1869.
39. Ibid.
40. Ibid.

Tuesday, April 15, 1869

Description

The Advance indicates that Moody led the meeting on this day, presenting the message. After reading the story of Stephen's martyrdom (Acts 7), Moody speaks, "If Stephen had lived in our day, and preached as he did, no doubt there are many professing Christians who would have said, 'I'm sorry for Stephen, but he ought to have known better.'"[41] Moody later says, "Let us not study policy. Let us be bold. Let us tell the truth right out if it does cut."[42] Following this brief summary of Moody's message, the paper went on to mention remarks of an unnamed man who spoke after Moody.

Evaluation

Normally when Moody chaired the meetings *The Advance* carried more of his words than are here recorded. On this occasion, they recorded very little of his message. In what is covered, it seems that Moody followed the pattern described by Daniels. Though he began by reading of Stephen's death, Moody chose to focus this attention on application without regard to explaining the text within its context. There is no record of Moody sharing the gospel on this occasion.

Wednesday, April 21, 1869

Description

This day's entire report focused on Moody's message. The report appears to be a summary of a larger sermon. Moody begins, "We all get the best we

---

41. *The Advance*, April 22, 1869.
42. Ibid.

can for our money. The world is looking after best things."[43] Moody indicated that everyone has a religion of some kind. He suggested that if Christians could show that their religion was the best, others would accept it. He says, "Now I confess, when I go into a meeting and see every body with their heads down and long faces, it chills me."[44] Later he said, "We've got to win men."[45] Moody went on to say, "When they see eternity written on our faces… when we show them Christ is better than anything else, then they will be won to Christ."[46] *The Advance* chose to conclude their coverage of Moody's remarks with these words.

Evaluation

Characteristic of the testimony of Daniels above, Moody's focus in these words was on passionate illustration and application. While this is likely only a summary of his message for the day, *The Advance* usually mentions if Moody read a passage or alluded to a text of Scripture. They did not mention any reference to Scripture at all in this report. Therefore, this report leads one to believe that Moody did not mention a passage of Scripture at all on this day. In addition, the extant portion of this message indicates a topical concern, but no biblical support. The gospel was not proclaimed.

Wednesday, May 5, 1869

Description

Moody commented on Hebrews 11, after another person read the text for the gathered crowd. He says, "We talk about faith; we think we know something about it. But, my brethren, when we look at these instances, when we look at the examples in this chapter—we don't know anything about it."[47] Moody then picked up the story of Abraham taking Isaac to Mt. Moriah.

---

43. *The Advance*, April 29, 1869.
44. Ibid.
45. Ibid.
46. Ibid.
47. *The Advance*, May 13, 1869.

The Advance does not give the full text of his message. Rather, it simply says, "He told the story of that three days' journey to the mount of sacrifice, as only Mr. Moody could tell it." [48] There is no indication of what Moody said in telling this story. We read very little about the journey in Genesis 22:3–8. There is no indication whether Moody read or quoted from the Bible but simply that he told the story, " as only Mr. Moody could tell it."[49] This statement seems to fit Daniels' testimony above, about Moody's passionate story telling. *The Advance* did record Moody's concluding words. He says, "How ashamed ought we to be!"[50] The story and the statement appears to have moved the audience. *The Advance* notes that this feeling [of shame], "had begun to take possession of us all."[51] No additional information is provided by the paper.

Evaluation

The report in *The Advance* once again offers only a little material for consideration. What can be noted is that the entire chapter of Hebrews 11 was read just prior to Moody's message. Moody did not focus on explaining the meaning of the text in context but quickly moved to application. He noted that reading this text reveals how little people know about faith. He then took one example from the chapter and offered a story of the three-day trip Abraham, Isaac, and two servants took to Mt. Moriah. Upon finishing the story, Moody drove home the idea that the gathered Christians should be ashamed of their weak faith. From the report of *The Advance*, it appears that Moody's message was a passionate story-telling event, with strong emotional appeal, but without regard to the overall context of the text for the day. We do not know if Moody shared the gospel on this occasion, though the story he told certainly lends itself to doing so.

---

48. *The Advance*, May 13, 1869.
49. Ibid.
50. Ibid.
51. Ibid.

D.L. MOODY: TURNING POINTS TOWARD TEXT-DRIVEN PREACHING

Thursday, May 6, 1869

Description

Moody was not the main speaker on this day. However, following the introduction of the subject of Elijah's faith on Mt. Carmel, Moody was given the floor to share a short message. He begins, "When prayers have been asked for those who are under the strong power of strong drink I have said to myself, 'I can't pray for them.'"[52] Moody indicated that when he did follow through with prayer, he was concerned about the person or the person's family. He contrasted his own practice with Elijah's practice. Moody says, "But Elijah wanted to show that 'twas God, and not Elijah. And when the sacrifice was consumed the people exclaimed, 'The Lord, he is God.'"[53] Moody then says, "If we can only get this cursed self out of the way we could have faith to prevail."[54] After a long silence Moody exclaims, "Lord, teach us how to pray!"[55] These are the final words *The Advance* records from Moody in this edition of the paper.

Evaluation

Moody picked up on a concept from the text of Elijah on Mt. Carmel. He focused his attention on Elijah's example of praying for all the people to recognize that the Lord is God. All of his comments centered on this concept, without regard for the specifics of the context of the story. With very little material to evaluate, the pattern seems to fit Daniels's testimony of passionate, but topical, messages from Moody in the early years. *The Advance* does not indicate that Moody shared the gospel on this occasion.

---

52. *The Advance*, May 13, 1869.
53. Ibid.
54. Ibid.
55. Ibid.

Wednesday, May 26, 1869

Description

Moody began the meeting by reading James 1:2. He then says, "This sounds somewhat strange. But if you will notice a plant grown in a hot-house, where it is subjected to no trials or exposures, you will find that it is a weak thing."[56] Moody contrasted these types of plants with those grown outside in the harsh elements. He then says, "It is the same way with hot-house Christians. A man isn't worth much as a Christian man until he has been tried."[57] There is no indication what else, if anything, Moody said at this meeting.

Evaluation

The Advance only offered one paragraph of Moody's message on this day. It seems he started the meeting, so he likely was the leader and said more than was recorded. With what we have to go on, Moody read a verse, illustrated the value of trials and applied it to his listeners. Without knowing everything Moody said, it is difficult to determine whether the message fits the pattern described by Daniels or if he may have presented a textual message. As far as one can tell from the material available, he did not present the gospel on this occasion.

Wednesday, June 30, 1869

Description

It appears Moody opened the noonday prayer meeting on this day. He says, "The devil trips a good many people."[58] *The Advance* reports that he read the story of "… those that wandered among the tombs and how they were thrown

---

56. *The Advance*, June 3, 1869.
57. Ibid.
58. *The Advance*, July 8, 1869.

down by the evil spirits before they went out of them."[59] Moody then says, "Many a man is prevented by his pride from coming to the Savior. Another man thinks he must earn salvation, and the devil throws him down. He has a snare for everyone, and the only way to come to Him is to come to Him now, and Just as you are."[60] Following this brief summary of Moody's words, the paper added an editorial comment concerning the struggle people face with the call to come just as they are.

Evaluation

This summary does not provide much for one to evaluate. The failure to include the text Moody read complicates the attempt at evaluation even more. It appears that he read from Matthew 8, Mark 5, or Luke 8. Without more information on his message, it is difficult to determine much. If *The Advance* included Moody's main emphasis, then Moody did not focus his message on the main point of the story that was read. In fact, it could be argued that he misapplied the text in his topical approach. He did not fully explain the gospel, but he did indicate that one could not earn salvation.

Wednesday, September 22, 1869

Description

Moody opened his comments by telling of two different teachers in his mission Sunday School that came to him the previous week intending to resign their class. Both men came indicating the reason they were stepping down was because they felt a keen sense of their own unworthiness. After describing the scene of his encounter with these two men, Moody responds, "Well, when men begin to feel in that way I know that God is present, and if we ever accomplish anything it is

---

59. Ibid. It should be noted that the paper does not indicate what passage Moody read. The description given likely indicates that he read Matthew 8:28–34, Mark 5:1–20, or Luke 8:26–39.

60. Ibid.

when Christians begin to say 'Unworthy, unworthy.'"[61] There is no indication of Scripture being read or of the gospel being shared in this message.

Evaluation

Other than a few editorial remarks following Moody's words, *The Advance* did not report on anything else said by Moody or others during this meeting. It is difficult to know if this indicates Moody's entire message was without Scripture reading. If so, the question would arise as to whether he stayed on one topic or if he mentioned a variety of topics. In the end, it appears that the message likely followed the pattern described by Daniels above. This message was a topical sermon, possibly without any references to a biblical text.

Friday, September 24, 1869

Description

The only speaker *The Advance* recorded this day was Moody. He began by saying, "A good many men think that if they were to be Christians at all they would be better than this or that one anyhow. I think that we misjudge a great many in the same way ourselves."[62] Moody indicated that people tend to judge others with partial information. He says, "We see his failures but we don't see his wrestlings."[63] Moody indicated that in contrast God knows one's struggles, but he sympathizes with human weaknesses.

Evaluation

The Advance only reported two paragraphs of Moody's message. They did not include any Bible reading. They gave no indication that Moody proclaimed the gospel message. Without more information one cannot be certain,

---

61. *The Advance*, September 30, 1869.
62. Ibid.
63. Ibid.

but from what is provided this seems to fit Daniels' testimony of Moody's early preaching habits.

Monday, October 10, 1869

Description

Moody led the prayer meeting on this day. The Scripture lesson was on the second half of the Ten Commandments. Moody indicated he believed the neglect of parents to be of great importance to the problems faced in Chicago.[64] After a few more words about children respecting their parents and a brief word about covetousness, Moody shifted his focus.

Moody indicated a great concern over the fact that he thought Christians in Chicago were like the disciples that tried to cast out the demon from a child, but were unable to do so. He took this story as his main lesson for the day. There is no indication as to whether he read the passage or simply told the story. He did apply the story to his own life as well as to those who had gathered for prayer. He pointed out that Christ rebuked the disciples for their lack of faith. Speaking of Moody, the editor of *The Advance* then writes, "He poured out one of his hot, warm exhortations, and said that as for himself he felt the need of something beside man-power."[65] The editor pointed out that others gathered for the prayer meeting expressed a kinship with Moody's message.

Evaluation

It is unclear how Moody moved from the discussion of the second half of the Ten Commandments to a discussion of a lack of faith and power. It is also unclear if either of the passages were read in the meeting, or simply alluded to and discussed. In the case of the Commandments, it does not appear that he walked through each of them with explanation, but focused only on two. In the case of the disciples' failure to cast out the demon, once again it appears that the

---

64. *The Advance*, October 21, 1869.
65. Ibid.

story was simply discussed and applied. There is no indication that the gospel was presented at this meeting.

Tuesday, October 12, 1869

Description

Moody related a story of a young girl for whom the group had been praying. The editor of the paper indicated that the girl had been living in Chicago and "pursuing a life of shame."[66] Moody was asked to go see the girl as she was staying at the "Erring Woman's Refuge." He did not want to go. Moody put off the visit most of the day. When he finally went, he indicated that he did not want to speak with her. However, when she came into the room, Moody attempted to convince her to not go back out on the streets. She responds that "she did not believe in God, or in hell, or in life beyond the grave, she was going to enjoy herself here while she could."[67] Moody indicated that he could have no effect on her until he took her by the hand and says, "Mary, I don't come to you as a stranger, nor as a friend, but as a brother. And won't you treat me like a brother?"[68] Moody indicated that her heart melted. She became open and indicated no one cared for her like that since her own dad had died. Moody then says, "And, Oh, my friends, Christ came to us not as a stranger nor as a friend but as a brother! How near it makes Him seem to me to-day that he came down to earth and pleaded with us that we would look upon him as a brother!"[69] This is the last of Moody's recorded words from the day.

Evaluation

There is no indication that Moody read a passage of Scripture at this meeting. Neither is there any indication that he proclaimed the gospel message directly. He told a moving story and applied it to himself and his listeners by

---

66. *The Advance*, October 21, 1869.
67. Ibid.
68. Ibid.
69. Ibid.

describing Christ stooping down to reach humans. This appears, from the summary given, to be a topical message.

Friday, October 15, 1869

Description

Moody began the prayer meeting by referring to time spent in prayer and confession of sin. He says, "It is not a waste of time to pray for ourselves. The disciples might have been in a hurry to get out into the world when Christ arose, and to tell the good news to every one. But Christ bade them wait in Jerusalem for the promise of the Father."[70] Moody went on to indicate that after the disciples waited ten days the Holy Spirit did more in a day than they could have in a whole year. He then says, "And so it will be with us."[71] Moody told about when Spurgeon first became pastor in London. He indicated they had a small group. According to Moody, Spurgeon focused on preaching to the deacons until they got right with the Lord. He concluded by saying, "And what is the result"—the largest church in the world."[72] This statement ended the report for the day.

Evaluation

There is no record that Moody read any Scripture. He simply mentioned the disciples waiting in Jerusalem for the coming of the Spirit. He applied this immediately to himself and the gathered group, without concern for the context of Acts 1 and 2. He illustrated his point with the story of Spurgeon and his church. Moody seems to have presented a topical message on this occasion. He did not share the gospel in this message.

---

70. *The Advance*, October 21, 1869.
71. Ibid.
72. Ibid.

Tuesday, October 19, 1869

Description

The editor of *The Advance* indicates that the Monday and Tuesday meetings were very solemn. He then turned his attention to a message Moody gave the day before, but for some reason was not recorded in that day's report. Moody says, "I'm tired of general prayers. I have no heart to pray for anybody but myself now. If I can get Moody right, others will get right without any difficulty."[73] Moody encouraged the gathered group to focus their prayers on themselves, seeking to get right with God. He then says, "I think I see the cloud rising that is to shed its healing."[74] There is no verse shared here, but it may be an allusion to 1 Kings 18:41–46, when Elijah prayed for rain until a small cloud began to rise up out of the sea. Moody then related a conversation he had with a Presbyterian minister the Sunday before the meeting. Following the illustration Moody says, "And now let us all send up one united prayer that God would send his Spirit down upon us."[75] This request concludes *The Advance's* report of the meeting.

Evaluation

As noted above, there is one possible allusion to the biblical account of Elijah praying for rain near the top of Mount Carmel. However, there is no other reference to the Bible in Moody's comments. Moody's focus was on praying for oneself and particularly in confession of sin. He begins with his own experience and related a conversation with another minister as an illustration. Moody concluded the message by inviting all present to ask the Lord to send His Spirit. The gospel was not presented in this message.

---

73. *The Advance*, October 28, 1869.
74. Ibid.
75. Ibid.

D.L. MOODY:
TURNING POINTS TOWARD TEXT-DRIVEN PREACHING

Friday, December 17, 1869

Description

Moody's message began *The Advance's* report of the noonday prayer meeting. Moody says, "There has been some talk in this meeting of loving God with all one's soul. The man who says that he does that deceives himself or Satan is deceiving him. The man don't live that does it."[76] Moody went on to discuss the fact that if one truly loved God with all his soul, he would have great power to accomplish the Lord's work. He contrasted this by indicating that often people fail to work for the Lord because they know that their lives are lacking. Moody says, "That is just where many make a mistake. Read the Bible through and find how many of the holiest men in it remained at all times steadfast."[77] Later Moody says, "We know we are sinful—but He is our righteousness. Men often say to me, 'Moody, you did wrong in this and that,' and I say, 'Perhaps I did, but my Master is worthy, if I ain't. Our failures should not keep us from work."[78] This statement concludes *The Advance's* record of the meeting.

Evaluation

Moody began his words by quoting a portion of the "Great Commandment" but without reference. He indicated that a lot of discussion had been going on among the participants of the noonday prayer meetings about the idea of loving God with one's whole soul. This portion of the Commandment guided Moody's comments. He indicated that no one could fulfill this command. He pointed to the righteousness of Christ as the remedy and encouraged Christians to work for the Lord, based on that, rather than on their own righteousness. While he did not explicitly share the gospel, he strongly alluded to justification. Yet, the message did not explain even a single verse of Scripture within its con-

---

76. *The Advance*, December 23, 1869.
77. Ibid.
78. Ibid.

text. It appears to fit well within the testimony of Daniels concerning the topical preaching style of Moody's early years of preaching.

Summary of Findings from Moody's Early Chicago Sermons

The messages Moody shared at the Chicago noonday prayer meetings from November 1867–December 1869 provide the only verifiable Moody material from the early years. By the testimony of both William Moody and D. L. Moody himself, Moody's sermons during this time were often as short as five to ten minutes in length. In addition, *The Advance* when reporting on the noonday prayer meetings often summarized his words. These circumstances provide one with little information for evaluation. However, the available material appears to fit Daniels' testimony that Moody's early messages contained very little biblical content.

Of the twenty-two messages recorded in *The Advance*, nine of them had no Scripture reference of any kind. Seven of the messages briefly referenced either a story, or a passage from the Bible without giving a direct reference. Only five of the twenty-two messages are clearly connected in some way to a Bible verse(s). The one remaining message, not accounted for in these numbers, was presented on October 19, 1869. This message may have had a very slight allusion to 1Kings 18:41–46. However, it is not certain that Moody intended this allusion at all. If so, this would mean that ten of the messages had no reference to Scripture.

Of the five messages that had a direct reference to Bible verses, none of them seek to explain the verse within its context. Only one of the five may have fit into the textual category of the sermon rubric. The message recorded in *The Advance* on May 26, 1869 began with a reading of James 1:2. In the report, Moody offered a brief explanation of the verse, illustrated it, and applied it to his hearers. However, this particular report is clearly a summary of Moody's message for the day. Thus one cannot be certain if this is a textual sermon or not. The other four messages that referenced Scripture clearly fall within the topical category of the sermon rubric.

Conclusion

This chapter sought to gain a sense of the biblical content of Moody's early sermons. The chapter began by considering the testimony of W. H. Daniels, one of Moody's contemporaries, who published a work about Moody in 1875. After extensive research, the only extant Moody material discovered before Moorhouse's visit came from the Chicago noonday prayer meetings reported in *The Advance*. Twenty-two of the reports included messages from Moody. Some of these may have been brief words of exhortation. Others were short messages. In some cases, only summaries of Moody's words were preserved. Each one of these messages was described and then evaluated in light of Chapter Three's sermon rubric. The extant material affirms Daniel's testimony that Moody's early messages contained very little biblical content.

Just a little over two years following the last of these reports, Moody traveled to England with Ira Sankey, along with their wives. In the spring of 1873 they began the British campaign. Though the campaign faced many challenges in the early days, soon things turned around. The extent of Moody's influence garnered the attention of all Britain. Soon, reporters were coming to the services taking down his words verbatim and then publishing them in the secular newspapers. Moody's popularity grew and when he returned to the United States this practice became normal, making the messages he preached after 1873 readily available. Therefore, Chapter Five will have ample material to demonstrate Moody's sermon content following his visit from Henry Moorhouse and Moody's British campaign.

Chapter Five

An Examination of Moody's Middle Sermons

Having gained a sense of Moody's preaching prior to his British campaign of 1873–1875, it is now time to consider his preaching during his most popular years of life. The sermons delivered between fall 1875 and summer 1892 were preached during the time when Henry Moorhouse's Bible study method was most influential in Moody's ministry. As noted in Chapter Two, after a short rest Moody began holding extended preaching campaigns in large cities across the United States.[1] One such campaign was held in Boston. These Boston sermons will be evaluated as representative of Moody's preaching during the seventeen years before his sermon content shifted for a final time.

The Boston campaign sermons have been chosen for a few reasons. First, while Moody came to the know the Lord in Boston, he left the city for Chicago feeling somewhat rejected. When he returned for his evangelistic crusade, the atmosphere had not changed much. He faced some of his most difficult opposition in Boston, but he faithfully preached, trusting God to do a great work.

Second, Moody's preaching was constantly developing throughout his ministry. Biographer Lyle Dorsett noted, "God had not opened the way for formal theological education, but in the 1850s Moody was given tutors as he needed them along the way."[2] Indeed, a careful look at Moody's life reveals that he was always a learner. Even in the last years of his life, he is reported to have

---

1. John Pollock, *Moody: The Biography* (Chicago: Moody Press, 1983), 204.
2. Lyle W. Dorsett, *A Passion for Souls* (Chicago: Moody Publishers, 1997), 77.

inquired and learned at the feet of those who would preach at his Northfield Bible Conferences.

Third, as previously noted, his preaching grew in its biblical content. The first significant change occurred after Henry Moorhouse's visit to Chicago.[3] Another change came when Henry Weston preached at Northfield.[4] Since Moody's preaching changed through the years, three specific segments of time needed to be chosen for analysis. His Boston campaign occurred at the height of his popularity and in the middle years of his preaching.

The following pages will examine twenty sermons from Moody's Boston campaign. Before examining the sermons, this chapter sets the Boston campaign in its historical context. Individual sermons will then be described and evaluated. A description of the contents and flow of the message will be presented for each message. Following the description, the sermon will be evaluated utilizing the rubric established in Chapter Three. A summary of the findings from the evaluation of the Boston campaign sermons will bring the chapter to a close.

The Context of the Boston Campaign Sermons

In the spring of 1854, Moody left his family behind in Northfield and set out for Boston to make his mark on the business world. Upon his arrival, the five dollars his brother had given him was gone. The first few weeks left him terribly disappointed, as he could not find any work. Finally, he humbled himself and went to an uncle who ran a shoe shop, asking for a job. Reluctantly, his uncle agreed upon several conditions, one of which was that he must attend church.[5] Moody's early move to Boston led him to attend church and prepared him to become a follower of Christ.

---

3. Dorsett, *Passion for Souls*, 140.

4. Paul D. Moody, *My Father* (Boston: Little, Brown and Company, 1938), 185.

5. William R. Moody, *The Life of Dwight L. Moody* (Chicago: Fleming Revell Company, 1900), 28–38. (For a more detailed account of these years, see pages 25–29, above—ed.)

After a time, his Sunday School teacher, Mr. Kimball, came to visit him at work. The visit ended with Dwight turning to Jesus in faith. Shortly thereafter, he applied for membership in the Boston congregation and was turned down, due to a lack of being able to explain his new relationship with the Lord to the committee's satisfaction. After some mentoring by three members of the committee, he was later admitted.[6] Moody's life would never be the same.

After two years of successful shoe salesmanship, Boston seemed too small for Moody. His great aim was to be a wealthy business man, and Chicago seemed the place to go.[7] The Bible says, "Delight yourself also in the Lord and He shall give you the desires of your heart" (Ps 37:4 NKJV). The more Moody delighted himself in the Lord, the more the Lord changed his desires. Chicago became his home for business, and today it remains the primary place one can see the impact of his ministry. Yet Moody's concern for Boston grew, and he would one day return to see the city experience spiritual revival.

After his fall 1876 Chicago campaign, Moody headed to Boston for a three-month stint. William described the start to the Boston campaign as difficult at best:

> On the close of the Chicago campaign Moody began a mission in Boston that in many respects presented peculiar difficulties. The 'hub' of New England culture and refinement is the centre of every new philosophy and fad, while materialism and rationalism are widely spread. The idea of revival in Boston was repugnant to many people and on many sides he was subjected to hostile criticism and false reports, often of a personal nature.[8]

Despite the opposition and some financial struggles, Moody had a temporary structure erected that would seat somewhere between six and seven thousand people. He preached, held "Bible readings," prayer-meeting talks, and temperance lectures, filling the building as many as five times a day for a period of more than two months.

---

6. William R. Moody, *Life of D. L. Moody*, 39–45.
7. Ibid., 46–54.
8. Ibid., 291.

D.L. MOODY: TURNING POINTS TOWARD TEXT-DRIVEN PREACHING

Also despite the opposition, Moody's Boston campaign was blessed in another way. *The Boston Daily Globe* sent reporters to the meetings to take verbatim notes. Most days, they would publish the sermons, Bible readings, prayer meeting talks, and temperance lectures in the paper the following day. Occasionally, it was determined there was not enough room in the paper to print the messages. Recognizing the accuracy of the verbatim accounts, the Globe agreed to have the accounts published by E. B. Treat. According to the announcement in the front of the book, occasionally mistakes were made in the original newspaper publications due to time constraints. These mistakes were corrected for the book publication. In addition, they added the addresses that never made the paper due to space limitations on busy news days.[9] This publication began the trend of publishing Moody's sermons that continued throughout the remainder of his life.

Today, one might question how accurate these "verbatim reports" were regarding Moody's actual preaching. Discussing his sermons, Paul Moody, Dwight's youngest son, commented, "Some sermons should be heard, not read, precisely as others should be read and not heard. . . . The newspapers of the day, which often reported him verbatim, much to his embarrassment, give the clearest impression."[10] Paul's comments are enlightening. He acknowledged the accuracy of the reports and suggested that by reading the "verbatim sermons," one could gain a clear impression of his father's preaching.

Because six to seven thousand people at a time heard the sermons from Moody's mouth, one can assume that if the reports were not accurate there would be some historical evidence of such. Paul's statements indicated that Moody was "embarrassed" by the reports but not that he considered them inaccurate. In fact, his son believed that if a person wanted to understand Moody's preaching, the best way to do so was to read the verbatim accounts.

The present writer has examined both actual newspaper verbatims in PDF files converted from microfilm and those printed in *To All Peoples*.[11] The ser-

---

9. D. L. Moody, *To All Peoples* (New York: E. B. Treat, 1877), 4.

10. Paul Moody, *Father*, 111.

11. D. L. Moody, *To All Peoples*. The back of the title page of this collection of sermons gives an announcement concerning the accuracy of the sermons, reading in part, "Moody's sermons in Boston have been reported in the *Boston Daily Globe*. . . .

mons contained in the book are much easier to read because the microfilm produced poor copies. When one enlarges the picture through computer or print, the image blurs so much that it becomes very difficult to read. Therefore, attention is now given to a consideration of Moody's Boston campaign sermons, as published in *To All Peoples*.[12]

Description and Evaluation of Twenty Boston Campaign Sermons

As noted above, *To All People* contains verbatim accounts of many of Moody's addresses during his 1876–1877 Boston campaign. The book contains twenty-five addresses titled "Sermons and Lectures." It also presents accounts of sixteen "Bible Readings" where Moody would have someone read a verse and then speak to it, followed by moving on to another verse. He gave three "convention talks" concerning reaching the lost, reviving the church, and conducting prayer meetings, each of which are reported in the book. Six temperance addresses were presented. Seventeen "prayer meeting talks" and four prayers are recorded.

The focus of this chapter concerns Moody's preaching. Therefore, twenty sermons will be considered.[13] The first and last sermon of the campaign will be examined. The other eighteen sermons were chosen because of their interest

---

Mr. Moody himself has said, in regard to the *Daily Globe* Reports, that he never had been so well reported in any part of the world by any newspaper." The announcement goes on to indicate that the book publisher was furnished with the reporter's notes and that only slight editing was done to correct obvious errors. Such careful attention along with Moody's own testimony remove doubt about the accuracy of these verbatim accounts. In addition, they give a much better sense of the actual sermon than do the later books which were often edited more heavily.

12. D. L. Moody, *To All Peoples*.

13. Twenty sermons from Moody's middle years give a strong sample of his sermon content at this stage of his ministry. Chapter five will demonstrate such a consistency that the addition of more sermons would not change the findings. For a full explanation of the number of sermons chosen for this dissertation please see footnote 34 in chapter one.

D.L. MOODY:
TURNING POINTS TOWARD TEXT-DRIVEN PREACHING

to the present writer. Below, the reader will see the sermon title, followed by a summary description of the sermon. Next the sermon content will be evaluated utilizing the rubric established in Chapter Three.

The Faith of Caleb and Joshua[14]

Sermon Description

The opening sermon of the Boston campaign was based on Numbers 13:30, "Let us go up at once, and possess it; for we are well able to overcome it." Having read the text, Moody commended the words of Caleb and the action of Caleb and Joshua to the people of Boston. He called for people in Boston not to look at the obstacles and difficulties of revival coming to the city, but to have faith like Caleb that God could do a great work, even in Boston.

Moody briefly described the context of Caleb's word by giving an overview of Numbers 13. He also recalled the many miracles the people of Israel had observed, and claimed they gave Caleb and Joshua the courage to possess the Promised Land in faith. One of his statements seems anachronistic. Notice his running list of miracles:

> Ten men were looking at these obstacles that this new land presented to them, while these two men, Caleb and Joshua, looked up yonder, and they saw God's face and remembered the waste in Egypt, the crossing of the Red Sea, the destruction that was brought upon the Philistines, the water from the flint rock, and they believed that God was able, as He certainly was, to give them that land He had promised.[15]

Upon reading the sentence above, one wonders if Moody threw the Philistines into the list, thinking of a later time when the Lord delivered the Philistines into Israel's hand.

Moody abruptly switched characters in the middle of his sermon and began talking about Gideon as another example of trusting God against all odds.

---

14. D. L. Moody, *To All Peoples*, 17–23.
15. Ibid., 21.

The switch to Gideon may account for the mention of the Philistines in the previous list. At any rate, the statement does not seem to fit in the context of the Caleb and Joshua narrative.

Throughout the sermon Moody called on the people of Boston to ignore the obstacles and believe God to send a revival to the city. Indeed, he frequently moved back and forth from Caleb, Joshua, and the unbelieving spies, to the people of Boston. When he shifted his focus to Gideon, he continued to move freely back and forth from Gideon to the people in Boston. He spoke of the need for revival in Boston. He said the revival would start with God's people and end with a great cry from the Bostonians, "What must we do to be saved?"[16] With this Moody concluded his opening sermon in Boston.

Sermon Evaluation

Moody drew on the example of Caleb and Joshua to call his audience to act in faith. Moody took Caleb's words calling on the Israelites to go into the promised land, and used these words to call on Bostonians to go out expecting a great revival in the city. Moody focused his sermon on the faith he believed to be revealed by Caleb's statement. He called on his hearers to exhibit this kind of faith, trusting God to do great things again. While D. L. Moody is known most for seeing countless numbers become Christians in his ministry, this sermon does not explicitly share the gospel.[17] Comparing the sermon to the rubric established in Chapter Three will demonstrate the category into which this message fits.

---

16. D. L. Moody, *To All Peoples*, 23.

17. Many who read his sermons are amazed at how few of them share the gospel explicitly. Moody's reputation is that of a constant evangelist who led many to Christ. The reason for this seeming discrepancy is cleared up when one understands Moody's practice. Following a sermon Moody would usually say a few words and then encourage people to go to an "after meeting" to learn how to be saved. He often referred instead to these meetings as "inquiry meetings." In the meetings, he and other trained men and women made themselves available to talk to individuals one-on-one. This is where Moody often led individuals to Jesus. He referred to this as "personal work" and believed it was of utmost importance. By his own testimony, after the Chicago fire Moody never preached without asking people to respond (William R. Moody, *The Life of D. L. Moody*, 145). However, he usually separated his invitation to receive Christ from his actual sermon.

D.L. MOODY: TURNING POINTS TOWARD TEXT-DRIVEN PREACHING

Expository or Textual?

First, it should be noted that one can quickly dismiss the first two categories on the rubric. Even a cursory reading will reveal that the sermon does not seek to explain the meaning of the text within its context. The sermon is also not based on a single verse or a running commentary of an extended passage.[18] Therefore, the opening sermon of the Boston campaign cannot be considered either expositional or textual.

Biographical?

The title of this sermon might suggest the sermon should be considered a biographical sermon. While the sermon begins with Caleb and Joshua, it does not fit the definition of a biographical sermon this monograph has adopted. Neither does this sermon fit the rubric criteria of a biographical sermon.[19] It does begin with a sentence from Caleb. It does speak of the example of Caleb and Joshua. However, it does not really develop even the characteristic of faith throughout their lives. As noted above, the sermon abruptly shifts focus to Gideon. Thus, while the sermon title may imply a biographical sermon, the message really does not fit this category.

Topical?

The question remains whether the first sermon of the Boston campaign should be categorized as a topical sermon. When one looks at the category descriptions in the sermon rubric, the answer is at first unclear. The answer is found in comparing the sermon to the three criteria of the rubric.[20] Consider the theme of the sermon.

The sermon begins with a focus on Caleb's statement, "Let us go up at once, and possess it; for we are well able to overcome it."[21] From this sentence, Moody picked up the statement, "Let us go up at once."[22] This statement served as the unifying theme of the sermon. Whether Moody spoke of Caleb and Josh-

---

18. All sermons are evaluated in light of the rubric defined in Chapter Three.
19. Ibid.
20. All sermons are evaluated in light of the rubric defined in Chapter Three.
21. D. L. Moody, *To All Peoples*, 17.
22. Ibid.

ua, the Bostonians, or Gideon, this statement directed his thoughts. While the sermon did not concern itself with explaining the text itself, it utilized this sentence from the text to call for Bostonians to have faith and overcome obstacles. The statement, "Let us go up at once" carried the entire sermon.[23]

While the preacher moved back and forth from Caleb and Joshua to the Bostonians, to Gideon, he carried the same central theme throughout his sermon. Indeed, in the final moments of the sermon Moody exclaimed, "Let us have faith. Let us go up and possess the land. In the name of God let there be no adverse criticism, no looking at difficulties. Let us come praying to God to move this city, and may there go up the great cry from Boston of 'What shall we do to be saved?' "[24] "The Faith of Caleb and Joshua" is therefore classified as a topical sermon.

Saved or Lost[25]

Sermon Description

Moody began this sermon with the question, "Saved or lost; in the fold or out of it. That is the question to-night."[26] The preacher announced no text for this sermon. Rather, he only announced the subject introduced by the opening words. He did refer to a handful of partial verses without giving references for them. In his day, the verses would have likely been recognized as Bible verses or as biblical allusions. In the first few moments he quoted, "The Son of Man has come to seek and save that which was lost." He then referred to Jesus' conversation with Nicodemus without mentioning his name or the passage and quoted both, "Except a man be born again he cannot see the kingdom of God" and, "You must be born again."[27] While there were two other biblical allusions without reference, most of the sermon was filled with stories that pressed home the reality of just how bad it is to be lost.

---

23. D. L. Moody, *To All Peoples*, 17.
24. Ibid., 23.
25. Ibid., 31–40.
26. Ibid., 31.
27. Ibid., 31.

D.L. MOODY:
TURNING POINTS TOWARD TEXT-DRIVEN PREACHING

Moody showed his hand on the theological front in this sermon. He said, "Some people think the Lord will seek them. They will not come until the Lord has sought them. They are waiting for Him to seek them out .... Is there anyone who can say to-night, 'The Son of God has never sought for me!'"[28] The preacher then launched into a string of statements and illustrations demonstrating ways he believed the Lord is seeking all men.

Moody's list of Christ's methods includes sermons heard, Scriptures read, tracts given, prayers of a mother, friends and strangers who have attempted to share the Gospel, and more. He says, "There are hundreds of ways in which the Son of God seeks to save."[29] Moody furthered his case by stating, "But I want to say right here, don't any one of you go out saying the Son of God never sought for your soul. The man don't live whom the Son of God never sought to save."[30] The preacher then turned his attention to helping his listeners understand the depth of lostness.

Moody encouraged believers to seek the lost, and he encouraged the lost to be saved. He concluded by quoting a portion of John 3:16, again without reference. He then called on everyone to pray for the lost who were present in the building.

Sermon Evaluation

The reader of this sermon may be captivated by the flow of thought. Even in print, the passion of the preacher can be observed. The gospel was shared in parts throughout the message. Moody constantly called people to respond to the gospel message throughout the sermon. Yet, the question at hand relates to the classification of the sermon based upon the level of biblical content of the message. Attention now turns to consider the message in light of the sermon rubric.

Expository or Textual?

The above sermon summary demonstrates that Moody's Boston sermon "Saved or Lost" cannot be considered an expository sermon. The sermon began with a topic, rather than a text. While Scriptural references and allusions were made, they did not guide the sermon. Rather than choosing a text and seeking to

---

28. D. L. Moody, *To All Peoples*, 33.
29. Ibid., 35.
30. Ibid.

explain it within its context, the preacher chose a topic and used biblical statements to support the topic.

Neither could it be suggested that this sermon rose to the level of being a textual sermon. It does not fit the definition adopted in the sermon rubric. Neither does it fit even one of the criteria of the textual sermon according the sermon rubric. Therefore, neither of the present categories will do for this message.

Biographical?

"Save or Lost" does not in any way fit the category of a biographical sermon. It does not follow a character's life. The primary person mentioned in this sermon is Jesus. Moody sought to demonstrate that Jesus sought the lost. However, he did not develop this sermon as a biographical sermon. Having ruled out three of the sermon categories on the sermon rubric, the message must be categorized as either a topical or a diving board sermon.[31]

Topical?

Moody based his Boston sermon, "Saved or Lost" on a topic rather than a text. The sermon utilized several Scripture references and allusions but failed to explain any of the verses utilized. Each simply provided support for the topic. The divisions of the sermon were clearly chosen by the preacher, rather than provided by a passage of Scripture. Therefore, this message must be classified as a topical sermon.

The Holy Spirit III[32]

Sermon Description

To All People notes that Moody had four sermons on the Holy Spirit but only the third and fourth are contained in the book. The first two sermons on

---

31. The present author uses the term "Diving Board Sermon" to describe a sermon where the preacher reads a text of Scripture at the beginning of his message and then "dives off" into whatever subject or subjects he chooses. Often there is little or no structure to the sermon, just random thoughts about the Christian topics.

32. D. L. Moody, *To All Peoples*, 41–53.

D.L. MOODY: TURNING POINTS TOWARD TEXT-DRIVEN PREACHING

the Holy Spirit can be read in *Glad Tidings*, another book of Moody's verbatim sermons.[33] Consider the summary of the present sermon.

Moody began this sermon by reading Galatians 5:18 as his text. The theme of the sermon was the need to be led by the Spirit. He began by calling on unbelievers to willingly yield themselves to be led by the Spirit and be saved.[34] Moody quickly turned his attention to believers, calling on them to be led by the Spirit rather than by their own desires: "Oh, Christians, if you will be led by the Spirit you will have peace and joy that will throw light on questions that you don't now understand."[35] The remainder of the sermon focuses on the believer's interaction with the Spirit.

Moody connected the idea of being led by the Spirit to memorizing the Word of God. Moody said, "The Holy Ghost always quotes the Word. You will find that a man who is full of the Holy Spirit is generally full of Scripture, and that will lead you aright."[36] Moody warned those who say the Spirit led them to do something that is against the Word.

Moody spoke of how those who are Spirit led will treat one another in the church, quoting from Ephesians 4. Concerning the church, Moody stated, "Now if we grieve the Spirit He cannot work through us and use us."[37] He also spoke of Spirit-led preaching as preaching that called out sin that needs to be dealt with by members of a congregation. He warned against preaching that only speaks of the sins of people in the Bible and ignores the sins present in his own congregation. Moody stated, "Many preachers bring up the sins of those that lived hundreds of years ago. But if we are going to honor the Holy Ghost, we must give the message just as God gives it to us."[38] Sin hinders the work of the Spirit in the church. Moody believed that Spirit-led believers repent of sin.

Moody warned his listeners not to quench the Spirit, quoting 1 Thessalonians 5:19. He then spoke of the convicting work of the Spirit in Acts 7 and

---

33. D. L. Moody, *Glad Tidings, Comprising Sermons and Prayer-Meeting Talks* (New York: E. B. Treat, 1876).
34. D. L. Moody, *To All Peoples*, 41.
35. Ibid., 42.
36. Ibid.
37. Ibid., 45.
38. Ibid., 46.

John 16.[39] He warned of "dead orthodoxy" by referring to 2 Corinthians 3:6.[40] Next, Moody came back to the theme of the Spirit and the Word by turning to Ephesians 6:7. He spent a considerable amount of time connecting the Bible as the Sword of the Spirit to the work of the Spirit.[41] He concluded by noting several metaphors for the Spirit including: water, fire, wind, oil, rain/dew, a dove, and a seal. He then prayed that all present would be led by the Spirit from that day forward.[42] While the sermon remained focused on the Holy Spirit throughout, it touched on numerous aspects of the relationship between the Spirit and the believer. Many of the biblical passages included could be preached within their contexts, but as a single sermon on one aspect of the Spirit.

Sermon Evaluation

Moody directed this message primarily toward Christians. He did not share the gospel explicitly in the sermon, though he alluded to it lightly. As noted earlier, he always held an "inquiry meeting" after the main service where the gospel was shared. Having gained an understanding of the content of this sermon, attention must now be given to evaluating it in light of the sermon rubric. Comparing the sermon to the descriptions and criteria for each of the sermon types will guide the evaluation process. We begin by looking at the expository and textual categories.

Expository or Textual?

"The Holy Spirit III" begins with the reading of a text of Scripture. However, the attempt to explain the meaning of the passage within its context does not occur in this message. Rather, the sermon is based on a presentation of various biblical truths revealed throughout the Bible. Therefore, this sermon is not an expository sermon.

The textual sermon category will not fit this message either. The preacher does not present a sermon focused on divisions of a verse or even a few verses

---

39. D. L. Moody, *To All Peoples*, 48.
40. Ibid., 50.
41. Ibid., 50–52.
42. Ibid., 52–53.

in Galatians chapter five. Neither did Moody provide a running commentary of the passage. Therefore, one must consider other categories within the sermon rubric to classify this message.

Biographical?

While the sermon is somewhat based on a person—the Holy Spirit, it does not fit the category of a biographical sermon. The message explains various aspects of the Holy Spirit's work in and through the life of the believer. The believer's relationship to the Holy Spirit serves as the primary concern in the sermon. This leaves the topical category for consideration.

Topical?

While the sermon considers several topics, the preacher did this in a fashion that kept the Holy Spirit's relationship to the believer as his primary focus. Each of the Bible verses quoted were related to the main theme in one way or another. The preacher's sermon divisions were thought out and made both doctrinal and practical points related to the main theme. Considering each of the sermon rubric criteria, this sermon should be classified as a topical sermon.

The Holy Spirit's Power, IV[43]

Sermon Description

Moody began by announcing the subject of his sermon, "We have for our subject this afternoon the [S]pirit of power and the [S]pirit of service."[44] He then turned to the Bible, drawing attention to two passages. He read John 14:17, followed by 1 Corinthians 3:16—17. Moody described the need for servants who are filled with the Holy Spirit. Moody spoke of Jesus' first thirty years, saying that he did not do anything highly noteworthy until the Holy Spirit came upon Him.[45] Having laid the foundation for his theme, the preacher turned his attention to the problem of the lack of power in the church.

---

43. D. L. Moody, *To All Peoples*, 54–61.
44. Ibid., 54.
45. Ibid., 54–55.

Moody indicated he believed people in the church are either like Nicodemus who doubted, the Samaritan woman who served out of joy, or better yet, those who have a spring of water flowing out of them.[46] With each of these examples he quoted partial verses from John 3, 4, 7. Moody also talked about the change that came to Peter after Pentecost and the need for continual filling like John and Peter experienced in Acts 4. As with all of Moody's sermons, this one was filled with numerous stories and illustrations to demonstrate his theme.

Moody expressed concern that the Holy Spirit empower not only his preaching but the lives of all believers. This empowerment is necessary for being fruitful in God's work. Moody said, "In the church ... you will find upon making an examination that they have dead leaders, dead deacons, dead superintendents and Sunday School teachers; they are all dead together; they have not the love and power of God resting upon them."[47] He connected fruitful labor with the power of the Spirit and was concerned that all believers be filled and empowered for service.

Moody believed the Lord was empowering him, even as he preached this message. He expected the Spirit to work in the lives of his listeners to bring about *life change* in them. He specifically demonstrated the purpose of this *life change*, by passionately calling on people to be filled with the Spirit. He concluded his sermon by saying, "Let us pray God to descend upon the churches of Boston, and baptize them with His Holy Spirit."[48] Moody believed the Spirit empowered his preaching of this message, and he preached so that his listeners' lives would be changed.

Sermon Evaluation

Moody once again directed this sermon to Christians. However, he did allude to the gospel several times. He described one of the works of the Spirit as the work of convincing people of sin. This gave him the opportunity to share the gospel and call people to respond in faith and repentance. While

---
46. D. L. Moody, *To All Peoples*, 55–56.
47. Ibid., 57.
48. Ibid., 61.

the sermon may be helpful to the reader, the question of its biblical content remains the focus of this monograph. Therefore, we must now examine the sermon considering the sermon rubric. Once again, the starting point will be exposition.

Expository or Textual?

While the sermon began with a topic, Moody quickly read two Bible passages. Yet, he failed to explain the meaning of these passages within their context. The verses were used simply to support the early thoughts of the message. This pattern continued throughout the sermon. Therefore, the sermon cannot be categorized as an expository message.

The verses read at the beginning of the sermon did not provide the divisions of the sermon to follow. Neither did the preacher walk through a passage, giving a running commentary of the text. Therefore, the sermon does not fit the textual sermon category.

Biographical?

Even more clear than the previous sermon on the Holy Spirit, this message cannot be considered biographical in nature. The focus here is specifically on the empowerment of the Holy Spirit for service. The researcher must look to the last category of the sermon rubric to classify this message.

Topical?

Moody's Boston Sermon, "The Holy Spirit's Power" clearly fits within the category of a topical sermon. The unifying theme of the sermon is stated in the title and in the first sentence. The topic carries the entire message. There is one single point the preacher makes: believers need the power of the Spirit for service. This sermon must be categorized as a topical sermon.

The Life and Character of Jacob[49]

Sermon Description

Moody began this sermon by saying, "We have for our subject, to-day, 'Jacob.'"[50] He explained that for a long time he struggled over why the Bible presents characters like Jacob. He quickly contrasted Jacob with Daniel and other Bible characters. Moody then says, "You will find there are more Jacobs in the Church of God to-day than there are Abrahams."[51] Moody believed that by studying Jacob, the believer could see the grace of God and learn to trust him more.

Having introduced the subject of his sermon, Moody began by simply describing much of the early life of Jacob. He then turned to Genesis 27:46 and began reading. From here, Moody traced Jacob's life all the way to him standing before Pharaoh in Egypt (Gen 47:9). He demonstrated that throughout Jacob's life he continually chose not to believe God, often despite God's direct promises. Instead of trusting the Lord, Jacob doubted, deceived, and tried to plot his own path to success.

In the conclusion to the sermon Moody said of Jacob, "If he had lived in a castle he might just as well have written over the door, 'doubting castle.' He all the time saw bears—trouble with Esau, trouble with his father-in-law, trouble all the way, because he wouldn't take God at His Word."[52] While he traced Jacob's life, sometimes reading Scripture and sometimes simply telling the story, Moody's focus was on warning his listeners to avoid doubt and trust God.

Throughout the sermon, Moody sought to encourage his listeners to stop trying to walk by sight and to make bargains with God. He also sought to encourage them to walk by faith: "These Christians who are trying to make bargains with the Lord, trying to and walking by sight, instead of by faith, are

---

49. D. L. Moody, *To All Peoples*, 253–265.
50. Ibid., 253.
51. Ibid., 254.
52. Ibid., 265. What Moody meant by "He all the time saw bears" is not clear. He likely meant to say, "He all the time saw beers," indicating one who lives in fear.

a great hindrance to the Church of God (*sic*)."[53] He concluded the sermon with the following statement: "Your Heavenly Father knows all your needs.... God will help us if we put our trust in Him. Have faith in God, and not be complaining all the time."[54] Jacob's life served as both a warning and a promise to Moody's hearers.

Sermon Evaluation

The reader of this sermon will be engaged quickly. Moody began with a brief introduction and jumped right into the story of Jacob's life. He wasted no time moving from gaining attention to laying out his theme. The primary question of this monograph relates not to Moody's ability to gain and keep the attention of his audience, but to the biblical content of his messages. In that light, we will now examine the sermon by utilizing the sermon rubric of Chapter Three. Before considering the sermon rubric it should be noted that Moody did not share the gospel in this sermon. There is little doubt that he followed the sermon with an inquiry meeting where the gospel was shared on-on-one with all willing to listen.

Expository or Textual?

The sermon included the reading of several passages of Scripture from Genesis 27–47. Each time these passages were read, Moody included some explanation. However, the explanation of the meaning of the text was not the primary focus of the preacher. Because Moody read several portions from twenty-one chapters of Genesis, some sense of the context was demonstrated. However, the texts were primarily used by the preacher to demonstrate a few specific themes from the life of Jacob. Therefore, this sermon cannot really be considered an expository sermon in accordance with our sermon rubric. Thus, another category must be sought for this message.

According to the rubric, a textual sermon is one that is based on a passage of Scripture. It may be either a single verse or a running commentary of a group of verses. The difference in this and the expository sermon is that the divisions

---

53. D. L. Moody, *To All Peoples*, 264.
54. Ibid., 265.

of the sermon are not based on the divisions of the text in the textual sermon. While the present sermon does indeed utilize several passages of Scripture, the sermon is not so much based on those passages. Rather, the passages read serve to accentuate both warnings and promises that Moody desired his listeners learn from the example of Jacob. Therefore, this sermon must not be categorized as a textual sermon.

Biographical?

The definition this monograph adopted for a biographical sermon states, "The sermon is based on the life of a Bible character. The sermon utilizes passages that demonstrate the specific characteristics the preacher wants to emphasize. Application is based on those characteristics."[55] Moody's Boston sermon, "The Life and Character of Jacob" fits this description. The description is supported by three criteria, which are all met by this sermon. Therefore, the sermon under consideration should be categorized as a biographical sermon.

Topical?

Having already established that the present sermon fits well in the biographical category, there is little reason to even examine the message considering topical criteria. However, it could be noted that there are similarities to a topical sermon. There is a two-fold central theme to the message. First, the preacher is concerned that his listeners stop doubting, deceiving, and attempting to bargain with God. Second, he desires that they trust God fully in every area of life.

Despite the similarities noted in the above paragraph, the major difference comes in the fact that the primary theme is based on a specific character—Jacob. The primary passages chosen to demonstrate the two-fold theme were chosen specifically from the life of one man, and were limited to twenty-one chapters of a single book of the Bible. These facts demonstrate that the sermon fits better into the biographical category.

---

55. D. L. Moody, *To All Peoples*, 265.

D.L. MOODY:
TURNING POINTS TOWARD TEXT-DRIVEN PREACHING

The Life and Character of Joshua[56]

Sermon Description

Moody began this sermon at the Boston campaign by reminding his listeners of his previous sermon on Jacob. He then indicated that he was going to preach on the life and character of Joshua and contrast it to that of Jacob.[57] In setting the stage for the sermon Moody said, "Joshua was a man that walked by faith, and you will find the key to his character in three words—courage, obedience, and faith."[58] The preacher made a few general comments about Joshua before telling the story of his life.

Moody said, "Where Joshua met the God of Israel first we are not told. We don't catch a glimpse of him till he is about forty years old."[59] From this point early in the sermon, Moody simply tells Joshua's story. He did not begin by reading a text. Instead, he recounted several events in Joshua's life. While it is clear Moody followed the general flow of the biblical narrative, he did not really quote or read Scripture to make his point.

The first time Moody did read Scripture in this sermon, he read from Moses' departing message to Israel. He read an extended portion of the address and encouraged his listeners to read it in its entirety later. He quickly mentioned the end of Moses' life and then quoted, "Joshua, arise, and go over this Jordan. Moses, my servant, is dead."[60] Following this short excursus, Moody went right back to telling the life story of Joshua.

Throughout the entire sermon, Moody's unifying theme remained the example of Joshua's faith. He used various events in Joshua's life to demonstrate that Joshua trusted God, acted courageously, and obeyed the Lord. Moody mentioned Joshua's first battle with the Amalekites.[61] Moody spoke of Joshua lead-

---

56. D. L. Moody, *To All Peoples*, 266–278.
57. Ibid., 266.
58. Ibid.
59. Ibid.
60. Ibid., 266–267.
61. Ibid., 267.

ing the people across the Jordan river.[62] He spoke of the victory at Jericho, the defeat at Ai, and the victory of the five kings.[63] In each case, Moody noted Joshua's faith, courage, and obedience. Often, he engaged his listeners in the middle of telling Joshua's story by referring to "the men of Boston" or to the "people of Boston." He called on his listeners to follow Joshua's example.

On the final page of the sermon, Moody read from Joshua's last address to the people. He said, "I am going the way of all the earth; and ye know in your hearts and in all your souls that not one thing hath failed of all the good things which the Lord your God spake concerning you."[64] Moody moved toward his close by saying, "My friends, let us take God at His word . . . All these men are trying to pick the Word of God to pieces, trying to destroy our confidence in the Word of God, tell us it is not true; but anyone who has ever tried God, who have ever proved God, have found Him to be true."[65] Moody's entire sermon called on the people of Boston to trust God and his Word.

Sermon Evaluation

Wayne McDill argues that the "fundamental objective of preaching is faith."[66] If a faith response is the main objective of the sermon, Moody reached the main objective with the present sermon. From beginning to end, the preacher sought to call the people of Boston to a life of faith. While Moody preached for faith, he did not share the gospel message during the sermon. The question remains as to exactly how this sermon should be classified.

Expository or Textual?

Moody read or quoted Scripture directly in this sermon very little. When he did quote the Bible, it was used to support his overall theme. As noted above, the longest portion of Scripture read did not relate directly to the sermon itself.

---

62. D. L. Moody, *To All Peoples*, 270–72.
63. Ibid., 272–276.
64. Ibid., 278.
65. Ibid.
66. Wayne McDill, *12 Essential Skills for Great Preaching* (Nashville: B&H Publishing Group, 2006), Kindle Location 4488.

D.L. MOODY:
TURNING POINTS TOWARD TEXT-DRIVEN PREACHING

However, Moody's telling of the story of Joshua's life was based on the book of Joshua. He followed the story line well.

Moody's purpose is neither to give a full accounting of Joshua's life, nor is his purpose to explain a text of Scripture within its context. Rather, he is attempting to draw on events in Joshua's life to demonstrate an example of faith, courage, and obedience. In the end, this sermon would not be classified as expositional or textual.

Biographical?

As the title implies, "The Life and Character of Joshua," this sermon fits the definition and criteria of a biographical sermon. It is based on a biblical character. With the brief exception of the excursus from Moses' farewell address, the sermon follows the theme of Joshua's faith. Moody indicated in his introduction that he was going to show that the key to Joshua's life was his, "courage, obedience, and faith." [67] The preacher accomplished his purpose. Throughout the sermon, Moody applied the character of Joshua to his Boston listeners. Considering the definition and the criteria, this message should be classified as a biographical sermon.

Topical?

Like the sermon on Jacob, this sermon has a topical element. The message followed a unifying theme and applied that theme to the hearers. However, the sermon fits better in the biographical category since, as noted above, it is based on the life of Joshua and it applied Joshua's faith, courage, and obedience to the people of Boston.

The Life and Character of Peter[68]

Sermon Description

Moody wasted no time getting into this sermon. He began, "The first glimpse we catch of Peter is when Andrew brought him to the Saviour. That

67. D. L. Moody, *To All Peoples*, 266.
68. Ibid., 279–294.

is John's account. That is when he became a disciple; but he didn't leave everything then and follow Christ."[69] The preacher then shared a few thoughts on his belief that all people are called to discipleship, but not everyone is called to leave business and preach full time. He encouraged his listeners to be careful not to leave business, unless they are sure of God's call. In fact, Moody suggested that the preachers that fail are the ones that were never truly called by God. He says, "I believe there are a great many self-made preachers, man-made preachers, and that is the reason why so many fail. No man who is called by God has ever failed."[70] With this argument, Moody began to examine the character of Peter and apply various events in Peter's life to his Boston listeners.

Having described Peter's call to discipleship, Moody turned his attention to Peter's call to full-time ministry. Noting it is recorded in both Matthew and Luke, Moody read Luke 5. He described Jesus' invitation, "follow me and I will make you fishers of men."[71] In considering this call, Moody observed that Jesus first gave them success in fishing before he called them. As to why Moody suggested, "Now the Lord wanted them to give up something,"[72] the preacher spoke of the fact that if someone is going to leave business and preach it is going to cost them something. He then applied this to all of Boston. He warned against people who were willing to follow only if there was no sacrifice involved.

The next characteristic Moody demonstrated from Peter's life is not flattering. He directed the listeners to turn to Matthew 14:22. Introducing the passage Moody says, "The next glimpse we catch of Peter he takes a doubting character."[73] Having read the story, Moody focused on Peter taking his eyes of Jesus, looking at his circumstances, and beginning to doubt. He called on his listeners to focus their attention on Jesus by quoting Isaiah 26:3.

Moody jumped to Matthew 16:24 ff. Here he focused on Peter's great confession. The preacher expressed his concern for people who try to have a private relationship with the Lord, but are unwilling to confess it. He read Romans 10:10, and called up his listeners to confess Jesus unashamedly before others.

---

69. D. L. Moody, *To All Peoples*, 279.
70. Ibid.
71. Ibid., 280–281.
72. Ibid., 281.
73. Ibid., 282.

Moody's next passage for consideration was Luke 9:28. The focus here was on Peter's mistake on the Mount of Transfiguration. Peter offered to make three tabernacles: one for Moses, one for Elijah, and one for Jesus. Moody made the point that Peter mistakenly lowered his view of the person of Jesus. He warned his listeners of people who would do the same thing in Boston.

Considering Luke 22:33, Moody warned his hearers to beware of self-confidence and pride. He explained that when Jesus told Peter he would deny Him, Peter should have humbly sought the Lord's help. However, he acted arrogantly and proclaimed he would never deny Jesus. Applying this lesson to his listeners Moody said, "If a man gets his eye off of God, and relies on his own strength, you may look for his fall."[74] Moody then called on "backsliders" to return to the Lord.

Moody not only spoke of Peter's arrogance but suggested that Peter's "falling asleep" caused him to fall further. He noted that in the Garden of Gethsemane while Jesus was praying, Peter fell asleep. If he would have watched and prayed as Jesus warned, Moody thought he may have resisted the temptation. But his failure to watch and pray ensured his downfall.[75] Moody warned his listeners to not fall asleep.

While Moody's sermon on the character of Peter demonstrated both good and bad characteristics, he concluded the sermon with a look at Peter's restoration. Moody noted that when the ladies were sent to the disciples to proclaim Jesus' resurrection, He singled out Peter. Moody said, "Tell Peter; put his name in; don't leave him out."[76] Moody then recounted the restoration by the sea with Peter's acknowledgement of love and Jesus' commission to care for his sheep. Moody concluded the sermon with a call to his hearers to return to the Lord.

Sermon Evaluation

This is the longest sermon the present researcher has read from D. L. Moody. In print form, the sermon took up sixteen pages. Moody focused on encouraging his hearers to follow the positive examples from Peter's life and

---

74 D. L. Moody, *To All Peoples*, 289.
75 Ibid., 289–292.
76 Ibid., 294.

shun the negative examples. Moody did speak of Jesus as the provider of redemption. He also spoke of the necessity to believe in one's heart and confess with the mouth to be saved. However, he did not explicitly share the gospel in this message

Expository or Textual?

D. L. Moody included several passages of Scripture in this sermon. Most of these were read in their entirety, or at least enough to get a sense of the general context of each text. However, rather than explain the meaning of the passages, Moody chose a characteristic from each passage that served as an example of some truth from Peter's life. Therefore, this sermon does not fit either the exposition or textual categories of the sermon rubric adopted in this monograph.

Biographical?

As noted in the sermon summary above, Moody jumped right into describing Peter. He began with the first introduction to Peter in John's Gospel. Throughout the sermon, Moody read and quoted passages from the Gospels that demonstrated various characteristics of Peter's life. Each of these characteristics were developed somewhat and then applied to Moody's Boston hearers. This sermon fits both the definition and the criteria of a biographical sermon.

Topical?

Unlike Moody's sermons on Jacob and Joseph, the sermon on Peter does not follow a single unifying topic throughout the life of the Bible character. Rather, this sermon considers several characteristics from the life of Peter. If there is a unifying theme in this sermon, it is Peter himself. Therefore, of the sermons considered thus far, this sermon is most distinctly not a topical sermon. There is no reason to view this sermon as anything other than a biographical message.

D.L. MOODY: TURNING POINTS TOWARD TEXT-DRIVEN PREACHING

Sowing and Reaping[77]

Sermon Description

Moody began this sermon by announcing his text: "You will find my text in the 6th chapter of Galatians, the 7th and 8th verses."[78] After reading these two verses he continued, "There are a good many men quarrelling with the Word of God nowadays, but I think all will admit that this text is true."[79] Moody then warned against deception. He spoke of deceiving others and deceiving oneself. Yet, he reminded his hearers that no one can deceive God.

Returning to his main topic of sowing and reaping, Moody suggested that everyone recognizes that whatever one sows is what he will reap. He provided several illustrations from everyday life that demonstrate this truth. The preacher said the law of sowing and reaping is true of nations as well as individuals. He noted Nineveh, Jerusalem, and Babylon.[80] Then he pointed to the United States sowing slavery and reaping the war that led more than half a million soldiers to their grave.[81] He returned to examples of individuals reaping what they sow.

Moody mentioned several biblical characters who learned the law of sowing and reaping. He spent a little time talking about David, who sinned, thought he got away with it, was confronted, repented, was forgiven, but still reaped what he had sown.[82] The preacher then quickly mentioned Cain, Ahab, Herod, and Joseph's brothers. Most of the time Moody simply told the story of these characters. However, in telling the story, he quoted verses or partial verses di-

---

77. D. L. Moody, *To All Peoples*, 295–302. It should be noted that "Sowing and Reaping" is one of the most well-known sermons Moody preached. Nearly every book of collected Moody sermons will present a message by this title. While the sermon was preached hundreds, if not thousands, of times, most biographers would note that it was never preached exactly in the same way. Therefore, it is important to note that this is the message as Moody preached it during the Boston campaign of 1875–1876.

78. Ibid., 295.
79. Ibid.
80. Ibid., 296.
81. Ibid., 297.
82. Ibid. 297–298.

rectly from the Bible. He did not usually give the reference. Having used several biblical examples, Moody then turned to direct and pointed confrontation with those who think they will get away with sin.

Moody declared that every preacher must confront sin and warn people of the truth. He used a handful of illustrations to make his point. Moody quoted, "Be sure your sin will find you out."[83] He called on the gathered Bostonians to cry out to God for mercy rather than attempt to hide sin. He concluded the sermon by saying, "Oh sinner come to-night! Confess your sins, ask God to blot them out, and He will do it now, this very hour."[84] Following those stirring words, Moody led the congregation to prayer.

Sermon Evaluation

Reading this sermon, one can appreciate the passion of the preacher. Moody preached this message often.[85] Anyone interested in Moody's preaching would be remiss not to read this sermon. However, this monograph does not focus on the passion in Moody's preaching.[86] Instead, attention must be given to examining the sermon category in accordance with the sermon rubric. However, it should first be noted that Moody did proclaim the gospel in this message. While he did not speak of the resurrection, he spoke of Christ taking our sin and suffering the wrath of God. He then spoke of God's mercy for those who would receive this salvation. He called on his hearers to turn to Christ for salvation in the sermon itself, which was not his usual practice. Typically, he saved that for the "inquiry meetings" that followed his preaching services.

---

83. D. L. Moody, *To All Peoples*, 298.

84. Ibid., 302.

85. This particular sermon is repeated in nearly every collection of Moody's sermons. It was even preached by Moody in his Northfield summer conferences. See Delevan L. Pierson, ed., *Northfield Echoes*, (East Northfield, MA: The Conference Book Store, 1895), 132–145; hereafter, *Echoes* (publication year).

86. For an examination of Moody's passion in preaching, along with other rhetorical factors, see Rollin Walker Quimby, "Dwight L. Moody: An Examination of the Historical Conditions and Rhetorical Factors which Contributed to His Effectiveness as a Speaker" (PhD diss., University of Michigan, Ann Arbor, MI: University Press, 1951),

D.L. MOODY:
TURNING POINTS TOWARD TEXT-DRIVEN PREACHING

Expository or Textual?

As noted above, D. L. Moody began this sermon by announcing and reading a text of Scripture. There is no question that the main thrust of the sermon came from the sentence, "Whatever a man sows, that shall he also reap" (Gal 6:7). However, the preacher failed to set the verse in its context and did not explain how it relates to the meaning of the paragraph and chapter in which it is found. Therefore, this sermon does not fit the criteria or description of an expository sermon.

At first glance, one may wonder if this sermon could be classified as a textual sermon, since it is based on two verses in Galatians chapter six. This possibility comes into even greater focus when Moody states, "Now I want to divide this text into four parts."[87] However, the question is quickly settled when he follows that statement with, "Not that I am going to speak on the divisions."[88] Even when one considers the divisions he made in the next few moments of the sermon, it becomes clear that these divisions did not come from the verse itself. Rather they were deductions about general principles of sowing and reaping in the natural world. Therefore, this sermon does not fit the description or the criteria of a textual sermon.

Biographical?

The sermon is not based on a biblical character. While several biblical characters are mentioned, they are utilized as supportive illustrations for the main topic. Thus, the sermon does not fit within the biographical category.

Topical?

"Sowing and Reaping" as preached during the Boston campaign should be categorized as a topical sermon. The sermon was based on a topic that was introduced from a phrase in Galatians 6:7. This concept served as the central theme of the sermon. This theme drove the content of the entire message without diversion into other topics.

---

87. D. L. Moody, *To All Peoples*, 296.
88. Ibid.

Every Scripture verse, Bible character, and biblical illusion mentioned serve to support the main theme of the message. While the topic came from a text of Scripture, the sermon was nonetheless based on a topic. That topic carried the sermon and was repeatedly applied to the listeners in Boston. Therefore, this message must be categorized as a topical sermon.

Sowing and Reaping II: The Life and Character of Ahab[89]

Sermon Description

The night after he preached his most famous sermon on "Sowing and Reaping," Moody announced that he was again going to preach on Galatians 6:7–8. He began with this statement, "I want to talk to you from the same text as that of last night, and I want to take as an illustration the character of Ahab."[90] Moody compared Ahab to others who have sold themselves for something. He mentioned Judas and Herod but quickly returned to Ahab.

Moody declared, "Ahab was a religious man, he thought. He had 850 prophets; and what king had more, what king did more for religion than he . . . There is a difference between religion and having Christ."[91] Moody then spoke of Ahab's wife Jezebel who had God's prophets killed. Moody suggested that Elijah was really a friend to Ahab, but the king thought of Elijah as an enemy.

Building upon the idea of friendship, Moody spoke of the praying mother and the faithful minister as friends of those they warn. He spent some time making strong application to the people of Boston. He followed this with several illustrations indicating the responsibility of the preacher to warn others that they will reap what they sow.[92] Moody returned to speak of Ahab.

The preacher recounted the story of Ahab's desire for the vineyard of Naboth. When Naboth would not sell his property, Ahab pouted. Jezebel told him she would get it and she had Naboth killed. A break came at this point in

---

89. D. L. Moody, *To All Peoples*, 303–308.
90. Ibid., 303.
91. Ibid.
92. Ibid., 304–305.

the text of the sermon as reported by the newspaper. The reporter taking down Moody's words shifted to a third-person summary of the full story of Naboth. The text reads, "Mr. Moody then related how Jezebel sent the letter to the elders, and gave the story in almost accurate Scriptural language."[93] The reporter then picked back up with Moody's words and continued the sermon.

Moody began making direct application to his congregation. Speaking of God watching all people Moody said, "He notices all of us, and there is not a hellish act that has been or is going to be committed to-night but that God knows all about it."[94] At this point in the sermon, there is another brief break. The reporter noted that a person fainted. Moody dismissed the fainting and encouraged the congregation to refocus on the message.

Moody returned to his focus on Ahab, demonstrating both a guilty conscience and the eventual judgment of God upon Ahab's life. Moody moved to the conclusion by making strong and direct application to his listeners. He concluded the sermon by stating, "It is a terrible truth that God is going to punish sin; you may laugh at it, but be not deceived; whatsoever a man soweth he must reap. Oh, may God wake up every one stumbling, sleeping here to-night!"[95] With that, Moody ended his message.

Sermon Evaluation

The present sermon served as a follow up message to the sermon of the previous night. The title indicates that in some ways this sermon could be considered the sequel to "Sowing and Reaping." However, as the opening sentence indicates the sermon seeks to present the life and character of Ahab as an example of sowing and reaping. The message is nearly as direct and confrontational as the previous night's sermon. Moody noted that having Christ and having religion were not the same thing. He emphasized the need to have Christ, but he did not explicitly share the gospel message itself during the message.

An interesting fact distinguishes this sermon from the others previously evaluated. Three times, the reporter acted as a narrator and broke into the flow

---

93. D. L. Moody, *To All Peoples*, 306.
94. Ibid.
95. Ibid., 308.

of the sermon. Two of the breaks were places where the reporter summarized Moody's presentation. Likely, this was done for space limitations in the paper. One time the reporter broke in to report that someone fainted. The fainting did not stop the service. Moody simply called the audience back to attention and continued his message.

Expository or Textual?

While Moody began by saying, "I want to talk to you from the same text as that of last night," he failed to read the passage. Rather, he quickly introduced Ahab as an illustration of the previous sermon. The sermon referred to many events in the life of Ahab and quoted a few verses here and there. The preacher failed to explain a text of Scripture within its context. Thus, this sermon cannot be considered expositional.

This sermon does not fit within the category of a textual sermon either. The sermon was based primarily on two things. First, it was somewhat based on the concept of sowing and reaping. Second, the message was primarily based on the life of Ahab. To find the proper category for this sermon, one will need to look beyond the textual column of the rubric.

Biographical?

Much of the content of this sermon points to the biographical category. The sermon is primarily based on the life of Ahab. Moody chose various passages that described Ahab's failures and the results to warn his audience. He attempted to draw out negative characteristics of the evil king and make application to the people of Boston.

The complication in classification of this sermon comes in the fact that Moody began by saying that he was taking up the text of Galatians 5:7. This problem is furthered by the fact that he concluded the sermon by quoting the phrase, "Whatsoever a man soweth, that shall he also reap."[96] Thus, while this sermon may be classified as biographical, it is best to withhold a final decision until we consider the topical category.

---

96. Galatians 6:7.

Topical?

According to the sermon rubric, a topical sermon must be based on a topic. The topic may be from a word, phrase, or concept from a verse of Scripture. Bible verses provide support for the topic and are not typically explained within context. All of these criteria somewhat fit the sermon under consideration.

As noted above, the sermon also fits the criteria of the biographical sermon. Considering Moody's opening sentence to the sermon, the reader should not be surprised that the sermon fits both categories, at least to some degree. If Moody accomplished his purpose, the sermon was based on both the topic of sowing and reaping, as well as, the life and character of Ahab. In the end, the present reader looked to how much time Moody spent on the topic, versus how much time he spent on Ahab. This helped determine the proper classification. While Moody began and ended the sermon with a topic, the bulk of his message focused on Ahab. Therefore, the sermon will be classified as a biographical message.

What Will You Do with Christ?[97]

Sermon Description

D. L. Moody began this sermon by directing his hearers to a verse of Scripture. He said, "I want to call you attention to the 27th chapter of Matthew and the 22nd verse."[98] Having read the verse Moody picked up the question, "What shall I do then with Jesus, which is called Christ?"[99] This question became the recurring theme that carried the entire sermon.

Having set the stage for the question, Moody focused on relating the question to Boston. He said, "It is a question that is disturbing a great many in this city at the present time."[100] Moody spoke of some outside Boston who questioned if the work was doing any good in the city. He responded by saying, "The

---

97. D. L. Moody, *To All Peoples*, 315–321.
98. Ibid., 315.
99. Ibid.
100. Ibid.

cry is coming up from all classes, 'What shall I do?'"[101] Moody then shifted his focus to Pilate.

As Moody spoke of Pilate, he offered a picture of what might have gone through Pilate's mind. Much of what he said about Pilate came from his imagination. There is nothing that is strikingly wrong, but much of it cannot be found in Scripture. He did speak of some scriptural facts intermingled within his story of Pilate's life. Some of what Moody added to the story can be deduced from history, some from Scripture, and much came from his imagination.

Throughout the sermon, Moody moved back and forth from speaking about Pilate to his hearers. Moody spoke of Pilate as one who did not want to decide. He pointed out that Pilate allowed himself to be backed into a corner and then gave in, while trying to maintain his own innocence. Moody then said, "There are a great many men now like Pilate, they think they can shift the responsibility. But bear in mind that God gave Himself up freely for us all. God sends Him to each one of us, and we must decide what we will do."[102] He then pressed his audience to consider what was keeping them from making a decision.

Moody briefly left his consideration of Pilate to speak of others involved in the conspiracy. He considered Annas, Judas, Caiaphas, and then returned to Pilate. He contrasted these four men with Peter, James, and John. Shifting his focus back to Pilate Moody stated, "Pilate was lost for lack of courage, for want of decision. Let this question come home to each one of us this very night, 'What shall I then do with Jesus which is called Christ?'"[103] With this, the preacher once again brought the question home to Boston and to his listeners.

In bringing the sermon to a close, Moody pressed his audience. He asked, "Will you have Him? Let the question go round. Now who will have Him to-night? Who will take Him to-night as God's gift to you? 'What shall I then do with Jesus who is called Christ?' Shall I reject Him or shall I receive Him?" After this series of questions, the preacher let the audience know that anyone could turn to Jesus if they would. He argued that even Pilate could have been saved. Moody's final appeal came, "O may we all receive a passion for Christ

---

101. D. L. Moody, *To All Peoples*, 315 .
102. Ibid., 316.
103. Ibid., 318.

D.L. MOODY:
TURNING POINTS TOWARD TEXT-DRIVEN PREACHING

that we may commence this night to love Him and serve Him."[104] From beginning to end this sermon used Pilate's question to appeal to the people of Boston.

Sermon Evaluation

This short sermon is filled with passion and appeal. Reading the sermon, one understands what James Findlay Jr. meant when he described the pace of Moody's preaching. Findlay said, "When reading Scripture the evangelist spoke slowly, as though repeating a difficult matter to a child.... When he began the sermon, the tempo picked up considerably."[105] Reading the present sermon, one cannot help but pick up the pace. Reading the short sentences, moving back and forth from the scene in Pilate's Judgment Hall in Jerusalem to Moody's Tabernacle in Boston, the pace becomes rapid and passionate. Elements of the gospel message were proclaimed throughout the sermon. Every few moments, Moody called on his hearers to turn to Christ.

Expository or Textual?

It should be noted that Moody began this sermon by reading a verse of Scripture. As the sermon progressed, Moody set the verse somewhat in context, by describing the scene. He included historical information pertinent to the context. However, he failed to explain the verse within that context. Moody primarily used the little context he offered, to find possible reasons for Pilate's question that he could apply to his hearers. The sermon does not fit within the description or the criteria of an expositional sermon.

While Moody did begin his sermon with a single verse, he failed to deal with the entirety of the verse. Rather, he drew on the question Pilate asked the people and this question became the driving theme of his entire message. Reading through the sermon one almost gets the sense that the question was posed to Pilate, rather than to the gathered crowd. The sermon was hardly based on the verse at all. Rather the focus was on the question contained within the verse. Therefore, the sermon fails to fit the category of a textual sermon.

---

104. D. L. Moody, *To All Peoples*, 321.

105. James F. Findlay Jr., *Dwight L. Moody: American Evangelist, 1837–1899* (Chicago: The University of Chicago Press, 1969), 222.

Biographical?

As noted in the sermon description above, Moody moved back and forth from speaking of Pilate to speaking to his audience. While he briefly considered a few other characters, Pilate was mentioned numerous times throughout the message. Yet, the message was not really presented as a biographical sermon of the life of Pilate. Rather the sermon focused on the question, "What shall I do with Jesus?"[106] Thus, while Pilate was mentioned often, the sermon fails to fit the category of a biographical sermon.

Topical?

The sermon, "What Will You Do With Jesus?" as preached by D. L. Moody during his Boston campaign, exhibited the characteristics of a topical sermon. The sermon was based on a concept, i.e., a question that came from the lips of Pilate as recorded in Matthew 27:22. This question was related to Pilate, to the crowd in Jerusalem, to Annas, to Judas, to Caiaphas, to Peter, James, and John, and to the gathered Boston crowd. The question served as the unifying theme, keeping Moody from diving off into numerous directions. Therefore, the message clearly fits the topical category of the sermon rubric.

God's Love for the Sinner[107]

Sermon Description

Moody began this sermon by stating, "We find a good many people in the inquiry room night after night that tell us they cannot pray …. Their sins are troubling them; they are weary and heavy laden, many of them cast down under their sins."[108] Moody told the gathered congregation that the reason people could not pray was that they did not really know that God loved them. The preacher read Romans 5:6–10, making brief comments about each verse to prove that the Bible teaches God loves sinners.

---

106. D. L. Moody, *To All Peoples*, 315.
107. Ibid., 322–334.
108. Ibid., 322.

D.L. MOODY:
TURNING POINTS TOWARD TEXT-DRIVEN PREACHING

Very quickly, Moody moved from his brief explanation of the passage into his sermon. He divided his comments under five ideas. In the first four divisions of the sermon, Moody talked about various categories of people who attended church in his day and how they relate to the concept of God's love. In the final section of the sermon, Moody discussed how the Christian who is under God's discipline should respond.

First, Moody spoke of those who believed they were too great of a sinner to be saved. He demonstrated that to think one is too evil and without strength to be saved is a false assumption. Moody said, "It is a good thing to know that we have no strength, and to bear in mind that Christ died for the ungodly."[109] Those who recognize their sin are ready to turn to the Savior and find real life.

Moody also spoke about those who think they are too good to need salvation. He told a couple of stories about encountering people who thought they were all good and did not need God's forgiveness. Moody used these two stories to show that all people are sinners and need Jesus. He briefly went back to Romans to show that Christ died for everyone while still in their sins. The preacher said, "Christ comes to bring reconciliation between God and the sinner."[110] Having expressed God's love for these people, Moody moved to discuss another class of people in the church.

In describing the next group of people, Moody used a term that is not often heard in our post-modern world. He said, "There is another class that we meet in the inquiry room—the backsliders. They say, 'We have wandered away from the Lord . . . and now we cannot pray.' If there is a backslider here this afternoon, I want to tell him he can pray."[111] Moody offered hope for backsliders to be reconciled to the Father; by referring to passages from Hosea and Jeremiah. Moody constantly held forth the love of God.

Having preached a considerable time on the concept of backsliding, Moody turned his attention to those who have never really been saved. He said, "There are many who would not class themselves among the backsliders, who make a profession of Christianity, but who have not the real love of God in their

---

109. D. L. Moody, *To All Peoples*, 322.
110. Ibid., 323.
111. Ibid., 324.

hearts."[112] Once again, Moody confronted the problem of false professors of Christianity and held out the love and forgiveness of God as the only hope for them. This section is one of the longest parts of the sermon.

In the final pages of this sermon, Moody focused his attention on the discipline of God. Moving into this section, Moody stated, "But I can imagine some mother saying: 'If God loves me, why does He chasten me?'"[113] The preacher began to deal with the question by quoting Hebrews 12:5. He then offered a story about disciplining his daughter.[114] Through the story he demonstrated that chastening is a sign of love.

Throughout the sermon, Moody sought to demonstrate that God loves sinners, saints, and backsliders. He constantly pointed his listeners to the opportunity to be forgiven. After two more stories were told, Moody moved to his conclusion. He said "Now is the accepted time of salvation. Come under the banner of love. May the God of grace help you to come under the banner now and recognize Him as your Lord and Saviour. May you come to-night and be saved."[115] With this appeal, Moody closed another Boston sermon.

Sermon Evaluation

As noted in chapter two, Moody's biographers are unanimous in recording that after Henry Moorhouse visited Chicago, Moody began preaching more on the love of God. However, some have suggested that Moody completely abandoned the idea of God's judgment on sin after the Moorhouse incident.[116]

---

112. D. L. Moody, *To All Peoples*, 327.
113. Ibid., 331.
114. Ibid., 331–332.
115. Ibid., 334.
116. While a few Moody observers have made claims about the idea of Moody abandoning the concept of God's judgment on sin, the strongest case was made by Elmer Powell. During the 1930s, a controversy arose between Moody Bible Institute and the Northfield Bible Conferences. The controversy centered around issues such as the verbal plenary inspiration of Scripture and the substitutionary atonement. These doctrines, among others, had been abandoned by Paul Moody and most of the speakers at the Northfield Conferences. Moody Bible Institute responded. Powell wrote a book to defend Paul through a "re-evaluation" of Dwight. The book never made it to broad

D.L. MOODY:
TURNING POINTS TOWARD TEXT-DRIVEN PREACHING

However as this sermon demonstrated, Moody did not abandon the concept of God's judgment. He simply balanced his preaching to explain that despite God's judgment on sin, he also loved sinners and offered forgiveness through the death and resurrection of Jesus. This sermon proves to be a classic example of Moody's understanding of God's love and justice. He clearly shared the gospel, including Christ's substitutionary atonement, and called people to respond.

Expository or Textual?

This sermon is not a "text-driven" sermon, fitting within either the expository or textual classification. Yet, Moody did more to interact with a passage of Scripture in this message than in any sermon yet evaluated. The first two pages of the message offered brief comments about Romans 5:6–10. He read a verse and said a few words. He then read the next verse, and so on. However, the comments Moody made were very brief and by page three he moved back to his typical sermon format consistent with this era of his ministry. With only two pages of explanation, followed by ten pages of stories and comments unrelated to the text, this message cannot be classified as either an exposition or a textual sermon.

Biographical?

There is no biblical character development in this sermon. Therefore, it cannot be classified as a biographical sermon. Another category must be sought for this message.

Topical?

As noted above, Moody divided his comments in this sermon under five concepts. He was careful to relate all five concepts to the love of God. Indeed, the love of God served as the driving force of the sermon content. He developed his topic using both Scripture and personal stories. He concluded with an appeal

---

publication. The author had a few copies bound. To this researcher's knowledge, the only extant copy is the copy its author gave to Paul Moody as a gift. Later, Paul's copy was given to the Northfield Mount Hermon Schools. The book is housed in the school's archives. The present researcher is indebted to Mr. Peter Weis for allowing access to the work. The bibliographic information is as follows: Elmer William Powell, "Moody of Northfield: A Re-evaluation in Light of Research," Unpublished.

to act upon the topic at hand. Therefore, this message should be classified as a topical sermon.

Christ in the Old Testament[117]

Sermon Description

Prior to beginning this sermon, Moody spoke of his concern that all the new believers should have a great love for the Bible. He said, "As the time begins to draw near for us to leave you, one feeling comes over me more and more, and that is, I would like to get all these young converts in love with their Bible, and especially with the *person* of Christ."[118] Moody then spoke of his thought that Boston had attacked the Bible more than any other city in the country and warned the new converts to believe and love the Bible. He then argued that those who love and read their Bible grow and serve the Lord, while those who do not fall away.

Following his opening concern, Moody began his sermon by saying, "This morning, I want to call your attention to Christ in the Old Testament."[119] He followed this by noting that he had been preaching in Boston for ten weeks and that he wanted to spend his last three Sunday mornings talking about Jesus.[120] He was going to begin with the testimony of Jesus found in the Old Testament.

Having introduced his topic, Moody read 2 Peter 1:14–21. He then said, "The thought I want to call your attention to is this: That when we take up this Bible let us bear in mind that it is true."[121] Moody made the point that though the Bible was written by many men over 1500 years, it is one book with a unified

---

117. D. L. Moody, *To All Peoples*, 349–360.
118. Ibid., 349.
119. Ibid., 350.
120. Contrary to the statement in his sermon, Moody preached this sermon and the following three Sundays. This sermon was on "Christ in the Old Testament." The next Sunday, he preached on "The Christ of the New Testament." The third Sunday, Moody preached on "John The Baptist." His final Sunday, and his final sermon, in Boston he preached on "The Second Coming of Christ."
121. Ibid., 351.

theme. Moody believed Jesus Christ to be the theme of Scripture from Genesis to Revelation.

This sermon focused on Jesus as the fulfiller of Old Testament prophecy. The preacher began with God's promises to Abraham. He then spoke of fulfillment from Jeremiah. Moody claimed there to be nearly two hundred Old Testament prophecies that were fulfilled in Jesus. He spoke of Abraham and Isaac, the Genesis 49:10 prophecy of Shiloh, the promise of the Jewish nation, many of the Psalms, Isaiah's prophecies, the fulfillment of John the Baptist's ministry, the birth in Bethlehem, the Triumphal entry, the thirty pieces of silver, and more. Some of these Bible themes were simply mentioned, while others were read from Scripture.

Each Old Testament passage read was used to demonstrate two truths. First, Moody wanted his listeners to understand that the Bible is true. Second, he emphasized Jesus as the overarching theme of the Bible. This two-fold emphasis guided the sermon from beginning to end. Moody concluded by saying,

> Let us keep in mind it is true. He says heaven and earth will pass away. But not one jot or tittle shall pass from the law till all be fulfilled. O, that Boston may be brought back to its Bible and that this city may come to know and love the person of the Lord Jesus Christ. And may we not set up our own law, but follow in the law of our Saviour.[122]

The sermon focused on the truthfulness of Scripture and the person of Jesus Christ as revealed in the Old Testament.

Sermon Evaluation

In the evaluation of the prior sermon, it was noted that the message clearly demonstrated that Moody never abandoned the idea of God's judgment of sin. Powell also claimed that Moody did not hold to the truthfulness and authority of the Bible as verbally inspired.[123] The present sermon dispels this misunderstanding as well.

122. D. L. Moody, *To All Peoples*, 360.
123. See footnote 126.

From the beginning to the end of this sermon, Moody spoke of the truthfulness of Scripture. He made it clear that he understood the Bible to have God as its ultimate author. Moody said, "Let us just bear in mind that the Word of God is true, and that we can rely upon it . . . It is one book written by one hand—by holy men, who speak as if they were moved by the Holy Ghost."[124] This sermon revealed Moody's view of Scripture as well as his belief that Jesus was the central theme of the entire Bible. On two occasions in the message, he spoke specifically of Christ dying in the place of sinners. Once again, he affirmed his view of the substitutionary atonement. He not only shared the good news of Jesus, he called on his listeners to respond to the gospel.

Expository or Textual?

Moody read quite a bit of Scripture in this sermon. He began by reading 2 Peter 1:14–21. While he read enough to gain some sense of the context of the passage, Moody failed to explain the text within its context. Rather, he used this passage to introduce his two-fold theme as noted in the sermon description above.

The many verses read from the Old Testament, throughout the sermon, were all used to support the concept that the Old Testament prophecies of Christ predicted things that were fulfilled in Jesus. Therefore, one should understand that the Bible is true and Jesus is the central theme of the entire Bible. Since the verses were used to support a topic rather than to guide the content of the message, this sermon should not be classified as either an expositional or textual sermon.

Biographical?

While Moody mentioned many Bible characters, including Abraham, Moses, David, Daniel, Esther, and others, none of them served as the central thrust of the message. Moody's two-fold theme included much information about Jesus. However, the information was not presented in a biographical fashion. Rather, the information about Jesus served to support the topic of the sermon. Therefore, the sermon cannot be classified as a biographical sermon.

---

124. D. L. Moody, *To All Peoples*, 351.

Topical?

The sermon now under consideration clearly fits within the topical sermon category. Moody began by introducing his two-fold topic. Every passage of Scripture referenced and every story told supported the theme. In the conclusion, Moody called on his listeners to believe the Bible and follow the Savior. The message should be classified as a topical sermon.

Christ of the New Testament[125]

Sermon Description

Moody began this sermon by referencing his previous week's sermon on Christ in the Old Testament. His focus was to demonstrate that Christ was wonderful and distinctive. Moody said, "Everything about Christ was wonderful. All these prophecies in the Old Testament concerning Christ were wonderful. Everything about His birth, about His life and about His death was wonderful."[126] Moody suggested that many people thought Jesus to be no different from any human. Moody intended to demonstrate the distinctiveness of Jesus by considering passages about him from the Gospels.

To make his point, Moody began with Gabriel. He argued that Gabriel gave three announcements in Scripture, and they were all about the Messiah.[127] First, he considered the angel's announcement to Daniel about the Messiah being cut off for man's sin. Second, he discussed Gabriel's announcement about John the Baptist being the forerunner of Jesus, when appearing to Zacharias in the Temple. Third, Moody spoke of Gabriel's announcement to Mary concerning Jesus' birth.

Moving on from Gabriel, the evangelist walked his audience through Mary's visit to Elizabeth, John's birth, Jesus' birth, Jesus in the temple, and the visit of the wise men from the East. Moody argued that the unique nature of each of these events demonstrated that Jesus was wonderful. The preacher then

---

125. D. L. Moody, *To All Peoples*, 361–374.
126. Ibid., 361.
127. Ibid., 361.

contrasted Jesus with Herod. Once again, his focus was to show that Jesus was distinctive when compared to other rulers.

Moody concluded the sermon with these words: "A stone cut out of the mountain is going to fall and crush all who war against Christ. Oh, may God help us to preach the coming of Christ. May He help each one of us to receive the Savior."[128] Moody desired his audience not to fall into the trap of reducing Jesus to a "good prophet." The preacher wanted them to understand that Jesus is the eternal Son of God and the only hope of salvation.

Sermon Evaluation

Moody opened his sermon with these words, "You that were here last Sunday remember I was speaking about Christ in the Old Testament, and how the prophecy of the Scripture was fulfilled in His birth. This morning I want to just take up the subject where I left off, and show that everything about Christ was wonderful."[129] This last phrase of his opening statement became Moody's topic. The topic was repeated several times in the message. In contrast to those of his day who were re-evaluating Jesus as simply a good man, Moody wanted to demonstrate that Jesus is the eternal Son of God. The message was a powerful testimony to Christ. Moody spoke of Christ's death on behalf of sinners and called people to respond in faith.

Expository or Textual?

Moody read several portions of Scripture in this message. He also made several biblical allusions. Most of the readings came from Matthew 1 and Luke 1–2. Moody commented on each of these passages in relationship to his main topic. With the extensive amount of reading Moody did from these chapters, one can gain some sense of the context of the passages. However, Moody's point was not to explain the meaning of each text within its context. Rather, he used each passage read as support for his main topic that "Christ was won-

---

128. D. L. Moody, *To All Peoples*, 374.
129. Ibid., 361.

derful."[130] Therefore, this passage does not fit within either the expository or textual sermon categories.

Biographical?

This sermon is about a single person—Jesus. However, the sermon is not presented like a biographical message. The sermon neither develops characteristics of Jesus, nor does it apply characteristics to the audience. Rather, Moody attempted to reinforce the idea that Jesus is wonderful and not like other men. The focus is to help people turn to Jesus in faith, not provide them with characteristics to emulate. Therefore, this message fails to fit the description and criteria of a biographical sermon.

Topical?

Moody began this sermon by announcing his topic for the message. The announced topic was carried throughout the sermon and brought unity of thought to the flow of the message. The passages read were offered as support for the main theme. The overriding application focused on turning to Jesus in faith for salvation. This sermon should be classified as a topical sermon.

Christ as a Shepherd[131]

Sermon Description

Moody opened this sermon by saying he was going to speak from John 10 but first wanted to point his listeners to Psalm 22 and 23. In Psalm 22:7, 16, he referred to the Good Shepherd suffering for the sin of his sheep. He then spoke of the "valley of the shadow of death" from Psalm 23.

Moody described Christ as going before his sheep through the "valley of the shadow of death." He stated, "There is the Good Shepherd leading His flock through death and judgment, and I do not know of any one passage in Scripture that is more misquoted than that. You hear people say, 'the dark val-

---

130. D. L. Moody, *To All Peoples*, 361.
131. Ibid., 375–382.

ley,' but the word 'dark' isn't there at all. All that death can do to the believer is just throw its shadow across his path."[132] The preacher briefly spoke about the last verse of Psalm 23, referencing the joy of "goodness and mercy" following the Lord's sheep.

Moody used Psalm 24 to speak of resurrection. Making a quick reference to Hebrews, he pointed out that Jesus provides peace. Moody then returned to Psalm 23 to describe the Shepherd giving his sheep rest. From here the preacher moved to Luke 15 to discuss the Good Shepherd seeking those sheep who go astray. He made specific application to those present who are "backsliding" and "wondering." He called on "backsliders" to return to the Lord, indicating the Shepherd's willingness to forgive.

Finally arriving at John 10, Moody spoke of the Good Shepherd knowing his sheep by name and holding them in his grasp so that no one can take them away. He illustrated his point with a story about an "Eastern shepherd" who called his sheep by name.[133] Moody went into an extended discussion of why he did not call out specific sins very often. He suggested that should be left to the Shepherd.

The sermon concluded with three illustrations. The first illustration was about a man who mistreated his dog. Being angry at the dog, the man put it into a lion's cage. Unexpectedly, the lion licked the wounds of the dog. The man could not get the dog to return to him. The lion keeper refused to help. Moody attempted to tie the story back into his theme. He said, "Now that may be a homely illustration, but I hope it will fasten on your minds the idea that we are no match for the devil." After some additional comments Moody said, "Why not to-night every one of us make the Lord our Shepherd."[134] He then moved on to two other illustrations.

The final two illustrations Moody used led to the close of the sermon. They both described the Shepherd carrying his children across the river and into the gates of Heaven. Following the illustrations Moody said, "If we have the Good Shepherd He will be with us in the dying hour, and what wilt thou do if He is not with thee in the swelling of Jordan? Oh! May God help each one of us to be

---

132. D. L. Moody, *To All Peoples*, 375–376.
133. Ibid., 378.
134. Ibid., 381.

wise and take Christ for our Shepherd to-night." These words of appeal brought the message to a close.

Sermon Evaluation

Moody effectively stayed on the topic of his sermon which was to demonstrate that Jesus is a good Shepherd. The sermon does not begin or end with Scripture. However, several verses are read and quoted. A few biblical allusions were also made. The main point of the sermon was that one should trust the Good Shepherd. While Moody alluded to the gospel in this sermon, he did not explicitly proclaim it.

Expository Or Textual?
As noted above, Moody read and quoted several verses of Scripture. However, he failed to explain those passages within their context. In reading the first few lines, one gains the idea that Moody was going to preach from John 10, but wanted to make a few quick comments about Psalm 23. However, the preacher ended up reading verses from several chapters, making comments on each. He said more about the passages in Psalms than he did about John 10. All the verses mentioned were used to support the topic at hand. Considering the sermon in light of the sermon rubric, it cannot be classified as either expositional or textual in nature.

Biographical?
This sermon was about Jesus. However, it did not develop his character. Neither did it present characteristics from Jesus' life as examples for the believer to follow. The message was focused on a single aspect of Jesus' ministry, that of being the Good Shepherd. This concept was applied to the hearers, not as an example to follow, but as motivation to turn to Jesus in faith. Therefore, this message does not fit the description or criteria necessary to be categorized as a biographical sermon.

Topical?

The topic of this sermon is clearly stated from the beginning. Moody wanted his hearers to see Jesus as the Good Shepherd and turn to him in faith. This topic serves to unify the theme, at least in a general fashion. Moody did seem to stray from his main theme a little more than the other sermons analyzed from the Boston campaign. However, he did attempt to get back on track and wrapped up the message by returning to the topic at hand. "Christ as a Shepherd", as preached during the Boston campaign, should be classified as a topical sermon.

The Blessed Gospel[135]

Sermon Description

Moody began this sermon by saying, "I want to call your attention to-night to a part of Luke ix. 18."[136] After reading his text Moody said, "You that have been attending the meetings for the past few months know that I have spoken upon this text before. I have tried to tell these audiences what the gospel is, but the other night, talking with quite an intelligent man in the inquiry-room, I thought I should have to begin all over."[137] The preacher then described two recent incidents in the inquiry-room where the counselee thought the gospel was about trying to be good. Therefore, Moody felt it necessary to address the topic again.

Following his introduction of the topic, Moody stated that the gospel was "represented in the Scripture as good news. 'Behold, I bring you tidings of great joy.' 'Unto you is born a Saviour.' That is the Gospel. God has given us a substitute, God has sent Christ to die for our sins."[138] According to Moody,

---

135. D. L. Moody, *To All Peoples*, 383–392.

136. Ibid., 383. It should be noted that the verse Moody actually read was Luke 4:18. However, either he announced it as Luke 9:18 or the reporter took it down wrong.

137. Ibid.

138. Ibid., 384. This statement provides further demonstration against Powell's argument noted in footnote 126. He indicated that Moody did not believe in the substitutionary atonement after his encounter with Moorhouse and his emphasis on the love of God. However, the Boston campaign was held subsequent to the Moorhouse

D.L. MOODY:
TURNING POINTS TOWARD TEXT-DRIVEN PREACHING

the gospel is about substitution. Jesus died as man's substitute, and he offers salvation as a gift.

After illustrating the free gift of salvation, the evangelist argued that all people have a debt, but God paid that debt through Christ. He said, "There isn't a sinner but that owes God a debt, a heavy debt. God can pay your debts this moment."[139] Moody then spoke of the desire everyone has for peace. He argued that true peace is only found in Jesus. He spoke for an extended period on peace using Scripture quotations and illustrations.

Moody sought to help his audience understand the necessity of being saved. He said, "You cannot work out your own salvation unless you are first saved."[140] To illustrate his point, the preacher told a story about wounded soldiers during the siege of Paris. In the story, as rescue workers came the wounded began calling out for help. Moody said, "If there is anyone in this assembly that will cry out, 'I am wounded; I need a Saviour,' He will come and help them to-night."[141] The preacher quickly moved to another illustration encouraging his listeners to be saved.

Moody turned his focus to tell his audience that God calls all people to turn to him. He said, "He gives out a universal call: not for one but for all. Christ calls you to Him. He will forgive all your sins."[142] Moody shifted his focus to demonstrate that Jesus heals the broken-hearted, while continuing to emphasis that he will heal the heart of anyone who will turn to Jesus.

In the final section of the sermon, Moody began to speak to those who allowed other things to get in the way of turning to Jesus. Moody spoke of another incident in the inquiry room where a lady first denied she had sinned but ended up acknowledging that she held her son up as an idol. Moody told a couple of illustrations encouraging parents to be careful not to let their children be an idol that keeps them from Christ.

---

incident, and here we have a direct statement of Moody regarding the substitutionary atonement of Christ.

139. D. L. Moody, *To All Peoples*, 385.

140. Ibid., 388.

141. Ibid. (The siege of Paris took place from 19 September 1870 to 28 January 1871 and ended in the consequent capture of the city by Prussian forces—ed.)

142. Ibid.

The preacher concluded the sermon by telling of a young boy who turned to Jesus. His dad was a drunk and would not stand for the boy praying in the house. Finally, the dad told him to either stop praying or to leave. The young boy would not deny Jesus and so the boy left. The dad was overcome with the resolve of his son, chased him down, bid him to return home, and was saved.[143] Moody said, "Oh, may God help us to realize this truth that God sent Christ into the world to heal the heart!"[144] He then concluded by encouraging the people of Boston to bring their hurts to Christ.

Sermon Evaluation

The reader will quickly note that Moody's primary concern in this sermon was to help his listeners understand that they need a Savior. He also wanted them to know that the Good News is that Christ can save and will save anyone who will call upon him for salvation. He spent most of his time using illustrations, brief Scripture quotations, and biblical allusions to speak to various things that might keep someone from coming to Jesus. Moody argued that some are carrying burdens and come to Christ, while others recognize something is missing and they find their desires fulfilled in Christ.[145] Moody continually and forcefully appealed to his audience to be saved.

Expository or Textual?

While Moody began by reading Luke 4:18, he focused his attention on the concept of the Gospel. After his introductory comments on the nature of the Gospel, he spent the balance of the sermon appealing to people to be saved. He failed to return to his verse, except for brief comments about "healing the brokenhearted" toward the end of the sermon. Moody did not seek to explain his text either by setting it in context or by breaking down the various portions of the verse he read. Therefore, this sermon cannot be classified as either expository or textual.

---

143. D. L. Moody, *To All Peoples*, 391.
144. Ibid., 392.
145. Ibid., 387.

D.L. MOODY:
TURNING POINTS TOWARD TEXT-DRIVEN PREACHING

Biographical?

The present sermon does not deal with a biblical character. The message seeks to help people understand that the gospel is not about works, but about Christ's substitutionary atonement. Moody encouraged everyone to call out to Christ for salvation. Therefore, this message cannot be classified as a biographical sermon.

Topical?

Moody started off by reading Luke 4:18. He focused in on one concept—the Gospel. He then attempted to define the gospel as Christ coming in the flesh and dying as the substitute for all sinners. However, by the middle of the second page of the sermon, Moody shifted his focus from the text to appealing to his audience to be saved.

In Moody's appeal, he covered numerous things that might keep someone from coming to Christ. With only one brief exception, noted above, the preacher never returned to his text. While he spoke all around the gospel, he really did not return to his topic either. The sermon utilized Scripture, but his comments were only vaguely related to his texts. He had a topic, but it did not serve as a theme unifying the sermon. Therefore, this sermon must be classified as a topical sermon that lacked unity and covered a multitude of topics.

Blind-Eyes[146]

Sermon Description

While Moody did not begin this sermon with a verse, his opening line indicated that he preached a few messages using Luke 4:18 as his starting point. The present sermon began with these words, "We have come to-night to the best clause of the verse we have been speaking about, of regeneration and healing of broken hearts and giving deliverance to the captives, and now we come to giv-

---

146. D. L. Moody, *To All Peoples*, 408–415.

ing sight to the blind."[147] After a quick reference to previous sermons on each of the phrases of the verse, Moody moved into talking about blindness.

Spiritual blindness served as the theme of this message; however, Moody began by briefly talking about physical blindness. He said, "There is no class of people that receive so much from Christ as the blind. There is not one solitary blind man that asked for sight and cried for mercy but that he got it."[148] This statement is obviously not a claim that every blind person who ever lived and prayed for physical sight received it. Indeed, he uses an illustration of one blind from birth that did not receive physical sight. Rather, Moody here referenced those who came to Jesus for sight while he was on earth.

Moody quickly shifted his focus to the theme of the sermon—spiritual blindness. He said, "If I know mine own heart, I would rather have natural blindness than be blinded spiritually and go down without hope in the Lord Jesus Christ. There are many that are blinded and don't know it."[149] The preacher than read Revelation 3:17 and spoke of those who have spiritual blindness but fail to realize their condition.

Moody began speaking about spiritual blindness in Boston. He said, "How much spiritual blindness there is in this city; men who are talking against God, who is trying to save them. Satan has blinded men. How many he has blinded in this audience."[150] The preacher spoke of those who were blinded by business, money, pleasure, and fashion. Moody then turned his attention to those who are blinded by a specific sin. They have a pet sin that they enjoy and do not want to give it up.

Moody talked about people being blinded in a moment of weakness and giving into sin. He warned of those who in financial difficulty choose to steal from their boss. This led Moody to share an extended illustration about a man he met in another city. The man had committed forgery and was on the run from the law. He ran far from home and ended up at one of Moody's meetings. He spoke to Moody about the matter. He had been blinded for a moment, and it cost

---

147. D. L. Moody, *To All Peoples*, 408.
148. Ibid.
149. Ibid., 409.
150. Ibid.

him so much. Moody read portions of a couple of letters he received from the man, making comments along the way.

Not only did this story make a profound point of the danger of spiritual blindness, but it also greatly moved the preacher as well. Having finished reading the last letter from the man Moody said, "Yet, we have men tell us that they will not give up sin. I wish I could say something here that would open the eyes of every man and woman in this assembly. I have not finished the sermon, but I cannot go on longer."[151] With this statement, Moody abruptly ended his message and prayed the closing prayer.

Sermon Evaluation

Many of the illustrations Moody used in this sermon speak of the dangers of spiritual blindness. Even reading the sermon today, one gains a sense of the passion of the preacher. This is no more evident than in the final illustration. It was so moving that the preacher abruptly ended his sermon early. While Moody warned of spiritual blindness throughout the sermon and made light allusions to the gospel, he never gave the gospel message itself during the sermon.

Expository or Textual?

Moody began this sermon by referencing the fact that Jesus came "to give sight to the blind." This clause came from Luke 4:18, which he had been using as his starting text for several nights. It appears he took a different phrase each night and used that phrase as the theme of his sermon. There was no attempt to set the verse in context, or to explain the meaning of the passage. Rather, the preacher focused his entire sermon on spiritual blindness. This sermon cannot be classified as expository or textual.

Biographical?

The present sermon does not fit the biographical sermon category. It does not fit either the description or the criteria from the sermon rubric. Rather, the

---

151. D. L. Moody, *To All Peoples*, 415.

sermon focuses on the concept of spiritual blindness. Therefore, it cannot be viewed as a biographical sermon.

Topical?

Moody began this sermon by introducing the topic of blindness. He quickly moved from Jesus' healing of physical blindness, to the need for healing of spiritual blindness. The entire sermon focused on various ways that Satan spiritually blinds people, whom Moody calls to come to Jesus for healing. The biblical references and allusions all point to the topic at hand. The illustrations were chosen to enhance the topic. Moody did not jump off into unrelated topics but kept the focus on spiritual blindness from beginning to end. Therefore, this sermon should be classified as a topical sermon.

God's Instrumentalities[152]

Sermon Description

Moody began this message by reading 1 Corinthians 1:18–31. He then read verse 27 a second time and declared that God uses the weak to accomplish His purpose. He said, "We very often hear people say that they have not got strength to work for God . . . This is just what the Lord wants; it is our weakness, not our strength."[153] He continued to emphasize that God has a pattern of using the weak not the strong.

As an example, Moody read a few verses from Revelation 5. He focused on the "Lion of the tribe of Judah" being a slain lamb. He said, "God's lion is always a lamb."[154] The preacher wanted his audience to realize that God's strength is perfect in human weaknesses.

Moody then called on his listeners to be used of God to reach the 75,000 homes in Boston. He says, "If they will not come to us, we have got to go to them, because that is the spirit of the Gospel."[155] He connected this call to reach

---

152. D. L. Moody, *To All Peoples*, 428–441.
153. Ibid., 430.
154. Ibid.
155. Ibid.

D.L. MOODY:
TURNING POINTS TOWARD TEXT-DRIVEN PREACHING

Boston with Christ seeking the lost. He said, "Why, any little boy, any man or woman, can carry some tracts or some word and message of the Gospel to these homes."[156] Moody followed this with an illustration of an eighty-five-year-old woman who went door to door in London while he was preaching there.

Going back to his theme of God using the weak, he reminded his hearers of Noah, Abraham, and Moses. Moody spoke of how God used Martin Luther and then described how God used Charles Spurgeon, even though he had no college degree. Moody warned his listeners to not think of any work of God as little. After speaking briefly of Elijah praying for rain and the little cloud that arose, the preacher said, "God takes up little things."[157] With that Moody used several illustrations, some biblical allusions and some personal illustrations, to call on everyone to serve the Lord by doing the "little things." Moody warned his audience that if they served the Lord opposition would come. Moody said, "When a man becomes filled with the love of God and works for God, there will be opposition, and if there is a true revival in Boston there will be opposition."[158] Moody followed this with a series of illustrations demonstrating opposition but also demonstrating victory as saints persevered in the Lord's work.

Moody concluded this sermon by calling his listeners to serve the Lord. Moody said, "May we all work for Him who died to redeem us, and come to Christ in our weaknesses, and we will be strong for others, and if they see us leading pure lives it will have great influence upon them. Let us be so full of the spirit of the Master that no one will doubt the genuineness of our Christianity."[159] Having attempted to remove all excuses, Moody expected his hearers to go out and begin telling others about Jesus.

Sermon Evaluation

Moody sought to move his listeners from the pew to the streets with this sermon. He attempted to remove excuses that are sometimes offered to keep folks from sharing their faith with others. He argued that weakness is good.

---

156. D. L. Moody, *To All Peoples,* 430.
157. Ibid., 435.
158. Ibid., 437.
159. Ibid., 441.

While the sermon may have motivated many to get busy sharing the gospel, Moody never actually proclaimed the gospel in the message.

Expository or Textual?

Moody began this sermon by reading two paragraphs from 1 Corinthians 1. He then re-read verse twenty-seven a second time to kick off the topic of his message. While he read the extended passage, giving somewhat of the context, Moody failed to explain the text within its context. Neither did he seek to explain the meaning of the single verse he read. Rather, he simply picked up on the concept of God using the weak. Therefore, this sermon cannot be classified as either an expositional or a textual sermon.

Biographical?

This message does not fit the description or any of the criteria of a biographical sermon. Rather, it is based on a concept found in 1 Corinthians 1:27. Therefore, this message cannot be classified as a biographical sermon.

Topical?

The entire sermon from beginning to end is based on the concept of God using the weak to accomplish his purposes. Moody examined various excuses people make to keep from serving the Lord but always came back to his main topic. The concept of God using the weak gave unity and direction to the message. The topic was applied to the audience by calling on everyone to get busy serving Jesus in Boston. Therefore, this sermon should be categorized as a topical sermon.

John the Baptist[160]

Sermon Description

Moody began this sermon by reminding his hearers in Boston of the last two Sunday messages he had delivered to them. One was on Christ in the Old

---

160. D. L. Moody, *To All Peoples*, 450–464.

D.L. MOODY:
TURNING POINTS TOWARD TEXT-DRIVEN PREACHING

Testament and the second was to demonstrate that the Christ of the New Testament was not a mere man, but the eternal Son of God and the only hope of salvation. He then announced his topic for the day by saying, "To-day I call your attention to John, His forerunner."[161] However, before speaking on John, Moody said a few words about Jesus.

In speaking of Jesus, Moody noted that Jesus was a carpenter in his early years. Speaking of Jesus as a carpenter Moody said, "And right here is one lesson that we ought to learn, and that is, when Christ was here He was an industrious man."[162] With this, the preacher spent the next page and a half talking about the perils of being lazy. It appears this section of the sermon was unplanned.

Having said a few words about Jesus and the problem of laziness, Moody now moved into the topic of the sermon. He said, "Now we find his forerunner comes."[163] Moody quoted from each of the Gospels as they introduce John the Baptist. He did not offer the references for the text, he simply quoted Matthew, Mark, Luke, and then John. The preacher noted that the last prophet of the Old Testament foretold of John's coming, and the four Gospel writers described his ministry.

The balance of the sermon is a presentation of the life of John the Baptist. Throughout the message, Moody moved back and forth from describing John to reading various passages about John from the Gospels and to applying characteristics of John to the believers in Boston. He emphasized that John began his ministry preaching for repentance and reform. He called sin, sin. He called on people to repent and prepare for the coming of the Messiah. However, when Jesus came on the scene, John focused his preaching on pointing people to Jesus. Moody said these two must go hand and hand. One should preach about sin and judgment, but one should also point people to Jesus for salvation.

Moody described John sending two of his disciples to ask Jesus if he was indeed the Christ. Moody suggested, "I don't know, but I have an idea that he wanted his disciples to leave him and go over to Jesus . . . I can't believe in his faith wavering; but if he was wavering he took the best way, and sent these men

---

161. D. L. Moody, *To All Peoples*, 450.
162. Ibid.
163. Ibid., 452.

to ask our Saviour."[164] Moody then finished the story of John by briefly describing his death. Speaking of John, he said, "His work was done."[165] Describing John's death, Moody began to move to the close of his sermon.

In the final paragraph of the sermon Moody said, "There was none greater than this same John."[166] From here Moody briefly spoke of both the death of Jesus and of John. He then compared John's death and burial to that of Moses. Moody concluded the sermon by saying, "Oh, that God would give us the spirit of John, that we might exalt God, forget ourselves, and cry out "Christ is everything."[167] Following these closing words, Moody led in prayer, asking the Father to help him and his hearers be like John.

Sermon Evaluation

Moody began this sermon by announcing his topic as John the Baptist, but quickly got off topic. A couple of pages in, the preacher returned to John and described his life and character. The balance of the sermon stayed on topic drawing lessons from John's life that were applied to the people of Boston. Moody referenced the gospel along the way, but he did not explicitly proclaim it.

Expository or Textual?

While Moody referenced and read several passages of Scripture, he did not seek to explain the meaning of any of them within their context. Rather, the preacher used each passage chosen to develop the listeners' understanding of the character of John the Baptist. Therefore, this sermon cannot be classified as either an expository or a textual sermon.

Biographical?

This sermon fits well within the biographical category of the sermon rubric. The message was based on a biblical character. The verses read and quoted were chosen to demonstrate some aspect of John's character to be emulated by

---

164. D. L. Moody, *To All Peoples*, 462.
165. Ibid.
166. Ibid., 463.
167. Ibid., 463.

the people of Boston. Several key characteristics were specifically applied to the people of Moody's day. Therefore, this message should be categorized as a biographical sermon.

Topical?

While the preacher announced his topic and then dove off into another almost unrelated topic, he quickly returned and most of the sermon followed the life and character of John the Baptist. The message was not a simple topical sermon. As noted above the topic was a person. Moody explained, developed, and applied John's character to the Bostonians.

Salvation[168]

Sermon Description

Moody began this sermon by stating that the topic of his message could be found everywhere in the Bible. He said, "You'll find my text most anywhere in the Bible. If you look carefully you can find it written on every page."[169] However, the sermon is not based on a text at all. Rather, it is based a topic. Moody's sermon topic was "salvation." More specifically, Moody desired his hearers to recognize that salvation is an instantaneous event. One moment a person is condemned, and the next that person is justified. He also desired his listeners to realize that salvation is available to everyone who will believe.

Moody began addressing his topic by acknowledging that this concept was controversial in Boston. Speaking of the concept of "sudden conversion" Moody said, "I don't think we have been in any city where there has been so much downright opposition to this doctrine as there has been in Boston."[170] Moody indicated that he was going to lead his audience to look to Scripture. If he could show them this was a scriptural truth, they must accept it. However, he also indicated that if it was not in Scripture, they should reject it.

---

168. D. L. Moody, *To All Peoples*, 465–476.
169. Ibid., 465.
170. Ibid.

Having acknowledged the controversy over "sudden conversion," Moody turned his attention to his belief in the doctrine and to proving it. He said, "I want to give you a number of illustrations."[171] From this point in the message, Moody began to offer illustrations to show that conversion is instantaneous and that is available to everyone who would believe. Some of his illustrations were Bible passages, while some were practical illustrations from life. The biblical illustrations came from several passages of Scripture. Most of these are simply described, referenced, or quoted. A few passages were read.

Moody's first illustration came from the story of Noah's Ark. He said, "There was a moment when he and his family were outside the ark, and there was another when he was inside. That is sudden conversion."[172] Moody focused his attention on applying this principle to his hearers. He called them to recognize that God wanted to save them. He indicated that the problem was their darkened heart and pride. He called on them to hear God calling and step into the ark. Moody followed up the ark illustration by speaking of an encounter he had with a man in Manchester, England.[173] He then told how the ark illustration helped the man come to faith in Jesus.

Moody called attention to his next biblical illustration. He read Exodus 12:22–24. Once again, the preacher pointed out the instantaneous aspect of this event. He said, "Now there must have been a moment when the blood was not there . . . but the moment the blood was put there that moment they were sheltered. They had then security and safety."[174] Moody followed this brief reference with a legend of a child and her dad on that night in Egypt. He acknowledged it to be a legend but said the story illustrated the point that one moment the child was in danger and the next moment the child was safe.

Attention then turned to the cities of refuge in the Old Testament. Moody did not read extended sections of Scripture but told the story of the cities of refuge. He followed this with two fictitious stories based on the concept of the cities of refuge. In both cases, Moody emphasized that one minute the person was outside the city, but the next they were across the border and safe. Moody

---

171. D. L. Moody, *To All Peoples,* 465.
172. Ibid.
173. Ibid., 466–467.
174. Ibid., 468.

followed this up by applying the concept to his hearers once again and calling them to cross the line to salvation.

Moody indicated that some in Boston might object to the doctrine based on Naaman. He said that they might argue that Naaman went into the water six times to no avail. But, the process of going into the water seven times is what saved him.[175] Moody acknowledged that Naaman had to obey God's direction. However, he also argued that the actual cleansing of his leprosy was instantaneous. He said, "There is one moment when Naaman was a leper. But he goes in the seventh time, and he comes out in a moment clean."[176] Moody followed this by telling of two condemned men who were pardoned at the last minute. He indicated that one moment they were each condemned, the next they were set free.

After quoting Isaiah 1:18, Moody gave several illustrations of instantaneous conversion and called on his listeners to be saved. Leading to his conclusion, the preacher read 1 John 5:9–11. Moody said, "He gives us eternal life, and if we get it we have got to get it through this Son . . . Have you got him? That is the question."[177] With this Moody called on his audience to believe on Jesus. He then read Revelation 22:17, asking, "Won't some one take Him today? Won't you take this cup that is offered you? If you are Christians pass it to your next neighbor and ask her if she is saved."[178] He then encouraged all believers present to speak to those near them about receiving Jesus. Moody concluded the sermon in prayer.

Sermon Evaluation

Moody's Boston sermon titled, "Salvation" is one of his fast paced messages where the preacher's passion is evident even when read. The message utilizes several biblical texts and allusions to call his audience to turn to Jesus for instantaneous justification. Moody addressed believers only in the final few sentences of the sermon, where he called on them to invite those near them to be saved. The passion of the sermon is obvious.

---

175. D. L. Moody, *To All Peoples*, 471.
176. Ibid.
177. Ibid., 476.
178. Ibid.

Expository or Textual?

The first two sentences of the sermon, indicate the reality that the sermon was not really based on any text of Scripture. Moody said, "You'll find my text most anywhere in the Bible. If you look carefully you can find it written on every page."[179] Moody really had no text. The passages read and quoted were verses used to support the topic and were never explained or set in context. Therefore, this sermon cannot be classified as a textual or an expositional sermon.

Biographical?

This sermon does not fit the description or criteria of a biographical sermon. While it speaks of a few Bible characters, they are utilized to support the topic. The characters were not developed. Neither were specific characteristics of the people mentioned applied to Moody's audience. Therefore, this message cannot be classified as a biographical sermon.

Topical?

This sermon must be classified as a topical sermon. It was based on a specific word—salvation. More specifically, as noted above, the message was about instantaneous salvation that is available to everyone who will believe. This topic drove the entire content of the sermon and served to unify the message from beginning to end.

Therefore, it should be classified as a topical sermon.

The Second Coming of Christ[180]

Sermon Description

Moody began his final sermon of the Boston Campaign by reminding the gathered congregation of his sermons from the past three Sundays. He then spoke of several sermons he had preached about various aspects of Christ throughout the campaign. Having spoken of the past sermons on Christ, Moody

---

179. D. L. Moody, *To All Peoples*, 465.
180. Ibid., 499–514.

D.L. MOODY:
TURNING POINTS TOWARD TEXT-DRIVEN PREACHING

introduced his topic for the present sermon. Moody said, "Now, this morning I want to talk about His coming again."[181] Having preached about Christ for three Sundays in a row, Moody's last sermon in Boston focused on preparing his hearers for Christ's return.

The preacher wanted to demonstrate the importance of the topic. He said, "There is more said in the Epistles about the Lord Jesus Christ returning to this earth than there is about baptism."[182] Moody then spoke of the churches who rarely mentioned the doctrine of Christ's return. He argued that no other topic could move churches to faithful service like the doctrine of the Second Coming.

Moody argued that if a doctrine is not Scriptural it should be shunned. But if the Scripture teaches something, it should be believed. Reading 2 Peter 1:19–21, Moody emphasized that Scripture is the final authority in the matter. He then read from the first chapter of Acts to remind his listeners of the promise of Jesus' return.

Having introduced the topic, Moody read passage after passage of Scripture, making a few comments here and there. The focus of the preacher in reading each text was to demonstrate the reality of Jesus' physical return. In fact, this sermon quotes Scripture more than any sermon this researcher has read from D. L. Moody.

Along the way, the evangelist distinguished between death and Jesus coming back for his children. Moody says, "Now, I can imagine some of you saying, 'He is coming for us when we die.' But that is not what is taught here. Death is not the coming of the Lord."[183] Moody spoke of "three dispensations represented by Enoch, Elijah, and Jesus."[184] According to Moody, believers died in each of these dispensations. But, when Jesus returns, the bodies of all believers will be raised from the dead.

Moody quoted several more passages, commenting on each one to emphasize that Jesus is coming back. Moody raised the question of post-millennialism. He indicated he once believed that the world was getting better and that when the millennium was complete Jesus would come back. He said, "Ah, my

---

181. D. L. Moody, *To All Peoples*, 499.
182. Ibid.
183. Ibid., 503.
184. Ibid.

friends, but since I have got a little better acquainted with the Word of God, I find that is not God's plan."[185] Moody read an extended passage from 2 Timothy 3 about the condition of the last days. He then read additional texts of Scripture demonstrating that the days before Jesus second coming would be days of growing evil in the world.

Moody turned his attention to the Lord's Supper. He wanted to emphasize that it is a meal of rejoicing and a meal that looks forward to Christ's return. After reading I Corinthians 11:26 Moody asked, "How many that ever go the Lord's table ever think of His return?"[186] He suggested that most people partake of the meal with dread. Moody indicated that previously he came to the Lord's table with that attitude, but now he comes to it with joy.

Moody ended his sermon by reading several passages of Scripture that mention Christ's return. The last passage he read was 1 Thessalonians 4:13–18. Moody spoke of the day when Satan will be bound and Jesus will assume the throne of David. Moody then issued another call for believers to pray for Christ to return soon, saying, "Let us pray that He may come quickly. Let that be the burden of our prayers."[187] With these words, D. L. Moody closed the sermon, and closed the Boston campaign of 1876–1877.

Sermon Evaluation

Having led the Boston campaign through three months of preaching 3–5 times a day, six days a week, Moody concluded with this sermon on Jesus' Second Coming.[188] The sermon was filled with Scripture readings and quotations. With each passage read, Moody made brief comments. Throughout the sermon

---

185. D. L. Moody, *To All Peoples*, 508.
186. Ibid., 511.
187. Ibid., 513.
188. This means that Moody preached more than 250 times during the campaign. Since the testimony of Moody himself and Wilbur Smith is that he only had a little over 250 sermons total and that only around 100–150 that were repeated, he must have preached some sermons more than once during this campaign. The Boston papers did not publish every sermon. So, to my knowledge, there is no way to confirm this other than the testimony of Moody and Smith.

D.L. MOODY:
TURNING POINTS TOWARD TEXT-DRIVEN PREACHING

Moody emphasized that Jesus was coming back and that his children should be watching for his return. He raised a few of the objections commonly lodged against the doctrine of the Second Coming. Yet, he tried to show the error of the objections. Moody mentioned the death of Christ several times, but focused primarily on His Second Coming. The gospel was not explicitly proclaimed with a call to salvation in the message. It is likely, however, that Moody followed his pattern of inviting people to the "inquiry room" to talk to someone about being saved. Moody consistently stayed on track with the theme of the sermon. The preacher made his point clear, direct, and passionate.

Expository or Textual?

As noted above in the Sermon Description, this message has more Scripture content than any Moody sermon the present researcher has read. However, the meaning of the passages within their context were never explained. Rather, the preacher used each chosen text to support his overall theme, that Jesus is coming back. Therefore, this sermon cannot be considered either textual or expositional in nature.

Biographical?

While this sermon is about Jesus, it is not biographical in nature. Rather, it seeks to demonstrate that Jesus is coming back to earth to set up his millennial reign. It does not develop the character of Jesus, nor does it seek to apply characteristics from his life to the audience. This message cannot be categorized as a biographical sermon.

Topical?

The final message of Moody's Boston campaign should be classified as a topical sermon. The sermon is based on the concept of the Jesus' Second Coming. The many Bible verses read were chosen by the preacher to support his overall theme and answer objections by his critics. The topic of the Second Coming provided both content and unity to the message. The author spoke of various sub-topics, but each of them related to the central theme. The only category that this message fits is that of a topical sermon.

Summary of Findings from Moody's Boston Campaign Sermons

D. L. Moody preached a three-month campaign in Boston from late 1876 through early 1877. During this time, he would preach or teach three times a day on Monday through Friday, take Saturday off, and preach as many as five times a day on Sundays. Despite early challenges and difficult circumstances, Moody persevered. The city heard the gospel. Lives were changed. Even the Boston newspapers moved from criticism to publishing Moody's sermons.

Fifty of Moody's addresses were recorded in the Boston newspapers as verbatim sermons. The reporters would take down his words verbatim. Occasionally they would add minor editorial comments. Twenty-five of these sermons were gathered from the newspapers and published in the book, *To All People*. Care was given to print as close to what Moody said as possible. This is evidenced by the fact that they even printed obvious errors in grammar and occasional errors in Scripture references. Reading the Boston sermons as recorded in *To All People* give one the clearest sense of Moody's preaching during his most popular years.

The present researcher chose twenty of the twenty-five published sermons from Boston for analysis. The sermons were read several times. Then each sermon was evaluated using the sermon rubric established in Chapter Three. With the help of the rubric, each sermon was classified as either, expositional, textual, biographical, or topical. The researcher discovered five biographical sermons, based on the life and characteristics of a biblical character. The remaining fifteen messages were all topical sermons.

All the sermons utilized Scripture. The amount of Scripture varied significantly. However, the way Scripture verses were used remained consistent from sermon to sermon. During this time Moody used Scripture to support his topic. This was true of his topical sermons, but it was equally true of his biographical sermons. At this stage of his preaching, Moody's sermons were driven more by his topic than by the meaning of his text(s).

D.L. MOODY:
TURNING POINTS TOWARD TEXT-DRIVEN PREACHING

Conclusion

This chapter sought to demonstrate the content of Moody's sermons during his most popular years. The chapter began by putting the Boston campaign within its historical context. Through this it was demonstrated that these sermons, as contained in *To All People*, give us an accurate picture of the preaching content of Moody from his return to the United States in 1875 until Henry Weston preached at a summer conference in 1892.

Twenty sermons were presented in this chapter. The content and flow of each sermon was summarized. Following the summary, each sermon was analyzed in accordance with the sermon rubric of chapter three. Each sermon was classified according to the description and criteria set forth in that rubric. A summary of the sermons was then offered as evidence of Moody's preaching content at this stage of his life and ministry. This chapter has demonstrated that most of Moody's sermons at this juncture were topical. These topical sermons used Scripture to support the topic, rather than to guide the content. The five biographical sermons utilized Scripture in a similar fashion.

Chapter four gave the reader a sense of the biblical content of Moody's sermons in the early years. This chapter has demonstrated some growth. However, the chapter has also demonstrated that Moody did not come close to preaching textual or expositional sermons at this point in his ministry. It is now time to consider sermons from the last few years of Moody's life to determine whether the growth in biblical content continued and to see if he ever preached a textual or expositional sermon.

Chapter Six

An Examination of Moody's Late Sermons

Dwight L. Moody made several significant confessions in his lifetime. The first came when he confessed Jesus as his Lord and Savior in the back of his uncle's shoe store.[1] Another great confession came when he declared his absolute dependence on the power of the Spirit to fulfill his ministry.[2] A third significant confession came at a summer conference in 1892 when Moody declared, "There goes one of my sermons."[3] As previously demonstrated, following this event Moody began calling for expositional preaching. This chapter seeks to discover whether he simply called for exposition or if his own preaching began to reflect his statements.

Moody lived and preached another seven years after he acknowledged his need to preach differently. To discover whether Moody ever preached an expositional or even a textual sermon, sermons were examined from the years 1894–1899. Despite Moody's pattern of repeating sermons, about thirty distinct sermons were discovered that he preached during the years of 1894–1899.

As in previous chapters, the focus remains on dealing with verbatim sermons. As previously noted, Moody's son Paul testifies that these verbatim re-

---

1. William R. Moody, *The Life of Dwight L. Moody* (New York: Fleming H. Revell Company, 1900), 41.

2. R. A. Torrey, *Why God Used D. L. Moody* (Kindle Edition), Location 2890–295.

3. Paul D. Moody, *My Father, An Intimate Portrait of Dwight Moody* (Boston: Little, Brown and Company, 1938), 185.

cords of his preaching give the strongest sense of his dad's preaching.[4] Newspaper verbatim reports continued to be sought and read. The newspapers are preserved in PDF format, having been produced from microfilm; the print is very small, and when enlarged, the page blurs so as to make it difficult to read. Due to this difficulty, an additional source of verbatim sermons was sought and discovered, with readable sermons useful for detailed examination.

During the years of 1894–1902, the Northfield Conference Bookstore published proceedings of the summer conferences under the title *Northfield Echoes*. These books contain verbatim accounts of sermons as well as other material related to the Northfield Summer Conferences. Each of the *Northfield Echoes* published from 1894–1899 contain sermons from Moody as well as from other conference speakers. Twenty-eight of Moody's sermons were gathered for evaluation.

Through the evaluation of twenty-eight sermons Moody preached during the summer conferences of 1894–1899, this chapter will demonstrate continued growth in the biblical content of Moody's preaching. The reader should not expect to see the kind of expositional sermons that reach the standards set in *Engaging Exposition*.[5] Indeed, Moody continued preaching topical sermons. However, this chapter will demonstrate that Moody continued to grow in the biblical content of his preaching and did indeed preach some text-driven sermons in the later years of his life. The extent to which some later sermons reach toward a text-driven model will be shown through the evaluations and summarized in the conclusion to the chapter.

The Context of the Northfield Sermons

Following the first conference held in September of 1880, the Northfield Seminary Campus became a gathering place for evangelical Christians. Each summer, college students, lay leaders, pastors, and other Christian leaders came

---

4. Paul D. Moody, *My Father*, 111.

5. Daniel L. Akin, Bill Curtis, and Stephen Rummage, *Engaging Exposition* (Nashville: B&H Academic, 2011).

from all over the United States and from as far away as England.⁶ Some of the most respected preachers from across denominational lines came to participate in these conferences. When one visits the birthplace of Moody, the pulpit used in the Northfield summer conferences may be viewed. On top of the pulpit sits a framed list of various preachers who spoke at the Northfield conferences. One may read names like G. Campbell Morgan, Henry Moorhouse, C. I. Scofield, Hudson Taylor, F. B. Meyer, and R. A. Torrey. Even Southern Baptists were represented at the conferences by men like John Broadus and others.

Believers came to Northfield to be refreshed, encouraged, and rejuvenated for another year of service to the Lord. The conferences were filled with inspirational singing, preaching, teaching, prayer, and times of fellowship.⁷ Some of the summer conferences focused specifically on college students. Other weeks focused on pastors and Christian leaders. Prayer meetings were held, as were special meetings just for men, and other meetings just for the ladies. An attendee was encouraged to make certain of his or her own salvation, to be filled with the Spirit, and to serve the Lord faithfully.

While Moody had some of the most respected preachers of his day speak at the conferences, he also brought sermons to the gathered crowd. The conferences provided opportunity for Moody to both minister to others and to receive ministry himself. Much of what happened and what was said at the conferences can be revisited today in writing. The *Northfield Echoes* provide a yearly publication of proceedings from the meetings and short descriptions of various events held at the conferences. The publications for the years 1894–1899 publish verbatim sermons of most of the conference preachers. Each book includes at least three sermons preached by Moody during the summer. The chapter will now consider twenty-eight sermons preached by Moody during the conferences and published in the *Northfield Echoes*.

---

6. For a brief introduction to the Northfield Summer Conferences, see Delevan L Pierson, ed., *Northfield Echoes* (East Northfield, MA: The Conference Book Store, 1894), 1–13.

7. Ibid., 11.

Description and Evaluation of Twenty-Eight Northfield Sermons

As with the sermons discussed in chapter five, the sermons examined below are verbatim accounts of Moody's preaching. These sermons were preached after Moody's confession before Henry Weston at the summer conferences of 1892.[8] These sermons were also preached during the years Moody began calling for expositional preaching.[9] While the *Northfield Echoes* (1894–1899) contains sermons by several preachers of the late nineteenth century, almost thirty of the sermons were preached by Moody. Some years the sermons were listed in a table of contents. The sermons for these years were examined alphabetically. Some years, the book collections fail to include a table of contents. In these cases, sermons were examined in the order in which they appear.

The present researcher intended to choose twenty sermons for evaluation. The plan was to simply take the sermons in the order in which they appear, according to the method described in the previous paragraph. However, the sermon on the Ten Commandments was delivered as two sermons preached by Moody during the 1897 conferences. Likewise, the sermon titled "Power in Prayer" was preached as a two-sermon series. Though "Power in Prayer" was presented as one message in the *Northfield Echoes*, the notes at the bottom of the page indicate the message was presented as a two-part sermon.[10] Also, in 1898 Moody preached a seven-sermon series on the Holy Spirit.[11] *Northfield Echoes*, again chose to present the sermon as one in the proceedings and simply indicate the dates of each sermon in the footnotes. Therefore, the reader will find twenty-eight sermons presented below. Each sermon will be shown with a sermon description followed by an evaluation of the message utilizing the sermon rubric. Attention now turns to the consideration of late Moody sermons preached at the Northfield summer conferences.

---

8. See footnote 100 in chapter two and footnote 17 in chapter three.

9. See footnote 36 in chapter one.

10. Delevan L. Pierson, ed., *Northfield Echoes* (East Northfield, MA: The Conference Book Store, 1897), 42–53, 124–138; hereafter *Echoes* (publication year).

11. Ibid., 248–270.

The Anointing of the Holy Spirit for Service[12]

Sermon Description

Moody opened this sermon by noting that the message was given in response to a request to preach on the topic at hand. He stated, "I have been asked to speak on the Holy Spirit as a help that we all need in order to do Christian work. He comes not only to help us in meetings like this, or when we are doing religious work, but Christ says that He shall *dwell* with you, *abide* with you, and *be in* you."[13] Moody went on to assert, "Every true child of God who has been cleansed by the blood of Christ becomes a dwelling place for the Holy Ghost."[14] Having introduced the idea of the Holy Spirit indwelling Christians, Moody argued that the Bible records three dwelling places for the Holy Spirit: Moses' Tabernacle, Solomon's Temple, and the life of "Every true believer."[15] This introduction set the stage for Moody's sermon.

Building on the idea of the Holy Spirit indwelling Christians, Moody quoted 1 Corinthians 6:19a. In explanation, Moody argued, "He dwells with the believer, not with the unbeliever, with a quickened man, not with a dead man."[16] Moody believed that every true Christian had the Holy Spirit dwelling within their very person.

Moody also wanted his hearers to understand that just because one is indwelt by the Spirit, it does not mean that person is walking in the power of the Spirit. He said, "The next point I want you bring to your mind is that you may be a son of God and have the Spirit of God dwelling in you, and yet not have the *fullness* of power (*sic*)."[17] Moody believed that a great many churches never sought the power of the Spirit to accomplish God's work. He said, "A man may

---

12. Delevan L. Pierson, ed., *Echoes* (1894), 322–328.
13. Ibid., 322.
14. Ibid.
15. Ibid., 323.
16. Ibid.
17. Ibid.

have *influence*, and yet not have *power*."[18] This statement launched Moody into a series of biblical allusions and quotations to demonstrate his point.

After a quick reference to the difference between David and Goliath, Moody suggested that each of his listeners could choose which of three different classes of Christians they wanted to be like. Moody said, "Take the third, fourth, and seventh chapters of John, and you will find three classes of Christians."[19] Nicodemus was Moody's first example. He argued that Nicodemus became a follower of Jesus, but never understood the power of the Spirit in his life. The women at the well in John 4:1–42, served as Moody's second example. Describing the woman, Moody said she, "Comes for a pot of water and gets the whole well full, a well that never dries up, and never freezes up."[20] Moody then looked to John 7:37–38 to describe his third type of Christian. Moody said, "If you get into the seventh chapter of John, you will be on fire three hundred and sixty-five days in the year. That spirit of lukewarmness will all be swept away."[21] Moody then sought to encourage his listeners to thirst after this filling of the Spirit's power.

Moody shifted his focus in the sermon to describing how Jesus' disciples were empowered by the Spirit on the Day of Pentecost. Moody emphasized that they waited for the power of the Spirit and then great things took place. Moody encouraged his listeners by saying, "Let us pray for this power."[22] He then spoke of the need for preachers to be empowered by the Spirit for effective service.

Moving toward the close of the sermon, Moody reminded his hearers, "Now, you notice the command to be filled. Are you full? If not, then are we not living beneath our privileges?"[23] He warned his listeners not to put the Spirit in a box by expecting him to come in a certain way. Moody said, "The Holy Ghost comes in his own way. If you expect Him to come in one way He will come in an opposite direction."[24] Moody then asked, "Do you want this power above

---

18. Delevan L. Pierson, ed., *Echoes* (1894), 323.
19. Ibid., 324.
20. Ibid., 325.
21. Ibid.
22. Ibid., 326.
23. Ibid., 327.
24. Ibid., 328.

everything else? …. He will do it, if you really desire it above everything else. Let us pray for this power."²⁵ With this, Moody concluded the sermon.

Sermon Evaluation

The present sermon relates specifically to the original purpose of the summer conferences. In telling the story of the conferences, the book quoted from the initial call to come to Northfield which Moody issued in 1880. Concerning the purpose of the gatherings, Moody wrote, "To plead God's promises, and to wait upon Him for a fresh anointment of power from on high."²⁶ Fourteen years later, Moody was again asked to preach on the anointing of the Holy Spirt. The purpose of this 1894 sermon was to fulfill that request. Moody did not explicitly share the gospel in this message.

Expository or Textual?
While the sermon referenced both biblical allusions, quotations, and readings, Moody did not explain a text within its context. The closest Moody came to keeping a text in its context came when he spoke from the book of John. He described three examples of people from John 3, 4, and 7. While he did set each example somewhat in context, he failed to explain the meaning of any of these chapters. Rather, he drew on allusions and quotes from these chapters to support his points concerning the relationship between individual Christians and the Holy Spirit. Throughout the rest of the sermon, verses of Scripture were used in a similar fashion, without regard for context. Therefore, this message cannot be considered an expositional sermon.

Moody did not base this sermon on an explanation of a single verse of Scripture. Neither did he present a running commentary of an extended section of Scripture. Therefore, this sermon does not fit the description or criteria of a textual sermon.

---

25. Delevan L. Pierson, ed., *Echoes* (1894), 328.
26. Ibid., 2.

D.L. MOODY: TURNING POINTS TOWARD TEXT-DRIVEN PREACHING

Biographical?

Throughout this sermon, Moody mentioned various biblical characters. However, he did not base his sermon on any individual. Rather, his references to various people were used as support for his topic. This message does not fit the description or the criteria of a biographical sermon.

Topical?

Moody based this sermon on a topic rather than a specific passage of Scripture. He utilized Scripture to support his theme by quoting, reading, and alluding to various biblical passages. Moody never explained a text of Scripture within its context in this message. The sermon was presented under the unified theme of living in the power of the Holy Spirit. Therefore, this message is classified as a topical sermon.

Studies in the Gospel of John[27]

Sermon Description

On Sunday night June 24, 1894, Moody preached the present sermon, "Studies in the Gospel of John."[28] Moody began the sermon by saying, "My great desire is to get you students into the Bible, and I want to impress that upon you to-night."[29] Moody then spent a few minutes talking about the importance of each Christian learning to study the Bible for themselves. Moody spoke of ways he sought to get his students at Northfield and Mount Hermon to study the Bible. Using his students as an example, Moody launched into an overview of the book of John.

Moody walked through the entire book. He noted major events and teachings. He also quoted specific verses from each chapter. From the first chapter Moody discussed verses eleven through thirteen. He then described the call of

---

27. Delevan L. Pierson, ed., *Echoes* (1894), 96–108.
28. Ibid., 96.
29. Ibid.

the first five disciples.[30] When he arrived at chapter two, Moody noted this was the beginning of the miracles. The verse he emphasized was "Whatever he saith unto you, do it."[31] He then applied this to his listeners by saying, "Obedience is the essential thought of that chapter."[32] With these first two chapters of John, Moody established the pattern he followed for the entire sermon.

Arriving at John 3:16, Moody emphasized this verse, but he also spoke of regeneration and the importance of the whole chapter. He said, "I believe that if every chapter in the Bible but one had to be blotted out, and God gave me my choice of one which I had to preach from all my life, I would say, Give me the third chapter of John."[33] Moody then continued on to the fourth chapter, noting the woman at the well.

In this manner, Moody continued to walk through the entire book of John. Some chapters of the Gospel were commented on more than others, but he indicated something important to understand from every chapter. Usually, he would give a verse or two and say a word about the context of the whole chapter. Occasionally, he would make a specific application to his audience. He used some illustrations, but for the most part he focused on describing a verse, an event, or both from each chapter.

Toward the end of the sermon, Moody picked up the pace. Having followed the pattern described above throughout the sermon, he simply summarized the final chapters in one long sentence. Moody said, "The *eighteenth* chapter is the one in which *Christ is arrested*, in the *nineteenth* chapter He is *crucified*, in the *twentieth* He has *risen*, and in the *twenty-first* chapter you find Him *calling His disciples* to that early breakfast by the sea."[34] Having finished his overview of the Gospel of John, Moody concluded with an appeal. He said, "O let us dine with him to-night, let us sup with Him; if we are willing to sup with Him, He will sup with us."[35]

---

30. Delevan L. Pierson, ed., *Echoes* (1894), 97.
31. Ibid., 98.
32. Ibid.
33. Ibid.
34. Ibid., 108.
35. Ibid. (Cf. Revelation 3:20).

D.L. MOODY:
TURNING POINTS TOWARD TEXT-DRIVEN PREACHING

Sermon Evaluation

A researcher who has read Moody's sermons from the previous years will notice a marked difference with even a cursory reading of this message. Moody took just a couple of minutes to speak of why it was important to study the Bible. He then walked through the Gospel of John chapter by chapter. Moody not only attempted to help his listeners get an overview of the book, but he also focused specific attention on the context of each chapter. On more than one occasion throughout the sermon, Moody shared the gospel with his listeners. The nature of this sermon demonstrates Moody's desire to grow in the biblical content of his preaching. This sermon demonstrates that he was not only calling for expositional preaching as previously noted, but he attempted to move in that direction.

Expository or Textual?

The present sermon is the first one examined in this monograph that has the possibility of being classified as either expositional or textual. Moody attempted to base his sermon on the entire book of John, rather than on a topic. He walked through the book, noting specific verses, events, and giving at least some context for each chapter. His words were guided by the contents of the chapters. All of these characteristics are true of both expositional and textual sermons.

The difference found on the sermon rubric between these two classifications comes in the author's divisions of his material. While Moody correctly drew his points from the text of each chapter, he failed to discuss the divisions of the text, as presented by its author. The sermon is basically a running commentary of the book of John. The divisions of the sermon are based on the preacher's choice, rather than on the grammatical structure employed by the author. Therefore, in accordance with the sermon rubric, this sermon should be classified as a textual sermon.

Biographical?

The present sermon mentions various characters in the Gospel of John. However, no character is developed beyond a brief mention. The sermon is not based on any one of the characters mentioned. Rather, they are mentioned because they come from the various chapters Moody walked through in his running commentary of the book. Therefore, this sermon cannot be classified as a biographical sermon.

Topical?

The sermon is not based on a topic. Rather, it is based on specific verses and events described in each chapter of the book of John. Therefore, this message cannot be classified as a topical sermon.

The Call of Moses[36]

Sermon Description

In a footnote to the sermon title reference is made to the fact that this sermon is based on two passages of Scripture, Exodus 3:10 and Deuteronomy 32:1. Moody read the Exodus verse and then began his sermon. Toward the end of the sermon Moody turned the attention of his audience to Deuteronomy 32:1–4 by reading the verses and making a few brief comments on Moses' growth in eloquence.

Moody's introduction to his sermon relates to the fact that more is said about the call of various men in the Bible than about their deaths. He then said, "Perhaps some of you young men don't know just what profession or work to take up, and so this morning I should like to take the call of Moses, and see if we cannot draw a lesson from it."[37] With these words, Moody set the stage for his message.

Starting with the burning bush, Moody began examining the exchange between God and Moses. He said, "You remember when God met him at that burning bush and called him to do as great a work as any man has ever been called to in this world, that Moses thought the Lord had made a mistake, that he was not the man."[38] Moody then noted Moses' question, "Who am I?"[39] Rec-

---

36. Delevan L. Pierson, ed., *Echoes* (1894), 273–278.
37. Ibid., 273.
38. Ibid.
39. Ibid.

ognizing that Moses was small in his own sight, Moody caused his listeners to remember how forty years earlier Moses thought he could handle the job of delivering the Jews in his own wisdom and strength. According to Moody, Moses better understood his limits and realized his need for God after forty years in the wilderness.[40] Moody indicated that he believed God knew that Moses was now ready to make a difference.

Moody pointed out that even though God knew Moses was ready, Moses did not think so. He said, "But Moses went on making excuses and said, 'When I get down there, who shall I say has sent me?'"[41] Moody described the exchange between God and Moses, at times quoting Scripture directly and then noting, "As long as God was with him, he could not fail."[42] Moody used John the Baptist as an illustration. Moody indicated that some might see John's beheading as failure, but he argued that John fulfilled the work the Father wanted him to complete. Moody then said, "Moses wasn't going to fail."[43] Moody then moved on to another of Moses' excuses.

Moody sought to help his listeners recognize that when God calls, one's excuses will not really excuse him or her from obeying God. He said, "Moses made another excuse and said, 'I am slow of speech, slow of tongue.'"[44] Again, Moody recounted the exchange between the Lord and Moses, occasionally quoting directly from the biblical account. Having recounted the exchange, including the addition of Aaron to the team as Moses' interpreter, Moody demonstrated to his hearers that over time Moses became eloquent.

Moody read Deuteronomy 32:1–4 to demonstrate that when he was one hundred and twenty years old, Moses demonstrated his eloquence. Having read the text Moody said, "He turned out to be one of the most eloquent men the world has ever seen. If God sends men and they go and deliver His message He will be with their mouth."[45] Moody then inserted a very brief illustration

---

40. Delevan L. Pierson, ed., *Echoes* (1894), 273–274.
41. Ibid., 275.
42. Ibid.
43. Ibid., 276.
44. Ibid.
45. Ibid., 277.

of Cicero and Demosthenes. He concluded that a messenger of God wants his hearers to forget about the messenger and remember the message.

Moody raised one more argument from Moses. Moody stated, "Then Moses said, 'Send whom thou wilt.' Did you ever stop to think what Moses would have lost if God had taken him at his word, and said, 'Very well, Moses, you may stay here in the desert, and I will send Aaron or Joshua or Caleb'?"[46] With this Moody moved to the conclusion of his sermon. He told his audience, "If God calls you consider it a great honor"[47] Moody then encouraged his listeners to look and listen for God's call. He said, "If we listen to His voice, we shall get a call, and if God calls us and sends us, there will be no such thing as failure, but there will be success all along the line."[48] With one sentence Moody closed by noting Moses' success owed to him moving forward in obedience to God's call.

Sermon Evaluation

As noted above, a footnote indicates this sermon was based on two verses of Scripture. Moody read, quoted, and alluded to several verses and partial verses of Scripture regarding Moses and his call to lead the people out of Egypt. In one sense, the sermon was based on Exodus 3:10. However, Moody covered quite a bit of the encounter at the burning bush. The Deuteronomy 32:1–4 text was read to demonstrate that one of Moody's objections at the time of his call was handled by God in such a way that Moses moved from a lack of eloquence to being very eloquent. Thus, most of Moody's sermon was based on Exodus 3:10–4:17. All along the way Moody made applications to his listeners based on Moses and his call to service. He did not share the gospel explicitly in this sermon.

Expository or Textual?

The sermon is said to be based on two verses, as previously noted. However, the sermon primarily follows the story of Moses' call from Exodus 3:10–4:17. Moody did follow the general flow of the passage. The fact that he walked

---

46. Delevan L. Pierson, ed., *Echoes* (1894), 278.
47. Ibid., 278.
48. Ibid.

through the test does not suggest that Moody recognized and emphasized the author's intent. Moody had a specific thing he wanted to draw from this extended passage. His entire sermon focused on Moses' call more than God's deliverance in the exodus. The sermon was clearly based on the text of Scripture, but it did not emphasis the author's theme or divisions of the text. This sermon comes close to exposition, as described in the sermon rubric. In the end, it must be classified as a textual sermon.

Biographical?

While Moses was emphasized in this sermon, Moody did not give a biographical sermon about Moses' life. Rather, Moody focused on one event in that life. Moody sought to help his listeners learn from Moses' call in order to consider God's call in their own lives. Therefore, this sermon cannot be classified as a biographical sermon.

Topical?

Moody's emphasis in this message was on the call of Moses. He based the sermon on a specific text of Scripture. The extended text of Exodus 3:10–4:17 moved the sermon along. The topic never overshadowed the text itself. Therefore, this message should not be classified as a topical sermon.

The Work of the Holy Spirit[49]

Sermon Description

Moody began this sermon by using his life as a testimony to lead into his subject. He said, "There are two epochs in my life that stand out above everything else, and the first was when I was born of the Spirit."[50] Moody briefly spoke of the importance of being regenerated. He then said, "The second great event in my life was when God baptized me with his Spirit for Service. That

---

49. Delevan L. Pierson, ed., *Echoes* (1894), 317–321.
50. Ibid., 315.

stands out as vividly to-day as in '71, when the power of God came upon me."[51] Having focused his audience's attention on the Spirit, Moody read John 14:17 as the text to introduce the subject of his sermon.

Moving past his introduction Moody announced his topic. He said, "Now we come to the work of the Spirit."[52] The rest of the sermon describes seven things the Spirit accomplishes. Moody states each action as a point and then makes his argument and his application. In most cases, he quotes Scripture to support his argument. Sometimes, he reads the supporting passage. At other times, he alludes to a biblical text. Only once does Moody credit the Holy Spirit with an action without any biblical reference.

The first work of the Spirit Moody described is the work of conviction. To support his argument, he quoted from John 16:8. The second work Moody attributes to the Spirit relates to love. He said, "The next work of the Spirit is to *shed abroad the love of God* in that man's heart."[53] While the statement itself comes directly from Scripture, Moody also quotes from 1 John reminding his readers, "God is love."[54] Moody then said, "The next work of the Holy Spirit is to *impart hope*."[55] Moody only offered five sentences regarding this work. He also did not give any biblical references in support of his argument. This is not to say his statement is false, he simply did not support this concept from the Bible.

Moody suggested another work of the Spirit. He said, "Another thing the Spirit of God does is to *give liberty*."[56] In support of his argument, Moody quoted a portion of 2 Corinthians 3:17, without offering the reference. He also illustrated his point without any biblical allusions. Moody said, "Another thing

---

51. Delevan L. Pierson, ed., *Echoes* (1894),While Moody used the phrase, "baptism of the Holy Spirit," he used it interchangeably with the "filling of the Holy Spirit." He never equated either phrase with things like speaking in tongues, entire sanctification, or a "second blessing." For more on this see, George and Donald Sweeting, *Lessons from the Life of Moody* (Chicago: Moody Press, 1989), 94—95.

52. Ibid., 318.

53. Ibid.

54. Ibid., 319.

55. Ibid.

56. Ibid.

the Spirit of God does is to *testify of Christ*."⁵⁷ Moody returned to supporting his argument with both Scripture quotation and biblical allusions. Moody's next point about the Spirit's work comes as a direct quote from John's Gospel. He said, "He shall *guide you into all truth*."⁵⁸ Once again, Moody did not give the exact reference; rather he simply quoted the verse.

Moody offered one final point about the work of the Spirit. This statement also arises out of Jesus' discourse in John 14–16. Moody quoted, *"He shall show you things to come."*⁵⁹ He contrasts the newspapers telling one of what has already happened, with the Spirit telling one what is going to happen. Leading to his conclusion Moody spoke of how the disciples had short memories prior to Pentecost, but after Pentecost, they remembered Christ's words.⁶⁰ He then ended the sermon abruptly.

Sermon Evaluation

Moody began the sermon with two paragraphs of personal testimony to direct his listeners to the subject of the Holy Spirit's work. In the third paragraph, he read John 14:17, which became his theme verse to move into the topic at hand. As noted above, Moody did not explain the passage of Scripture as such. Rather, he chose seven different activities of the Spirit to emphasize to his listeners. Moody did share the gospel in this message.

Expository or Textual?

While Moody moved quickly from getting the attention of his listeners to pointing them to a verse of Scripture, he did not explain the verse, or set it in its context. Moody used several Scripture quotations and biblical allusions in his message, but failed to set any of them in their context. His focus was to use them to support the various works of the Spirit. This sermon cannot be considered either an expositional or a textual sermon.

---

57. Delevan L. Pierson, ed., *Echoes* (1894), 320.
58. Ibid.
59. Ibid., 321.
60. Ibid.

Biographical?

While the sermon is about the person of the Holy Spirit, it is not a biographical presentation. Moody does speak of the work of the Spirit, but not of the characteristics of the Spirit. The message does not fit the description or criteria of the biographical sermon found in the sermon rubric. We must look to the topical category to find a classification for this sermon.

Topical?

Moody dealt with a single topic under the unified theme of the work of the Spirit. He described seven different activities carried out by the Spirit. These were supported by reading, quoting, and alluding to Bible passages. The points were also supported by illustrations and personal arguments. This message fits well into the topical sermon category.

Assurance of Salvation[61]

Sermon Description

Moody began this sermon by recounting John Wesley's struggle with assurance of salvation. Moody quoted Wesley being asked about this assurance, "'But are you sure, Wesley, that you are saved?' It went like an arrow to his heart, and he had no rest nor power until that question was settled."[62] Following the introductory story of Wesley, Moody attempted to help his listeners realize that before an individual can be useful in the Lord's service, he or she must have assurance of his or her own salvation.

Having set forth the subject of his message, Moody began to speak of three types of people who claim to be Christians. He said, "There are three classes among Christian people that do not have assurance, and I do not believe it is the will of God that they should have it."[63] Moody described the first type of person as one who is a church member, but has never truly been born again. The second type of person Moody discussed was the person who

---

61. Delevan L. Pierson, ed., *Echoes* (1895), 277–285.
62. Ibid., 277.
63. Ibid., 278.

has trusted Christ but is not willing to confess him before men each day. The third group Moody identified are the people who are saved, but they are not willing to work for the Lord.[64] Moody believes that all three of these will not find assurance of salvation.

Having thoroughly described the need for assurance, Moody turned his attention to 1 John. First, he pointed out that John wrote, "These things have I written unto you that believe on the name of the Son of God; that ye may know that ye have eternal life."[65] Moody then focused his attention specifically on 1 John 3. He said, "In the third chapter there are mentioned six things worth knowing."[66] Each of the six things Moody pointed out came directly from the text of the chapter.

The majority of Moody's sermon came from verses in 1 John 3. He began, "The fifth verse says, 'And ye know that he was manifested to take away our sins; and in him was no sin.'"[67] Moody then explained the verse emphasizing both Jesus' sinless nature and His substitutionary atonement. He then said, "Then, the nineteenth verse reads, 'Hereby we know that we are of the truth, and shall assure our hearts before him.'"[68] In explanation of this verse, Moody argued that truth matters. He indicated that one cannot simply be sincere in their belief, one must believe the truth to be saved.

Moody backed up to the fourteenth verse for his next point. He said, "Look at the fourteenth verse, 'We know that we have passed from death unto life, because we hate our sisters.'"[69] The preacher acknowledged everyone's laugh and then explained that he read the verse like many practice it. Moody then reread the verse correctly and spoke of the fact that when a Christian loves other Christians, he or she enjoys assurance of salvation. Building on this idea, Moody read verse fifteen and emphasized that if one hates in his or heart, he or she is guilty of murder.

---

64. Delevan L. Pierson, ed., *Echoes* (1894), 278.
65. Ibid., 279.
66. Ibid., 280.
67. Ibid.
68. Ibid.
69. Ibid.

Moody looked to verse twenty-four for his next point, "He that keepeth his commandments dwelleth in him, and he in him. And hereby we know that he abideth in us by the Spirit which he hath given us."[70] Moody offered explanation of this verse by encouraging his listeners to examine their lives to see if they bear the kind of fruit Jesus bore. He then said, "Now, we have kept the best until the last. This is the second verse, 'Beloved, now are we the sons of God, and it doth not yet appear what we shall be; but we know that when he shall appear, we shall be like him, for we shall see him as he is.'"[71] Explaining this verse, Moody focused on two aspects. First, he wanted his readers to understand that believers are already children of God. Second, he wanted to give his readers hope for the future, when sin and time will be no more.

The final point above led Moody into a discussion of how the Christian should deal with sin. He quoted 1 John 1:9. He then quoted Romans 8:33, indicating that forgiveness is available for God's children. Anticipating some objections, Moody read 1 Corinthians 9:24–27 and explained that rewards, not salvation, are in view in this passage. He then returned to Romans 8:35–39 and emphasized that Paul had assurance of salvation. Having read the text, Moody encouraged his listeners to recognize the importance of assurance of salvation. He said, "Let us pray God to keep us in perfect peace assured of salvation."[72] The message concluded.

Sermon Evaluation

The present sermon was not easy to categorize. As the reader will see below, the message fit some criteria in two different categories. This fact may be a sign of Moody's growth towards exposition during his later years. The early paragraphs sound as if he is going to preach a topical sermon. However, most of his sermon is based on 1 John 3. Toward the end of the sermon, Moody briefly

---

70. Ibid., 282.

71. Ibid.

72. Ibid., 284. While in the book this sermon concludes here, there is a footnote which indicates Moody continued preaching, by adding more to the message that was not recorded. Presumably, the additional material was left out for space.

discussed two other passages. These texts fit his overall theme of assurance. Moody did present the gospel explicitly in this sermon.

Expository or Textual?

The message is not an expositional sermon. Moody did not explain a passage giving emphasis to the intent or divisions of the original author. However, most of the sermon was based on a single chapter in the Bible. Moody chose six verses from 1 John 3. He read each verse and offered explanation of the verse. He applied the passage to his listeners. If the majority of the sermon is the factor determining its category, then this would be classified as a textual sermon.

Biographical?

The sermon does not present the life of a Bible character. The message does not fit the description or criteria of a biographical sermon. This is not a biographical sermon.

Topical?

Moody introduced this sermon as he would one of his topical sermons during the middle years of his preaching. He began with several illustrations and a few Scripture quotations. However, as noted above Moody moved to 1 John 3 and presented most of his message by explaining six verses from the chapter. In the final paragraphs, Moody returned to a close like his previous topical messages. One might be tempted to classify this as a topical sermon. Yet, the majority of the message is clearly textual.

Daniel in Babylon[73]

Sermon Description

In this sermon, Moody presented the life of Daniel, making application to his listeners all along the way. However, Moody did not tell the story of Daniel exclusively. Rather, he walked through the story of the first six chapters of the

---

73. Delevan L. Pierson, ed., *Echoes* (1895), 370–380.

book of Daniel. Consequently, when he arrived at chapter three, the emphasis was on Daniel's three Hebrew friends. Moody allowed the text to determine his emphasis, making the message unlike his earlier biographical sermons. Rather than limiting the message to the man, he focused more on the flow of the text of Scripture. This fact is reinforced when the reader considers the way Moody told about Nebuchadnezzar and his son Belshazzar as well. He followed the narrative of the first six chapters of the book.

While Moody's emphasis was on Daniel's role, he followed the narrative, giving attention to each person or group of people mentioned in the text. The sermon style was one that fits the text itself. Moody preached this sermon by telling the story. He did quote and read specific verses occasionally. Generally, however, he simply told the story in the order it occurred in the Bible.

Moody began with Daniel being taken captive. He said, "This young man, who was taken as a captive by Nebuchadnezzar, was about twenty years old, some say seventeen."[74] Following this statement, Moody set the stage historically helping his audience to gain a sense of the trials Daniel might face. Moody quickly moved to discuss the first major event in Babylon when Daniel was tempted to eat the king's food and drink his wine. He demonstrated how Daniel and his three Hebrew friends remained firm in their resolve to obey God.

Moody turned his attention to Nebuchadnezzar's first dream and the danger it posed to Daniel.[75] Walking through the story, Moody demonstrated Daniel's faith in God and showed how the Lord used Daniel to answer the king and save many lives, including his own. Moody then turned his attention to the trial of Shadrach, Meshach, and Abednego. He told how they were faced with worshiping Nebuchadnezzar's image or face the fiery furnace. Having described their faithfulness, Moody said, "Thank God for such men! I would rather have one man like that than a thousand that will run when the first temptation comes and yield to it and give up."[76] Moody then described God's amazing intervention to save the lives of the three Hebrews.

Moody then considered Nebuchadnezzar's second dream. While Moody spoke of Daniel's interpretation, the sermon emphasized the arrogance and

---

74. Delevan L. Pierson, ed., *Echoes* (1894), 370.
75. Ibid., 371–373.
76. Ibid., 375.

struggle of the king. Moody concluded this portion of the story by indicating that in the end Daniel won the old Babylonian king to worship the God of the Hebrews.[77] Moody turned his attention to the fall of the Babylonian empire during the short reign of Belshazzar. He quickly moved to a consideration of the story of Daniel in the lions' den.[78] Concluding the message Moody said, "In the evening of Daniel's life Gabriel was sent out of heaven twice to tell this man that he was greatly beloved. He was very popular in heaven."[79] Throughout the sermon, Moody encouraged his hearers to be like Daniel and his three Hebrew friends while avoiding the bad examples of others described in the narrative.

Sermon Evaluation

While this message focused on Daniel's life, it was not exclusively about Daniel. As noted above, rather than following Moody's previous pattern of a biographical sermon, this message walked the listeners through the first six chapters of the book of Daniel. Even though Daniel was not mentioned in chapter three, Moody did not skip the chapter. He presented the story of Daniel's three friends facing the fiery furnace. Moody also dealt with Nebuchadnezzar and his son Belshazzar. Therefore, rather than simply choosing to emphasize only passages about Daniel, Moody covered the whole story.

While Moody walked through the first six chapters of Daniel, he only read a few verses along the way. He preached this message by telling the story. These chapters clearly fall into a narrative genre. In keeping with this reality, Moody presented the message of these chapters as a narrative. He told the story in order, as it appears in the Bible. Moody focused on encouraging Christians to faithfulness and did not share the gospel explicitly in this message. It is now time to consider the sermon using the sermon rubric.

Expository or Textual?

While this sermon is primarily about a Bible character, it also contains elements that fit with both the expositional and textual sermon categories. For

---

77. Delevan L. Pierson, ed., *Echoes* (1894), 376.
78. Ibid., 376–380.
79. Ibid., 380.

instance, the divisions of the sermon were based on the divisions of the narrative of Daniel 1–6. Unlike biographical sermons from Moody's earlier years, he did not ignore the passages that did not directly mention Daniel. Rather, Moody followed the text itself. This fits the third criteria of an expository sermon in the sermon rubric.[80] The message also fits the second criteria of a textual sermon. It could be considered a running commentary of an extended passage of Scripture. The sermon certainly is based on six continuous chapters in Daniel, as much as the sermon is based on Daniel's life.

Biographical?

The title indicates that this message is likely a biographical sermon. To a large degree, biographical could be considered a correct categorization. The sermon is primarily about Daniel, his life, and ministry. However, the divisions come from the text of Scripture, more than from the preacher's choice of characteristics from Daniel's life. Certainly, Moody sought to apply characteristics of Daniel to his listeners. However, he also sought to apply the passages where Daniel was not the focus. Therefore, in the end, this sermon should be categorized as a biographical sermon with a heavy textual emphasis.

Topical?

This message does not fit the category of a topical sermon. Two other rubric categories provide criteria that guide the classification of this message. As noted above, this must be considered a biographical sermon with a heavy textual emphasis.

The Overcoming Life[81]

Sermon Description

Moody began this sermon by emphasizing salvation as a free gift from God that cannot be earned by good works. He said, "Salvation is as free as the

---

80. Delevan L. Pierson, ed., *Echoes* (1894), 380.
81. Ibid., 452–460.

air we breathe; it is a gift, to be obtained without money and without price."[82] However, Moody quickly contrasted the gift of salvation with the idea of receiving rewards when one gets to heaven. He said, "But, on the other hand, if we are to have a crown, we must work for it."[83] With this statement Moody set the stage for his opening text and the theme of his message.

Moody read 1 Corinthians 3:11–15. He then said, "We see clearly from this that we may be saved, but all our works burned up. I may have a wretched, miserable voyage through life, with no victory, and no reward at the end; saved yet so as by fire, or as Job puts it, by 'the skin of my teeth.' "[84] Moody encouraged his hearers by telling them that they can overcome and receive a crown at the end of life. He then argued that to overcome the world, one must rely on God's strength.

Moody spoke of the battle within a Christian. He described the Christian as one who has a new nature given by God that is able to overcome the world. He also reminded his audience that the old nature has not yet gone away. Therefore, the Christian struggles between the two natures. Moody indicated that the battle is both internal and external. There are enemies outside the person and enemies within the person. To introduce his audience to the enemies of living the overcoming life, Moody compared 1 John 2:15 and Genesis 3:6.[85] He noted, "the lust of the flesh, the lust of eyes, and the pride of life" as the things that lead the Christian into sin.[86] Moody said, "I must overcome sin, or sin will overcome me. God puts the power in my hands so that I can overcome. He puts the crown within reach of everyone."[87] Moody turned his attention to identifying enemies of the Christian.

Moody spoke about the struggles with sin that come from within the Christian. He said, "If a man gains the victory over himself, it is easy to win the victory over the world."[88] He warned of the appetites and desires within a per-

---

82. Delevan L. Pierson, ed., *Echoes* (1894), 452.
83. Ibid., 452.
84. Ibid. (Cf. Job 19:20.)
85. Ibid., 454–455.
86. Ibid.
87. Ibid., 455.
88. Ibid.

son. He also warned of the danger of yielding to a bad temper. Moody spoke of overcoming these temptations both by quoting Scripture and giving illustrations from everyday life.

In speaking about outside enemies, Moody mentioned several possible temptations including customs, pleasures, and amusements. He dealt with these temptations by the use of a series of illustrations. His longest illustration in this section was about a woman who did not want to give up going to the theater. He encouraged her to come to Christ and let him take care of the desire to go to the theater. Quoting the Bible, he encouraged her to proceed only if she could go to the theatre for the glory of God. After attending again with her husband, the lady lost all her appetite for the theater.[89] In the end of this section Moody said, "There is no objection to these things unless they get the mastery over you or are a hindrance to you."[90] Moody's concern was that if things in this life cause one to fall into sin, they should be avoided. He desired that his audience focus on overcoming sin.

Moody moved toward the conclusion of his message by pointing his listeners to the book of Revelation. He said, "Let me give you the eight 'overcomes' of Revelation."[91] The first seven "overcomes" that Moody pointed his listeners to consider come from the conclusion to the messages to the Seven Churches of Asia in Revelation 2–3. Most of them are simply listed without comment. Moody did make a brief comment on the first, the second, and the seventh promises. The eighth "overcome" Moody shared came from Revelation 21:7, "He that overcometh shall inherit all things; and I will be his God and he shall be my son." Moody noted, "This is the best. Perhaps you didn't know that I was a millionaire."[92] Moody emphasized that the Christian is a joint heir with Jesus. He said, "Find out what Jesus Christ is worth, and I will tell you what I am worth."[93] Moody encouraged his audience that since Christians are joint

---

89. Delevan L. Pierson, ed., *Echoes* (1894), 457–459.
90. Ibid., 459.
91. Ibid.
92. Ibid., 460.
93. Ibid.

D.L. MOODY:
TURNING POINTS TOWARD TEXT-DRIVEN PREACHING

heirs with Jesus, they are to represent him on earth. He said, "Let us go out and represent Him."[94] With this invitation, Moody concluded the sermon.

Sermon Evaluation

Moody began this sermon by establishing that salvation is a free gift of God, but he indicated that rewards are based on good works. He quickly moved to the Bible, reading 1 Corinthians 3:11–15. All along the way Moody referred to Scripture, he concluded the sermon by surveying Revelation 2–3 and Revelation 21:7. Other than his initial statement about salvation being a free gift, Moody did not share the gospel explicitly in this sermon. The question is whether Moody used these passages to support his topic, or whether the passages directed his comments. The sermon rubric proves helpful in evaluating this question.

Expository or Textual?

As noted above, this message contains Scripture reading and quotations. While Moody began with 1 Corinthians 3:11–15 as his primary text, he never explained the passage in detail or within its context. Rather, he used the text to support his claim that rewards are based on works. The passages Moody quoted throughout the sermon were used in the same manner. In his conclusion, Moody surveyed the promises to the overcomers of the Seven Churches of Asia. He also briefly considered the promise found in Revelation 21:7. However, none of these passages are explained within their context. Neither are they the primary focus of the sermon. Rather, they are each offered as support for the main theme of working to overcome in this life. This sermon cannot be considered an expository or a textual sermon.

Biographical?

The sermon is not based on a Bible character. It does not fit the description of a biographical sermon. None of the criteria for categorizing a sermon as a biographical sermon were met. Therefore, this message cannot be considered biographical.

---

94. Delevan L. Pierson, ed., *Echoes* (1894), 460.

Topical?

The sermon was based on a specific topic of concern, rather than on a single text of Scripture. While several passages of Scripture were read, quoted, or referenced, none of them were explained within their context. The divisions of the sermon arose from Moody's choice, rather than from a text of Scripture. The message had a basic unifying theme. This sermon fits within the topical sermon category.

Confession of Christ[95]

Sermon Description

Moody began this sermon by pointing his audience to Romans 10:9. He said, "I think that he [Paul] has put the way of life as clearly as it has ever been put on earth, and I believe that if he were to come back from heaven, he could not put it any plainer than he has."[96] After these brief introductory remarks, Moody read Romans 10:9–11. Using this passage as a starting point for his sermon, Moody briefly commented on the verses themselves.

He said, "You may notice three things in those three verses—believe on the Lord, confess it with the mouth, and be not ashamed of it. When a man or woman is willing to take those three steps I believe that they will enter into the fullness of Calvary."[97] After noting these three concepts, Moody focused the rest of his sermon on the idea of not being ashamed of Jesus.

Moody began his discussion by contrasting people of false religions with people who claim to believe in Jesus. He said, "I do not believe there is any false religion in the world which men are not proud of. The only religion in the world which I have ever heard of, that men were ashamed of is the religion of Jesus Christ."[98] Moody then contrasted Mormons, disciples of Confucius, and

---

95. Delevan L. Pierson, ed., *Echoes* (1896), 9–19.
96. Ibid., 9.
97. Ibid.
98. Ibid.

D.L. MOODY:
TURNING POINTS TOWARD TEXT-DRIVEN PREACHING

Muslims with Christians, claiming none of these false religions are ashamed of what they believe, but Christians are often ashamed of Jesus.

Moody quoted portions of Peter's great confession recorded in Matthew 16:13–17. He then said, "I tell you, my friends, I have never in my life seen a man confess Christ when he was not blessed in the very act of confessing."[99] Moody contrasted this confession with Peter's denial during Jesus' trial. He said, "It is when we are ashamed to own Jesus Christ that we get away from the Lord."[100] To further emphasize his point, Moody read Luke 9:23–26. Moody illustrated his point by speaking of a man wanting to be a soldier but unwilling to put on the uniform.

Introducing another concept, Moody told of a lady he met in London. She read to a man who was prone to drinking. Moody noted, "[She] felt she could not speak much for Christ."[101] Yet, through her reading to the man, she confessed Christ. Using this to refocus his audience, Moody shared several examples of people who were not gifted speakers, but found a way to confess Christ before men. He encouraged his listeners to find ways to confess Jesus. He said, "Watch for opportunities to let the world know on whose side you stand."[102] With this Moody returned to emphasizing the importance of confessing Jesus.

Moody read Luke 12:8–9. He then said, "I believe down deep in my heart that the reason a great many men do not make any progress in their Christian life is because they are constantly denying Christ by some act or other."[103] Moody told a story of two men who were afraid to confess Christ during one of his campaigns in New York City. Moody concluded this illustration by warning men to never be ashamed of Jesus.

Moody contrasted two men mentioned in the Gospels. He began by telling the story of the man born blind.[104] He followed the story closely, as it is presented in John 9. Occasionally, Moody quoted from the chapter directly. He then

---

99. Delevan L. Pierson, ed., *Echoes* (1894), 10.
100. Ibid., 11.
101. Ibid.
102. Ibid., 12.
103. Ibid.
104. Ibid., 14–16.

introduced the second man, Joseph of Arimathea. In telling the story of Joseph, Moody quoted from a few verses of Scripture. Since the Scripture says very little, Moody added a lot from his imagination. He acknowledged this along the way. The primary point of contrast came in the fact that the man born blind immediately confessed Jesus. Moody noted that Joseph was a "secret disciple."[105] Yet, Moody believed that it was during Jesus' trial before the Sanhedrin that Joseph likely spoke up. He said, "He first got his lips open for the Son of God on that night when Jesus was on trial for his life."[106] After continuing in his imaginative story for a while, Moody went back to the biblical story and spoke of Joseph and Nicodemus preparing Jesus for the tomb.

Moving toward his conclusion, Moody began to describe what he thought it might have been like on the day Joseph of Arimathea died. He imagined Jesus confessing Joseph before the Father and the angels.[107] Moody then said, "The best act Joseph of Arimathea ever did on this earth was to confess the Son of God."[108] Moody encouraged his listeners to follow Joseph's example. He said, "Let people know whom you follow, and whenever you can get hold of one who is not a Christian, speak a word for Christ, and the blessing of God will continually rest upon you."[109] This final exhortation concluded the sermon.

Sermon Evaluation

As noted above, Moody began the sermon by reading Romans 10:9–11. He then offered a few brief comments on the passage. However, Moody quickly contrasted being ashamed of Jesus and confessing Jesus. This contrast became his theme throughout the sermon. He supported his theme by reading and quoting Scripture as well as by sharing several stories to emphasize his main point. Moody shared the gospel explicitly in this message.

---

105. Delevan L. Pierson, ed., *Echoes* (1894), 16.
106. Ibid., 17.
107. Ibid., 18–19.
108. Ibid., 19.
109. Ibid.

D.L. MOODY:
TURNING POINTS TOWARD TEXT-DRIVEN PREACHING

Expository or Textual?

Reading the first few paragraphs, one might expect to find another textual sermon from Moody. He read a passage of Scripture. He then offered brief comments about the three verses he read. He did not explain the passage within its context. Rather, he used this passage to introduce his audience to the topic he would discuss in the message. While Moody read several additional passages throughout the sermon, each one was used to provide additional support for his topic. Therefore, this sermon cannot be classified as either an exposition or a textual sermon.

Biographical?

The message is not based on a biblical character. The Bible characters mentioned are used to illustrate and support Moody's main topic. The divisions of the sermon were not based on various characteristics in a biblical character's life. This sermon does not fit the biographical category.

Topical?

Moody based this sermon on a concept found in Romans 10:9–11. He focused his attention on two concepts: confession and being ashamed. Had Moody read verse eleven in today's more popular translations, he may not have found the contrast within the verses he read.[110] He chose to view verse eleven as a contrast to verse ten. He then used this contrast as the theme of his message. Every passage he read or quoted was used by Moody to support his topic. His topic was the driving force behind the sermon. The topic also unified the message. The sermon fits well within the topical category.

---

110. The New King James renders Romans 10:11 as, "For the Scripture says, "Whoever believes on Him will not be put to shame." This rendering would indicate a further statement of confidence for the one who believes and confesses, rather than a contrast of confessing versus being ashamed.

True Wisdom[111]

Sermon Description

Moody began this sermon by reading Daniel 12:3. He read, "And they that be wise shall shine as the brightness of the firmament; and they that turn many to righteousness, as the stars for ever and ever."[112] Moody introduced his sermon by saying, "I believe if a man is going to shine forever, the only way is by working for God."[113] Moody argued that all people want to do well, to stand out, and to shine. He did attempt to set his opening verse in the context of Daniel's life. Moody spoke of Daniel's trials and triumphs. He attempted to bring the concept to bear on his audience by indicating Daniel would recognize the great opportunity that was before his audience. He quickly moved to application by stating, "Gentlemen! [D]on't wait till you get back to college. Lift up your eyes; the field is already white for harvest. Look right around you for opportunities."[114] Moody then introduced the theme of his message.

Moody encouraged his listeners to get busy for the Lord in whatever task the Lord put before them. He said, "Don't call it little." He argued that his listeners might lead someone like Whitefield or Wesley to the Lord, if they would just take the opportunities that God placed before them. Moody said, "Men! [T]ake any position God offers you, and take the first thing that comes to your hand."[115] He encouraged them to not make excuses or worry about leaving their business plans. Moody used Peter and Paul as examples of people willing to leave comfort behind for the service of the Lord.

Moody turned his attention to the importance of removing sin from one's life to be a more effective servant. Quoting Titus 3:1, he encouraged his listeners to get ready to be used of the Lord. He said, "I have never seen a man ready yet that God did not use him. And what is a man good for if he is not ready?"[116]

---

111. Delevan L. Pierson, ed., *Echoes* (1896), 110–117.
112. Ibid., 110.
113. Ibid.
114. Ibid., 111.
115. Ibid., 112.
116. Ibid., 113.

D.L. MOODY:
TURNING POINTS TOWARD TEXT-DRIVEN PREACHING

Moody called on his hearers to avoid selfishness. He described a picture where one person was about to go under the water but one arm was around the cross, providing her salvation, and the other arm was reaching to pull someone up with her. He said, "First, give yourself up fully, wholly, and unreservedly to the Lord, and then put your life into some channel where you can be used."[117] Moody added another illustration to encourage Christians to win others to Christ.

Moody encouraged people to join the Lord's cause. He said, "There is a glorious battle going on between the powers of light and darkness, and the Lord wants volunteers."[118] Moody contrasted the Christians of his day with the Apostle Paul. He then said, "What we want is that old fire back again; willing to suffer, and willing to die, if need be, for our Christ."[119] Moody returned to Paul as an example, recounting his steadfast courage to press on toward the goal and continue serving the Lord despite all his trials. He began to describe what it might have been like when Paul was executed for his faithfulness. He asked his audience whether they were willing to serve Christ at all costs. After quoting Daniel 12:3 again, Moody said, "I tell you what I wish you would do. Say down deep in your heart, 'I will not rest day or night until God gives me one soul for my hire.'"[120] With this statement, Moody concluded his sermon.

Sermon Evaluation

Moody began this message by reading Daniel 12:3. While he did try to set the verse within the context of Daniel's life, he did not seek to explain the verse. Rather, he used the verse as an introduction to the concept he desired to press home to his audience. He spoke directly and often called his hearers to action throughout the sermon. The verses chosen, biblical references made, and the illustrations all served to call his listeners to action. Moody focused on encouraging Christians to share the gospel, but he did not explicitly share the gospel himself during this message.

---

117. Delevan L. Pierson, ed., *Echoes* (1894), 113.
118. Ibid., 114.
119. Ibid., 115.
120. Ibid., 117.

Expository or Textual?

Moody not only began by reading a Bible verse, he also attempted to set that verse within the context of Daniel's life. However, the verse did not guide his sermon content. Rather, the verse gave Moody a theme, which he developed by supporting the topic with various passages of Scripture and illustrations. This sermon cannot be categorized as either an expository or a textual sermon.

Biographical?

Daniel's life provided context for the verse Moody read. However, he never attempted to develop the life of Daniel, reveal specific characteristics from Daniel's life, or apply Daniel's characteristics to others. The message does not fit the description or the criteria of the biographical sermon category.

Topical?

The sermon is based on a concept from the text Moody read to start the sermon. However, the concept then becomes the driving force of the sermon and all Scripture references are simply used to support the topic at hand. The divisions of the sermon are based on what Moody chose to say about serving God, rather than on a text of Scripture. The unifying theme of the sermon is to serve God and be rewarded. This sermon fits well within the topical category.

Heart Service[121]

Sermon Description

D. L. Moody began this sermon by reading Exodus 25:2–3. The text describes how the Lord told Moses to receive an offering from the children of Israel to make the tabernacle. Having read the text, Moody began to emphasize that the Lord called people to give what they had, not what they did not have. He said, "If a man hadn't gold and only brought silver, it was just as acceptable

---

121. Delevan L. Pierson, ed., *Echoes* (1894), 331–337.

to God as if he brought a whole bag of gold."[122] This statement set the stage for the entire sermon.

Moody wanted everyone to consider what they could do for God, and then do it. He said, "Now, you notice that God has a work for everyone to do, and when you can't do a great thing, do some little thing; in other words, do what you can, not what you can't do."[123] Moody pointed out that through all of time God has used foolish and weak things to accomplish his purposes. Moody even pointed to the scene in Revelation 5 where no one was worthy to open the scroll except the Lamb of God. He said, "Well, that is God's way. He takes the weak things to confound the mighty."[124] Moody encouraged his listeners that God could use them, despite the weaknesses they may possess.

To further make his point, Moody discussed the call of Moses. Moody spoke of the stick in Moses' hand. After describing several things the Lord did with that stick Moody said, "My dear friends, if God can use an old dried up stick, He can use any one of us, can't He?"[125] Moody then offered several biblical illustrations of God using people and things that seem to be of no value.[126] He suggested that when people rely on the power of God, they accomplished much.

Moving toward the close of the message, Moody began talking about the filling of the Spirit. He called on everyone to seek the filling of the Spirit to empower them for service. He encouraged them to trust that the Spirit would fill them and then they should get to work. Moody said, "I believe if we sit down and pray to God to fill us with the Spirit, and don't go forth and go to work, we are going to be disappointed."[127] Moody encouraged his audience to get alone with God and ask him what work he wanted them to accomplish. He said, "My dear friends, don't you go to any man or woman on earth and ask them to set you to work. Get your orders from someone higher."[128] He concluded the message by encouraging them that God could use one with a heart willing to work.

---

122. Delevan L. Pierson, ed., *Echoes* (1894), 331.
123. Ibid., 332.
124. Ibid.
125. Ibid., 334.
126. Ibid., 334–335.
127. Ibid., 337.
128. Ibid.

Sermon Evaluation

As noted above, Moody began this sermon by reading Scripture. He also described several people throughout the Bible that God used. Each passage read, quoted, or referenced was used to support his main theme. Moody used this sermon to call on his hearers to serve God. Moody did not share the gospel during the message.

Expository or Textual?
While the sermon began with reading from the Bible, the sermon did not seek to explain the verse read or to set it within its context. The message was not a running commentary of an extended passage, nor was it based on the details of a single verse. Rather, the sermon was based on a concept deduced from the verse read at the beginning of the sermon. Other passages of Scripture and numerous illustrations were used to support Moody's call of his listeners to serve God. The message cannot be categorized as an expository or a textual sermon.

Biographical?
While several Bible characters were mentioned in this sermon, none of them were developed. Specific characteristics were not explained or applied to the listeners. Therefore, this sermon does not meet the criteria or the description of a biographical sermon.

Topical?
The category of topical sermon best fits this message. It was based on a concept deduced from Exodus 25:2–3. The sermon divisions were based on the preacher's choice of various ways to reinforce his topic. None of the passages referenced were truly set in context. This sermon fits well within the topical category.

Power in Prayer[129]

Sermon Description

Moody began this sermon by going straight to his topic. He said, "If a man knows how to pray, he generally knows how to live, and how to work. Prayer is sort of a pendulum that regulates our whole life."[130] Moody spoke of praying like Daniel. He then spoke of the role of prayer in Jesus' life and ministry. Moody concluded his introduction to the sermon by telling a story about a trip he made to England for rest in 1872. He intended not to preach on the trip. However, he ended up conceding to preach one Sunday. The morning service appeared dead. However, in the evening he saw many come to faith in Jesus. The meeting continued for a few more days and before it was over 400 came to Christ. Moody traced the success to a bedridden lady who had been praying for months that Moody would come and preach in the church she once attended. Sunday afternoon she learned he had done so in the morning. She spent the rest of the day fasting and praying that her church would be revived.[131] Having introduced his topic, Moody began describing key elements he believed necessary for effective prayer.

Moody indicated the starting point of prayer should be *Adoration*. He warned of rushing into prayer without due respect. Turning to Jesus' example, Moody said, "When Christ prayed He said, 'Holy Father,' and He taught His disciples to pray, 'Hallowed be Thy name.' When we go into the presence of God let us be filled with holy awe."[132] Moody moved to another key to effective prayer.

Moody noted that when we really understand God's holiness, we recognize our own sinfulness. He believed this will automatically lead us to *Confession of Sin*. He said, "Hidden sin hinders prayer."[133] Moody reinforced this statement

---

129. Delevan L. Pierson, ed., *Echoes* (1897), 42–53.
130. Ibid., 43.
131. Ibid., 43–44.
132. Ibid., 45.
133. Ibid.

with two illustrations. He did not quote any Scripture for this point. He followed the illustrations by applying the principle to his listeners.

Moody continued to suggest actions that lead to power in prayer. He said, "Another element of true prayer is *Restitution*."[134] Once again, Moody did not look to a Bible verse to support this principle. He relied on illustrations to make his point. Following the illustrations Moody said, "If there is anything wrong in your life, make it right."[135] He continued with his next principle.

Moody's next key to effective prayer was to maintain a *Spirit of Forgiveness*. He immediately quoted Matthew 6:15 to convey the seriousness of unforgiveness to his audience. To illustrate the importance of this Moody told a story of two preachers he knew. After a quarrel, they both refused to forgive one another and it destroyed their ministries.[136] Moody quoted Matthew 5:24 and encouraged his hearers to forgive one another.

Moody identified *Unity* as the next key principle for effective prayer. He said, "[P]rayers are cold and cheerless if there is not unity."[137] He referred to the day of Pentecost and described the disciples as being of "one mind and one spirit."[138] Moody said, "What Christians need is to be united in brotherly love and then they may expect to have power."[139] He moved to his next principle.

Moody focused his audience's attention on the importance of living a life of *Thanksgiving*. He quoted from Philippians 4:6, "With thanksgiving let your requests be made known unto God."[140] Moody made his point by the use of three illustrations, one of which comes from the life of Paul and Silas in the Philippian jail (Acts 16). He applied the principle, calling on his hearers to be thankful.

Faith was the next element Moody claimed necessary for effective prayer. He said, "If you have complied with all the conditions expect an answer."[141]

---

134. Delevan L. Pierson, ed., *Echoes* (1894), 47.
135. Ibid., 48.
136. Ibid.
137. Ibid.
138. Ibid.
139. Ibid., 49.
140. Ibid.
141. Ibid.

D.L. MOODY:
TURNING POINTS TOWARD TEXT-DRIVEN PREACHING

Moody described both *yes* and *no* answers from God. He emphasized that both of these were real answers. This emphasis led Moody to his next principle for effective prayer.

Moody indicated that true faith in prayer leads the Christian to *Submission*. He said, "Spread out your petition before God, and then say, 'Thy will, not mine, be done.'"[142] Giving further explanation to this Moody said, "The sweetest lesson I have learned in God's school is to let the Lord choose for me, especially in regard to temporal things."[143] Moody encouraged his listeners to submit their prayers to the Lord's will.

Moody spoke of the importance of *Importunity*. He said, "Never give a man or woman up as long as you live."[144] He encouraged his audience to continue in prayer. Giving further support to this idea, Moody said, "If there is anything that we dislike, it is to have a person nagging us all the time, but the Lord encourages it in our relation to Him... He tells us 'always to pray and not to faint.'"[145] He used illustrations to further make his point. Following the illustrations Moody said, "My dear friend, never stop praying; do not be discouraged. God wants you to 'pray without ceasing.'"[146] Moody moved to his last principle for effective prayer.

The word, *Petition*, was Moody's final point in the sermon. After introducing the word, Moody quoted a portion of Philippians 4:6 again, "Make your requests known."[147] He warned of praying without making a petition. He drew the sermon to a close by saying, "It is a good thing to plead for what we want, and if it is for God's glory and we have complied with the conditions, we may surely look for the answer, and we will not be disappointed."[148] Though his comments on *Petition* were short, he made his point and ended the message.

---

142. Delevan L. Pierson, ed., *Echoes* (1894), 51.
143. Ibid.
144. Ibid., 51–52.
145. Ibid., 52.
146. Ibid., 53.
147. Ibid.
148. Ibid.

Sermon Evaluation

Moody preached this sermon as a two-part message. He began the sermon on July 23, 1895 and concluded it the next day. The proceedings of the conference make note of this fact in the page footer on the first page of the message. However, the editor did not indicate where Moody stopped that first night in listing the prayer principles. Rather, he combined the two sermons into one. While this could be considered two sermons, it will be treated as one in this monograph. Moody did not preach the gospel explicitly in either portion of this sermon.

Expository or Textual?

The sermon does not begin with a text of Scripture. While several verses or parts of verses are quoted throughout the sermon, no verse is explained. The context of the verses quoted are ignored by Moody in this message. This sermon clearly does not fit any of the criteria for either an expository or textual sermon.

Biographical?

While various Bible characters are mentioned in the sermon, none of them are developed. Moody used the characters mentioned as brief illustrations but did not describe their personal characteristics. This sermon does not fit the description or the criteria of a biographical sermon.

Topical?

The sermon was clearly unified around the central theme of praying with power. Moody sought to teach his listeners key principles he believed were required for one to pray with power. The concept of effective prayer guided the message. The divisions of the sermon were based on the preacher's choice of principles to emphasize. Verses that were read or quoted were used to support Moody points. This sermon fits well within the topical sermon category.

D.L. MOODY:
TURNING POINTS TOWARD TEXT-DRIVEN PREACHING

The Ten Commandments[149]

Sermon Description

It should be noted that two sermons are presented under the title "The Ten Commandments" in the book *Northfield Echoes*. The editor of the conference proceedings noted in the footer, "Addresses delivered Saturday evening and Sunday morning, June 26 and 27, 1897."[150] However, the proceedings give no indications as to where he stopped on Saturday night or where he began on Sunday morning. While it is recognized that Moody delivered two sermons, they will be treated as one.

Moody introduced his message by pointing out the uniqueness of the Ten Commandments being written directly God. He said, "If it were known that a message was coming to us to-night direct from God, a great awe and solemnity would be over the meeting. Every soul would listen as God spake.... These commandments were written in the handwriting of God Himself."[151] Moody quoted Howard Crosby's comments about the unique way in which God spoke and then wrote these laws.

Moody responded to people who thought Christians no longer needed to be concerned with the commandments. He asked, "What did Christ say? 'Think not that I am come to destroy the law and the prophets; I am not come to destroy, but to fulfill. For verily I say unto you, Till heaven and earth pass, one jot or one tittle shall in no wise pass from the law, till all be fulfilled.'"[152] Moody demonstrated the importance of the Ten Commandments to his audience by speaking of the commandments' influence on the laws of many countries around the world. He read Psalm 19:8–11, emphasizing the perfection of God's law. After a few more words of exhortation, he began walking through the commandments.

---

149. Delevan L. Pierson, ed., *Echoes* (1894), 124–148.
150. Ibid., 124.
151. Ibid.
152. Ibid., 125.

Having introduced his message, Moody began to consider Exodus 20:1–17 by reading each commandment followed with comments and application. He began his walk through the text by saying, "Let us take up these Ten Commandments one by one and examine our lives in light of them."[153] While this chapter will not consider each of the commandments, looking at a few will demonstrate the pattern by which Moody dealt with each one. We begin with the first commandment.

Moody read the text, "Thou shalt have no other gods before Me" (Exodus 20:3). Commenting on the command he said, "If God created us, isn't it right that He should have the first place in our hearts? Love to God won't admit any other god to take His place."[154] Moody reminded his audience that God punished the Jews for serving false gods. He then pointed out that anything that one puts before God becomes a false god. Moody listed several things that he believed were common false gods in his day. After quoting the commandment again, Moody said, "If we let some false god come in and steal our love away from the God of heaven, we shall have no power."[155] Following this statement, Moody moved on to the next commandment in the text.

Moody considered each commandment. However, he did not give equal time to them. Some were only briefly explained, illustrated, and applied. In other instances, Moody gave an extended explanation or used a longer illustration to make his point. For instance, he spent quite of bit of time dealing with the third commandment. He read the commandment, "Thou shalt not take the Name of the LORD thy God in vain; for the LORD will not hold him guiltless that taketh His Name in vain" (Exodus 20:7). Moody then began his comments on the verse. He said, "Perhaps some of you think that there is no use touching upon that commandment, because there is none of you who swears. I was greatly amazed not long ago in talking to a man who was quite active in Christian work, to find that once in a while, when he got angry, he would swear."[156] After relating a little more about his interaction with the man, Moody spoke of the necessity of being born again to overcome any sin. He argued that when a per-

---

153. Delevan L. Pierson, ed., *Echoes* (1894), 125.
154. Ibid.
155. Ibid., 126.
156. Ibid.

son tries to overcome sin in his own strength, he will always fail, but if he will come to Jesus and is born again, the person will find victory.

Moody returned to the context of Exodus 20, describing how the people agreed to follow the commandments, but quickly turned away while Moses was on the mountain with God. Moody said, "The natural man cannot serve God.... If you are going to serve God you must be born of the Spirt."[157] To further illustrate his point, Moody related an incident he experienced when preaching somewhere "out West" in 1862.[158] Having finished this extended illustration, Moody said, "Take Christ in your heart and you will love God too well to take His name in vain."[159] Moody moved on to considering the next commandment.

While Moody spent more time on the third commandment than any other, he also spent considerable time considering the fourth and fifth commands. He offered explanation, illustration, and application of each one. When Moody arrived at the last two commandments, he seemed to be running out of time. He said, "I have not time to dwell upon these other two, but there are those Ten Commandments."[160] He then briefly commented on the final two commandments.

Moving to the close of the sermon Moody pointed to Romans 13:9–10 and then read, "Love is the fulfilling of the law." He read a document from an unnamed author which took each of the Ten Commandments and cast them in light of love. For instance, He read, "Love to God will admit no other god.... Love will give, but never steal.... Love will not slander or lie.... Love's eye is not covetous."[161] Moody then said, "Now face these Ten Commandments honestly and prayerfully. See if your life is right, and if you are treating God fairly.... Let us get alone with God and read that law."[162] Encouraging his listeners to examine their lives, Moody concluded the message.

---

157. Delevan L. Pierson, ed., *Echoes* (1894), 127.
158. Ibid., 127–129.
159. Ibid., 130.
160. Ibid., 138.
161. Ibid.
162. Ibid.

Sermon Evaluation

Moody introduced his message by pointing to the uniqueness of the giving of the Ten Commandments, by quoting a recognized scholar of his day, and by quoting a few Bible verses. He quickly moved to Exodus 20:1–17 and began walking through each of the Ten Commandments. Each commandment was read, explained, illustrated, and applied to his listeners. Moody did not share the gospel explicitly in this sermon, although he did allude to it. Evangelical expositors of today may take issue with some of Moody's explanations.[163] However, one must admit that Moody attempted to explain, illustrate, and apply each commandment in the text. The difficulty in evaluating this sermon comes in determining whether it should be categorized as an expositional or a textual sermon. The sermon rubric proves helpful in this regard.

Expository or Textual?

Following his introduction to the sermon, Moody walked his audience through a consideration of each of the Ten Commandments from Exodus 20:1–17. Even on the first reading of this sermon, this researcher recognized this message to be the most text-driven sermon studied to date. Determining whether this message should be classified as an expository or a textual sermon requires careful examination.

At first glance, the sermon appears to be simply a running commentary through an extended passage of Scripture. This description seems to fit the first portion of the textual sermon description in our rubric. However, the balance of the description says, "but the divisions and the structure of the text do not guide the divisions of the sermon."[164] A careful analysis of Moody's sermon reveals that he did indeed let the divisions of Exodus 20:1–17 guide the divisions of his sermon. Even more revealing is the second criteria on the sermon rubric. It states, "The sermon is a running commentary of a text without regard to the

---

163. Delevan L. Pierson, ed., *Echoes* (1897), 130–132. An example of this concern is found in Moody's explanation of the fourth commandment. Moody saw the trolley car, the bicycle, and the Sunday newspaper as "great temptations of Sabbath breaking."

164. Ibid.

divisions of the paragraph."[165] An analysis of Moody's sermon on the Ten Commandments reveals that he did indeed regard the divisions of the paragraph of the passage from which he preached.

When one looks at the expository sermon column of the sermon rubric, one finds several characteristics evident in this sermon. The description in the rubric states, "The sermon seeks to explain the meaning of its text within its context, prioritizing the author's intended meaning, and then applies the text to himself and his listeners in the power of the Spirit."[166] Moody sought to explain the meaning of the text. He attempted to keep the focus on the context of the passage. As noted above, expositors today may question his treatment of the Sabbath and possibly other explanations. However, he did attempt to explain the text and apply it to himself and his hearers.

Each of the three criteria of the rubric also provide helpful information in the analysis. The first criterion calls for the sermon to be based on a specific text. The second criterion insists that the theme of the message be based on the theme of the text. The third criterion requires that the divisions of the sermon be based on the divisions of the text. Moody's sermon on the Ten Commandments meets all these criteria. In light of the descriptions and criteria of both the expository and textual sermons, we must classify the sermon as exposition.

Biographical?

This sermon does not fit the description or the criteria of a biographical sermon. Moody does not discuss a biblical character, other than the brief mention of Moses in the sermon. Therefore, the sermon cannot be classified as biographical.

Topical?

This sermon does not fit the description or the criteria of a topical sermon. It is not based on a topic but on a text of Scripture. The divisions of the sermon are based on the divisions of the passages under consideration. The sermon has a unified theme and does not move into unrelated topics. In the end it must be recognized that this sermon does not fit into the topical sermon category.

---

165. Delevan L. Pierson, ed., *Echoes* (1894), 130–132.
166. Ibid., 130–132.

The Transfiguration[167]

Sermon Description

As the title implies, Moody based this sermon on the Transfiguration of Jesus. He introduced the sermon by saying, "It is a singular fact that John, the one of the four evangelists that was with Christ on the Mount of Transfiguration, is the only one who does not give an account of it."[168] He offered a suggestion as to why this might be the case. Moody then focused on Peter's mention of the event in his second epistle, by reading 2 Peter 1:16b–18.

Moody attempted to set the story of the Transfiguration in context. He said, "It is a good thing to see what happened just before this wonderful scene, and also what followed."[169] After reading Matthew 16:24–28 Moody declared, "Then He takes them up into the mountain, and the transfiguration scene follows. First, the cross, then the transfiguration, and after that service, when they came down and found the man possessed with an evil spirit."[170] Having introduced the sermon, Moody began to tell the story of the event.

Moody spoke about the Transfiguration by pointing out who was on the mountain and what they were doing there. He said, "Jesus took Peter and John and James and went up into a mountain to pray. Every one of the six men who met on that mountain was eminently a man of prayer."[171] Moody spoke of famous councils in history. He discussed Lincoln and Grant meeting with the Vice President of the Confederacy to agree on terms of ending the Civil War. Moody spoke of Napoleon and Alexander of Russia meeting on a river raft. Then Moody said, "We can recall other critical councils in the history of the world, when the destiny of nations hung in the balances. But never was there held so important a council as this on the Mount of Transfiguration."[172] Moody pointed out that despite the fact there was no great fanfare for this meeting, the

---

167. Delevan L. Pierson, ed., *Echoes* (1894), 238–247.
168. Ibid., 238.
169. Ibid.
170. Ibid., 238–239.
171. Ibid., 239.
172. Ibid., 240.

subject matter was of importance to all of creation. He said, "Moses and Elias appeared and talked with Christ of 'His decease which He should accomplish at Jerusalem.' "[173] Moody pointed out that Luke is the only Gospel that records the content of the conversation between Jesus and the two Old Testament Prophets.

Returning to the six men gathered on the mountain, Moody pointed out that they were men who prayed. Moody spoke of Moses spending forty days on the mountain with God. Moody also spoke of Elijah's forty days alone with God. He pointed out that the other three men were to carry on Christ's work after He returned to heaven.[174] Moody imagined that Peter wanted Moses to go down to Jerusalem and tell the people that Jesus was the Messiah. Moody pointed out that Peter did not realize that he would be used greatly in "winning people to Christ."[175] Moody used this to call on his audience to seek to be used by the Lord to bring others to Christ. He said, "The idea that others can be more used than we ourselves has been the great hindrance to the church in all ages."[176] Moody pressed on his audience the idea that each person should seek to be used by God and not miss out on the joy the Lord has for them in that service.

Moody turned his attention to the fact that the disciples recognized Moses and Elijah, even though they had never seen them before. He pointed out that one's identity is not lost in death. He illustrated this with a story and said, "So I believe that when we meet in eternity there will be no introduction needed, but that we shall know Moses just as those apostles did on that mountain."[177] Moody moved on to the next point he wanted to make from the Transfiguration event.

Moody pointed out that the Father spoke on this occasion. He told how that the Father wanted the disciples to understand that a greater person than Moses was on the scene. Moody discussed the importance of Christ being the center of all Christian work. He said, "He excels the lawgiver and the prophets. He is above every other name under heaven."[178] Moody indicated that he would like to have been with them on the mountain and stayed there like Peter

---

173. Delevan L. Pierson, ed., *Echoes* (1894), 240.
174. Ibid., 242.
175. Ibid.
176. Ibid.
177. Ibid., 243.
178. Ibid., 245.

suggested. Then he said, "But there was work below the mountain."[179] With this Moody spoke briefly of the boy who was delivered from demon possession as they descended from the mountain top experience. He said,

> Do not expect to be always abiding in idleness on the Mount of Transfiguration, but go down into the world and bring souls to the Master. It is good to be on the mountain top, in spiritual communion, and occupied *with* Jesus; but it is not good to remain there—we must descend to the plain, and be occupied *for* Jesus in the practical affairs of our everyday life.[180]

Moody then concluded his sermon.

Sermon Evaluation

After introducing his sermon, Moody began to walk through the story of the Transfiguration. Moody set the story within the context of Matthew's Gospel, but he pointed out differences in the other two Gospel accounts. He would describe a portion of the event, illustrate some point from the story, and then make an application to his hearers. While Moody spoke of Christ's death, he did not explicitly preach the Gospel.

Expository or Textual?

Moody based this sermon primarily on Matthew's account of the Transfiguration in Matthew 17:1–13. He set the story in context by pointing out the paragraphs before and after the event. Moody also considered the parallel accounts in Mark and Luke, specifically noting Luke's addition of the content of the conversation held between Jesus, Moses, and Elijah. He followed the storyline, making applications along the way. Moody's sermon divisions followed the basic divisions of the narrative. So, while he presented the message by telling the story, the divisions of the text guided the divisions of Moody's sermons. Utilizing our sermon rubric as our guide, this sermon fits within the expository sermon category.

---

179. Delevan L. Pierson, ed., *Echoes* (1894), 245.
180. Ibid.

Biographical?

This sermon speaks about six Bible characters, including Jesus. However, the sermon does not develop the characters or seek to apply their characteristics to the audience. Rather, the sermon follows the basic flow of the biblical narrative. The message does not fit within the biographical sermon category.

Topical?

Moody did not base this sermon on a topic. Rather he walked his audience through the biblical account of the Transfiguration. The message does not fit the description or criteria of a topical sermon. The content of the sermon is clearly text-driven.

Abraham's Four Surrenders[181]

Sermon Description

Moody introduced this sermon by talking about the will of God. He said, "A great many people are afraid of the will of God, and yet I believe that one of the sweetest lessons that we can learn in the school of Christ is the surrender of our wills to God, letting Him plan for us and rule our lives."[182] Moody spoke of his own life and his desire to let God choose for him. Having introduced the theme of surrendering to God's will, Moody said, "Abraham found this out, and I want to call your attention to four surrenders that he was called to make. I think that they give us a pretty good key to his life."[183] The rest of the sermon was built around four key events in Abraham's life.

Moody began with God's call for Abraham to leave his country. He said, "While men were busy building Babylon, God called this man out of that nation of the Chaldeans."[184] With this, Moody drew the attention of his audience to Genesis 12:1–4. After reading the text, Moody set it in context by telling his

---

181. Delevan L. Pierson, ed., *Echoes* (1898), 3–14.
182. Ibid., 3.
183. Ibid.
184. Ibid.

listeners that prior to these words the Lord had led him to leave and he went as far as Haran. Moody applied this to his hearers by saying, "I believe that there are a great many Christians who are what might be called Haran Christians. They go to Haran, and there they stay. They only half obey."[185] Moody pointed out that it was not until Abraham's dad died that he headed to the promise land.

Moody spoke of a second surrender required of Abraham. Having described Abraham's short move to Egypt, Moody pointed out that when Abraham returned to the Promised Land, he was wealthy. Moody described the trouble that arose between Abraham and Lot. Moody pointed out that Abraham surrendered his rights to choose the best land. Moody said, "Instead of standing up for his rights, he surrenders them, and says to the nephew: 'Take your choice.'"[186] Moody spoke briefly of Lot saying, "He walked by sight, instead of by faith."[187] Lot walking by sight gave Moody a negative example to apply to his hearers, while at the same time calling his hearers to walk by faith. Contrasting Lot with Abraham, Moody returned to the result of Abraham's surrender, pointing out that then the Lord came to him and promised that he would give Abraham all the land his eye could see.

Moody described how that Abraham and his three hundred and eighteen men rescued Lot and the kings of the region. Having told this story, Moody was ready to explain Abraham's third surrender. Moody spoke of Abraham's meeting Melchizedek, who blessed the Patriarch. Moody told how the king of Sodom offered Abraham wealth for rescuing the people of his city. Moody quoted Abraham's response, "Not a thing will I take" (Genesis 14:23).[188] Moody said, "There is another surrender. There was a temptation to get rich at the hands of the King of Sodom. But the King of Salem had blessed him, and this world did not tempt him."[189] Moody applied this to his listeners encouraging them to surrender to God. Returning to Abraham, Moody spoke of God's promise to bless the whole world through him. Moody assigned this blessing to Abraham's willingness to surrender.

---

185. Delevan L. Pierson, ed., *Echoes* (1894), 4.
186. Ibid., 5.
187. Ibid.
188. Ibid., 8.
189. Ibid.

Moody introduced his listeners to his final point, saying, "The last surrender is perhaps the most touching and the hardest of all to understand."[190] Moody pointed out that the Lord had used the previous steps of surrender to prepare Abraham for this last surrender. Moody began to describe the call of God for Abraham to sacrifice Isaac. He told how the Lord provided Isaac and described Isaac as deeply loved by his mother and father. He described the command of the Lord and the journey to Moriah. In his characteristic vivid story-telling style, Moody described the trip, demonstrating the battle that must have raged inside of Abraham. He then described the climb up Moriah, the building of the altar, and the preparation of the wood. Moody described a possible scene of Abraham explaining to Isaac what he was about to do.

Moody broke into the midst of the story to speak of the great love of the Father. He confessed that once he had devalued the Father's love and emphasized only the love of Jesus. But having become a father, Moody said, "[I]t takes more love for the father to give up the son than it does for the son to die."[191] Moody indicated that a good father would rather die than have his son die.

Returning to the story, Moody described Abraham raising the knife and God's intervention. After describing God's intervention, Moody turned his attention to the cross of Jesus. He said, "You remember that Christ said, 'Abraham saw my day, and was glad.' I have an idea that God then and there just lifted the curtain of time on Abraham, and he looked down into the future, saw God's Son coming up Calvary, bearing his sins and the sins of all posterity."[192] Moody concluded his look at the fourth surrender and moved to the close of his message.

Closing the sermon, Moody was concerned that his listeners surrender to the Lord. He described his own struggles to surrender. Moody said, "Now, my friends, notice; whenever God has been calling me to higher service, there has always been a conflict with my will, and I have fought against it, but God's will has been done instead of mine."[193] Moody described three battles of surrender he faced at different times in his life. He then encouraged his hearers, "Make

---

190. Delevan L. Pierson, ed., *Echoes* (1894), 10.
191. Ibid., 13.
192. Ibid., 14.
193. Ibid.

a full and complete surrender, and the sweet messages of heaven will come to you."[194] With a few more sentences of encouragement along this line, Moody closed his sermon.

Sermon Evaluation

Moody began this sermon by connecting to his audience and helping them to think about surrendering to the will of God. Moody spoke of Abraham in terms of four times in his life that God called him to surrender something. Moody quickly read Genesis 12:1–4 as the basis of his introduction to Abraham. He set the passage in context and talked about Abraham's first surrender. From here, Moody told Abraham's story covering the major highlights of his life. The primary emphasis remained on moments of surrender. Moody simply told the story. Along the way, he would quote a verse or partial verse of Scripture. Moody illustrated each point he made and applied the message to his listeners throughout the sermon. Moody alluded to the Gospel a few times in this sermon. The clearest reference came when he described God's intervention on top of Mt. Moriah.

Expository or Textual?
Shortly into the sermon, Moody read Genesis 12:1–4. He explained the passage and set it within its textual and historical context. In addition, he illustrated the text and applied it to his listeners. However, this sermon was not solely based on this passage. Rather, the sermon was based on a specific aspect of Abraham's life. Moody wanted to demonstrate the necessity of surrendering one's life to God, by speaking of four specific moments of surrender in Abraham's life. Because the sermon was not driven specifically by this text, it does not really fit into the category of an expository or a textual sermon. However, it should be noted that overall the sermon did accurately follow the story of Abraham's life from his call to leave Ur to his visit on Mt. Moriah with Isaac.

---

194 Delevan L. Pierson, ed., *Echoes* (1894), 14.

D.L. MOODY:
TURNING POINTS TOWARD TEXT-DRIVEN PREACHING

Biographical?

This sermon fits well in the biographical sermon category of our sermon rubric. It is based on a Bible character. It utilizes Bible passages that reveal the surrender of Abraham to the Lord. This characteristic is applied to the hearers in each of the four moments of surrender considered. The sermon meets both the description and the criteria of the biographical sermon category.

Topical?

While surrendering to the will of God is a theme carried throughout the sermon, it is the story of Abraham's life itself that provides the content to the message. In the sermon rubric the topical category indicates that the topic of the sermon is emphasized, "without regard to the context."[195] Moody worked hard to set the entire message in both its textual and historical context. The sermon was driven more by the content of the biblical story than by the topic. Therefore, the sermon does not fit the topical category.

The Sure Word of Prophecy[196]

Sermon Description

Moody began this sermon by reading 2 Peter 1:19. After reading the verse, Moody began speaking, "I would rather have faith in the Bible than all the gold of the Klondike. Faith in God's Word will carry us through many a storm and many a conflict, and I pity any man who has lost this faith."[197] Moody encouraged his listeners to trust the Bible. To demonstrate its trustworthiness Moody pointed his audience to fulfilled prophecy. He said, "I don't know of any portion of Scripture that will tone up a man's faith in the Bible like the fulfilled proph-

---

195. Delevan L. Pierson, ed., *Echoes* (1894), 14.
196. Ibid., 135–145.
197. Ibid., 135. A note gives context: "the Klondike referred to a discovery made in August 1896. Three men found gold in a tributary of the Klondike River in Canada this discovery set off a gold rush in Canada and Alaska." For more on this, visit https://www.nps.gov/klgo/learn/goldrush.htm.

ecies."[198] Moody claimed that there were more than six hundred in the Old Testament that were fulfilled. Two hundred of these Moody claimed were already fulfilled in Christ. Moody gave a few quick examples of fulfilled prophecies then emphasized the importance of trusting the Bible.

Moody read prophecies from the Old Testament and described their fulfillment. He began with prophecies related to Babylon, Tyre, and Nineveh.[199] Moody considered prophecies God made to Abraham.[200] He also spoke of prophecies to Moses and Daniel.[201] With each prophecy Moody read the text where the prophecy was given and described its fulfillment. In some instances, the fulfillment was read from later passages of Scripture. On other occasions, the fulfillment was simply described by Moody. He supported each point with an illustration. He applied each fulfillment to his listeners. He concluded the sermon by saying, "I thank God for this old Book—a 'sure word of prophecy.' "[202] With this final statement Moody brought the sermon full circle, ending where he started with 2 Peter 1:19.

Sermon Evaluation

The sermon began with Moody reading 2 Peter 1:19 and emphasizing that the Bible gives a sure word. The truthfulness of Scripture was Moody's unifying theme for this sermon. He picked up on Peter's statement concerning "a sure word of prophecy" and launched into a series of Old Testament prophecies that have been fulfilled. While he did not share the Gospel directly in this sermon, Moody was in the habit of encouraging people to turn to Christ following his sermons.

Expository or Textual?

While Moody began this sermon by reading a passage of Scripture, he really did not explain the verse or set it in its context. Rather, he picked up on a

---

198. Delevan L. Pierson, ed., *Echoes* (1894), 135.
199. Ibid., 137–139.
200. Ibid., 139–142.
201. Ibid., 142–145.
202. Ibid., 145.

phrase from the verse which became the topic of his message. The sermon does not fit the description or criteria of either an expository or a textual sermon.

Biographical?

While the sermon mentions a handful of biblical characters, it does not describe their lives. The sermon also does not apply a person's characteristics to Moody's hearers. The message cannot be classified as a biographical sermon.

Topical?

This sermon is based on a phrase from 2 Peter 1:19. The phrase served as the unifying theme of the message. The divisions of the sermon were chosen by Moody to emphasize the main theme. Numerous verses of Scripture were read, but they were used to demonstrate the main topic of the sermon—that fulfilled Bible prophecies provide a "sure word." This topic was used to encourage the listeners to trust the Bible. The sermon clearly fits within the topical sermon category.

Emblems of the Holy Spirit[203]

At the summer conferences in 1898, Moody preached a series of seven sermons under the title *Emblems of the Holy Spirit*. He defined what he meant by the term "emblems" in the opening sermon. He said, "The best definition I can find of 'emblems of the Holy Spirit' is: God's chosen illustrations from natural things to help us to understand the work of the Holy Spirit, whereby, through the physical senses, we may get a clear grasp of important spiritual truth."[204] Each of the seven sermons took one "emblem" Moody identified and attempted to use to help conference attendees understand more about the work of the Spirit. In each sermon, Moody suggested actions of the Spirit that he believed were demonstrated by the "emblem" under consideration. To each of these actions, Moody connected various verses of Scripture.

The book *Northfield Echoes* presents all seven sermons together. The date and approximate time of day is given for each of the seven sermons. Moody preached on each "emblem" separately even though this caused some of the

---
203. Delevan L. Pierson, ed., *Echoes* (1894), 248–270.
204. Ibid., 248.

messages to be relatively short in length. It should be noted that the sermons are presented in the book of proceedings in a logical rather than a chronological order. This chapter will consider the sermons together, as *Northfield Echoes* does. In the sermon description section below, each message will be described individually under the sub-title of the "emblem" considered. However, the entire series will be examined as a unit in the Sermon Evaluation section.

Sermon Description

Fire

Having given a brief explanation introducing the sermon series, Moody began the first sermon. He said, "The first emblem of which I want to speak is fire. There are three things that this holy fire does—it *searches*, it *purifies*, it *illuminates*."[205] Moody then described how fire represents the Holy Spirit. Beginning with the searching activity, Moody told a story about a previous conference in Northfield where he led the gathered crowd to consider Psalm 139:23–24. He said, "This is precisely what God's holy fire does: it searches."[206] Moody then spoke about the purifying work of fire. Using examples such as John the Baptist, the sons of Zebedee, Moses, and Isaiah, Moody emphasized the purifying work of the Spirit's fire. Moody also spoke of the illuminating work of the Holy Spirit's fire. Quoting from Hebrews, Acts, and mentioning Jeremiah, Moody illustrated and applied this principle.

Water

The second sermon focused on water as an emblem of the Spirit's work. Moody began, "Water has three characteristics as an emblem of the Spirit—*cleansing, fertilizing*, and *refreshing*."[207] He read Ezekiel 36:25–28. After a brief comment, Moody read John 4:10, 13–14. Moody then began to speak about the cleansing power of water. After an illustration, he supported his thought with Ephesians 5:26 and Psalm 119:9, 11. Moody said, "God wants purity of heart; and His Spirit will cleanse and purify every one who seeks Him above every-

---

205. Delevan L. Pierson, ed., *Echoes* (1894), 248.
206. Ibid.
207. Ibid., 252.

thing else."[208] Moody then focused on the fertilizing effect of water. Reading John 7:37–39, Moody discussed living in abundance. Speaking of the water Jesus shared with the Samaritan woman, Moody said, "You can have all this water you want. It is abundant, and God wants to give it to us."[209] Moody described the refreshing work of the Spirit. He read Revelation 7:17 along with a few other passages from the last book of the Bible. Moody said, "I believe God will give every one of us salvation, and then He will give us His Spirit to work out this salvation."[210] With this statement, he concluded the second sermon on the *Emblems of the Spirit*.

Rain and Dew

Moody began his third sermon in the series by focusing on rain and dew. He said, "Rain and dew are emblems of the Spirit. They are *refreshing* and they are *abundant*."[211] Moody did not begin with a passage of Scripture in this sermon. Rather, he emphasized his point through several back-to-back illustrations. Moving to his close he read Scripture for the first time in the message. He read Hosea 14:5–8 and listed seven results from the dew of God resting on Israel.

Wind

Moody's fourth sermon on the *Emblems of the Spirit* considered wind as an illustration of the Spirit's work. Moody opened the sermon by saying, "The emblem of wind has four characteristics that I want to call your attention to. It is independent, reviving, sensible in its effects, and powerful."[212] After quoting from John 3:8, Moody said, "You cannot understand the workings of the Spirit."[213] Speaking of the independence of the wind Moody said, "No man can control it; no man can measure it; no man can buy it or sell it."[214] Moody turned his attention to the reviving work of the wind. He read from Ezekiel 37 and Acts

---

208. Delevan L. Pierson, ed., *Echoes* (1894), 254.
209. Ibid., 256.
210. Ibid., 258.
211. Ibid.
212. Ibid., 260.
213. Ibid., 260–261.
214. Ibid., 261.

1. Moody said that wind was sensible in its effect.[215] He did not use Scripture to make this point. Instead, he used an illustration and attempted to apply the concept to his hearers.

The Seal

The fifth sermon Moody preached on the *Emblems of the Spirit* considered the concept of the seal. He made two points about the seal. He indicated that the seal impresses and secures.[216] In this sermon Moody read Ephesians 1:13 and Ephesians 4:29–30. This message lasted only a few minutes. After the sermon, Moody later pointed out nine different things indicated by the seal of the Spirit in the life of the believer. These are included in a footnote to the sermon but were not shared during the message. Therefore, the additional material will not be considered as part of this sermon.

The Dove

Moody considered the dove as an emblem of the Spirit in his sixth sermon on the topic. He said, "The next emblem of which I want to speak is the dove: *gentle, meek[,] innocent*."[217] The only Scripture read or quoted in this message came from Jeremiah 48:28. The message is completely supported by illustrations and the preacher's own thoughts.

Oil

Oil stands as the last *Emblem of the Spirit* Moody chose for this sermon series. Moody said, "Oil, as an emblem of the Spirit, stands for four things—consecration, comfort, healing, life."[218] Moody immediately read 1 John 2:20 and spoke of the "unction" of the Spirit. He then began speaking about the concept of consecration. After describing various people anointed by oil in the Bible, Moody read 1 John 2:27. He also read Leviticus 14:28–31. Moody then focused on the comfort and healing elements of oil in conjunction with the work of the Spirit. He began by reading Isaiah 61:1–3, speaking of healing and joy using il-

---

215. Delevan L. Pierson, ed., *Echoes* (1894), 262–263.
216. Ibid., 264.
217. Ibid., 265.
218. Ibid., 266.

lustrations and a few references from Psalms. Moody never spoke of the fourth characteristic of oil he introduced above. He concluded the sermon by saying, Thank God for this blessed anointing for service."[219] This statement not only concluded the sermon, but also the series as printed in the *Northfield Echoes*.

Sermon Evaluation

As noted above, Moody preached seven sermons during the 1898 summer conferences on the *Emblems of the Spirit*. All of these sermons were shorter in length than most of his messages during this era of his preaching career. He focused each sermon on one "emblem." These sermons will be categorized together. They all follow the same pattern. Moody would announce the emblem and then list two to four actions of the Spirit which he planned to relate to the emblem in the sermon. He spoke on each action, often connecting the action with a passage of Scripture. He would illustrate the emblem and actions, and apply the concepts to his audience. While none of these sermons specifically share the Gospel, there are allusions to the Gospel. While Moody typically held his invitation to respond to the Gospel for his "inquiry meetings," he did on occasion in these sermons call people to respond even during the message.

Expository or Textual?

Not one of the seven sermons in this series could be considered either expositional or textual. Though Moody read, quoted, and often alluded to Scripture, he did not seek to explain the meaning of any of the texts within their context. Rather, he used Scripture to support the various points he chose to make about the work of the Spirit.

Biographical?

While most of the sermons mention at least one Bible character, none of them develop a character. Instead, references to biblical characters simply supported whatever aspect of the Spirit's work Moody was trying to empha-

---

219. Delevan L. Pierson, ed., *Echoes* (1894), 270.

size at the time. Therefore, none of these messages could be biographical sermons.

Topical?

Not only did Moody keep each sermon unified but the entire series of sermons presents a strongly unified testimony to the work of the Holy Spirit. All seven messages are topical sermons. Each sermon fits both the description and the criteria of the topical category. They are all based on the general topic—*Emblems of the Spirit*. Each individual sermon has its own sub-topic like, *fire, water, oil*, and so on. Bible verses abound in most of these sermons. However, the verses are simply used to support Moody's ideas without regard to the context of the verse(s). The sermon divisions do not arise out of a text of Scripture, but from Moody's choice. All seven messages must be classified as topical sermons.

Fellowship with God[220]

Sermon Description

Moody began this sermon by reading Leviticus 36:3–4, 12, 21. He then said, "No man has a real desire to walk with God until he has been redeemed by the blood of Christ, and so has been brought into fellowship with God."[221] Having stated that fellowship with God begins with salvation, Moody turned his focus to Christians who were not enjoying fellowship with God. Moody quoted Psalm 84:11, "No good thing will He withhold from them that walk uprightly."[222] He told the audience that if God was withholding good things from them, they should find out why. The balance of the sermon suggested things that hinder the Christian's fellowship with God.

Moody began by suggesting that one reason some struggle in their walk with God is that they are downplaying the Gospel. He said, "[T]here is a ten-

---

220. Delevan L. Pierson, ed., *Echoes* (1899), 23–27.
221. Ibid., 23.
222. It should be noted that in the sermon Moody said this verse was found in Psalm 8.

dency among some people to get away from the old gospel."[223] He spoke specifically of two concerns. First, Moody pointed out the problems with avoiding repentance. Second, he briefly discussed the move away from the idea of substitutionary atonement. He said, "A man who has broken away from the great fundamental doctrines is like a blasted tree in the desert; there is no life and no power in him."[224] Moody turned his attention to activities that he believed hindered fellowship with God.

Quoting from the first portion of Jeremiah 6:16, Moody encouraged his listeners to return to the old paths. He turned his attention to 2 Corinthians 6:14 and emphasized that Christians must not be yoked with unbelievers but be separate from the world. Moody declared that he believed the Sunday newspapers to be tools that were turning people away from the Lord. He called on his hearers to separate themselves from the things of this life. Moving toward the end of his message Moody said, "Our home is in heaven and we are only here as our Lord's representatives. 'He that saith he abideth in Him, ought himself also so to walk even as He walked.' "[225] Moody concluded this sermon.

Sermon Evaluation

While Moody began the sermon with reading Scripture, he quickly moved to his topic of concern. In the early moments of the message, Moody briefly pointed to the Gospel, but quickly turned his attention to doctrinal and moral concerns. This sermon seems out of character for Moody's preaching during this era. From the summer conference of 1892, there was noticeable growth toward text-driven preaching. However, this sermon content seemed to fit more with Moody's pre-Moorhouse sermon style. It had very little Scripture. The message focused more on trying to be good, than on trusting in the grace, mercy, and love of God.

Expository or Textual?

There is nothing in this sermon to commend it to either the expository or textual sermon category. Moody did not explain the few verses he used. Neither

---

223. Delevan L. Pierson, ed., *Echoes* (1894), 24.
224. Ibid.
225. Ibid., 27.

was he concerned with the context of the verses. The few Scripture verses referenced were used to bolster the preacher's ideas.

Biographical?

No biblical character was in view in this sermon. It does not meet the description or any of the criteria of a biographical sermon. We must look elsewhere to classify this message.

Topical?

The sermon was based on a topic of concern, rather than on a passage of Scripture. The sermon used a few verses from the Bible to offer support for Moody's ideas. The divisions of the sermon came from Moody's choice, rather than from any passage from the Bible. The verses utilized in the sermon were used without regard to context. However, the sermon did indeed have a unifying theme. This message clearly fits into the topical sermon category.

Mary and Martha[226]

Sermon Description

While the present sermon is titled, "Mary and Martha," Moody clearly emphasized the life of Mary in this message. He began by saying, "Mary of Bethany is one of the most famous women in history, and yet there is very little that she ever did that the world would call great. I can find only ten words recorded that fell from her lips."[227] Moody listed several things that might cause someone to note a person, but concluded that none of these were the case for Mary. Despite this Moody pointed out, "All four evangelists have something to say about Mary."[228] Moody read Luke 10:38–42 and noted the difference between Mary and her sister. He briefly spoke of the text, illustrated it, and applied it to his listeners.

---

226. Delevan L. Pierson, ed., *Echoes* (1894), 227–238.
227. Ibid., 228.
228. Ibid.

Moody continued in the sermon with a specific focus on Mary. He spoke of Mary by saying, "I imagine that Mary was in the habit of slipping off to the temple very often to hear Christ." He later said, "I do not think that Mary was a shirk. Jesus never made people lazy, and never will."[229] Moody presented Mary as one who balanced communing with Jesus and working for Jesus. He contrasted her with Martha, suggesting that Martha worried herself with work. Moody attempted to apply Mary's example to his hearers, encouraging them to balance communion, rest, and service.

Moody turned his attention to times of trouble. He said, "Mary's communion with Jesus brought her so near to His heart that when the time of trouble came she knew where to go for comfort."[230] Turning to John 11:32, Moody noted the ten words Scripture records that Mary spoke, "Lord, if Thou hadst been here, my brother had not died."[231] Moody told the story of Lazarus, his sickness, his death, and his raising to life again. He spoke of Mary as communing with Jesus after raising Lazarus.

Moody considered one more event recorded in Scripture. He spoke of the Mary that anointed Jesus' feet with costly oil. Moody believed this to be Mary of Bethany. He described the story with very few Bible quotations. He sought to apply this event to his listeners. He insisted that Mary gave her gift knowing that Jesus was going to die. Moody encouraged his audience to not wait until someone has died to say nice things about them. He encouraged them to give their gifts and say kind words while the person was alive. He quoted from Mark without specific reference, saying, " 'She hath done what she could: she is come aforehand to anoint my body to the burying. She has done what she could!' God does not ask any man or woman to do more than that."[232] After telling a story about a missionary's son, Moody imagined what it was like when Mary arrived in heaven. He then said, "May God help each one of us to do what we can! Life will soon be over; it is short at the longest. Let us rise and follow in the footsteps of Mary of Bethany."[233] The sermon concluded.

---

229. Ibid., 229.
230. Ibid., 231.
231. Ibid.
232. Ibid., 236.
233. Ibid., 238.

Sermon Evaluation

Mary of Bethany was the primary focus of this sermon. Moody began with the story of Mary sitting at Jesus' feet, by reading Luke 10:38–42. He described two other biblical events in which he emphasized Mary's role. Moody also described how he imagined Mary's entrance into heaven upon her death. He sought to demonstrate Mary's life as a balance of communion, service, and sacrifice. Moody applied Mary's actions to his audience along the way. The gospel was not explicitly shared, though briefly alluded to in the story of the anointing of Jesus' feet.

Expository or Textual?

Most of Moody's material for this sermon came directly from the Bible. However, he also shared thoughts he had about Mary that were from his own imagination. The verses Moody read and/or quoted were set in context. However, the sermon was not based on a passage of Scripture. This message does not fit with the expository or textual sermon categories of the sermon rubric.

Biographical?

The sermon fits well into the biographical sermon category. It is based on a specific Bible character. It seeks to demonstrate specific characteristics of that person and to apply the characteristics to the hearers. While Scripture is generally presented in its textual and historical context, the sermon is driven more by the life of Mary than by a specific passage from the Bible. Therefore, this sermon will be classified as a biographical sermon.

Topical?

The unifying theme of this sermon is the life and character of Mary of Bethany. Moody's presentation of her life followed the flow of scripture, rather than a simple topical concern. Therefore, the message cannot be considered a topical sermon.

D.L. MOODY: TURNING POINTS TOWARD TEXT-DRIVEN PREACHING

Revivals[234]

Sermon Description

This is the last Moody sermon from summer conferences recoded in the 1899 edition of the *Northfield Echoes*. It was preached on August 2, 1899. While not every sermon preached at the conferences is recorded in the proceedings, it is possible that this was Moody's last time to address the summer conferences before his death later that year. Moody spoke on a topic he believed to be of great importance. He opened the message by saying, "There is nothing I am more concerned about just now than that God should revive His church in America. I believe it is the only hope for our republic."[235] With this introduction, Moody moved into the body of his sermon.

Moody wanted his hearers to recognize that revival is a biblical concept. He said, "In all ages God has been quickening His people."[236] After mentioning a few different moments in time when God brought revival, Moody read 1 Samuel 7:3–4, 11. Moody spoke of the results of there not being a revival in Elijah's day. Having laid this biblical foundation, Moody turned his attention to various topics related to revival.

Moody spoke of the enemies of God's work. He urged his audience to realize that if God does a work, the devil will try to attack it. Yet, he encouraged them to persevere. Moody pointed out that many denominations began during a revival. He argued the Catholic and Episcopal churches should see themselves as born out of Pentecost.[237] He suggested that Lutherans were born out of the revival of the Reformation.[238] He then pointed to Methodists, Quakers, and the YMCA as all coming forth from revivals of the past.[239] Moody turned his focus to respond to those who object to revivals.

---

234. Delevan L. Pierson, ed., *Echoes* (1894), 375–382.
235. Ibid., 375.
236. Ibid.
237. Ibid., 376.
238. Ibid.
239. Ibid., 376–377.

Moody raised two major objections against holding revival services. The first objection was the lack of perseverance among the converts. Moody countered this by arguing that many regular church members do not persevere as well. He also described several people he knew that had been converted at revivals and did continue in faithful service to the Lord. The second objection Moody raised was that revivals often had too much excitement. He countered this objection by contrasting people being excited about sin, versus being excited about the Lord. Moody then related several stories and illustrations arguing for revival.

Moving toward the close of the sermon, Moody spoke of the need for revival. He talked about the rampant sin, increasing crime, the growing divorce rate, and other indicators that the United States needed revival at the turn of the century. Another indicator of the need for revival was a counterfeit gospel that Moody saw as a growing threat in the final months of his life. He suggested that people were watering down the gospel, but the old gospel story was the need of the hour. Moody said, "What we want is to cry down sin and lift up Jesus Christ, God's remedy for sin, and we will find that the gospel has as much power to save men as ever."[240] Despite the challenges of his day, Moody saw hopeful signs. He mentioned a few specific meetings, and an increase in Bible reading. He said, "Why shouldn't we have in the closing year of this old century, a great shaking up and a mighty wave from heaven? Is there anything to hinder? Are you doing anything to hinder it?"[241] In what is likely his last summer conference sermon, Moody sought to compel his hearers to go forth, pray, and work for a nationwide revival of God's people.

Sermon Evaluation

While Moody attempted to demonstrate that revival is a biblical concept, he quickly turned to practical matters of revival. He read and quoted a few passages in the opening moments of his message. However, most of the sermon presented argumentation, illustration, and application related to the general concept of revival. The gospel was discussed a few times in the sermon, but not explicitly presented.

240. Delevan L. Pierson, ed., *Echoes* (1894), 382.
241. Ibid.

D.L. MOODY: TURNING POINTS TOWARD TEXT-DRIVEN PREACHING

Expository or Textual?

The sermon read, quoted, and alluded to Scripture. Moody began by trying to demonstrate that the concept of revival is a biblical idea. However, no passages were explained. Rather, the focus was on giving a foundation for his message. The sermon used a few verses early on to support Moody's ideas. It clearly does not fit the descriptions or the criteria of either an expository or a textual sermon.

Biographical?

This sermon is not based on a biblical character. It does not fit the description or the criteria of a biographical sermon. The sermon rubric clearly demonstrates this is not a biographical message.

Topical?

The concept of revival serves as the unifying theme of this sermon. Moody did not present unrelated ideas but stayed on track with his theme. The theme was chosen by Moody as was each point of the message. The topic guided the content of the sermon and Bible passages were only used in the beginning to lay a foundation to support Moody's idea. This sermon fits well in the topical sermon category.

Temptation[242]

Sermon Description

Preaching to college students, *Temptation* served as the topic of this sermon. Moody opened by saying, "One of the most real things in this world is temptation, and the quicker we find it out the better."[243] Moody turned to Mark 14:38 emphasizing Jesus' warning to His disciples about temptation, and the weakness of the flesh. The phrase, "The spirit is willing, but the flesh is weak" became a recurring phrase in the message. Moody pointed out, "No man is be-

---

242. Delevan L. Pierson, ed., *Echoes* (1894), 115–121.
243. Ibid., 115.

yond the tempter."[244] He encouraged his audience to recognize that they were in a war. He said, "Christianity is no dress parade."[245] Moody reminded his listeners that everyone faces temptation and no one can claim his or her situation to be unique. He quoted 1 Corinthians 10:13 to make this point.

Moody turned his attention specifically to his audience of students. He warned them of temptations he believed they would face at college. He warned of going to the theatre.[246] Moody also warned his audience of the temptation to attain to power and influence, using Abraham, Lot, and Daniel as examples. Moody then warned his audience of "Sunday Bicycling and Sunday Newspapers."[247] He believed the devil was using these two things to keep students from observing the Sabbath. He said, "Do not turn God's holy day into a holiday."[248] Finally, he warned the students of false teachers. Moving towards his close he said, "The temptations are all around us, but blessed is he that endureth temptation."[249] He concluded the sermon by quoting a portion of James 1:12.

Sermon Evaluation

Moody quickly introduced his topic and then went straight to Scripture. Having read Mark 14:38, he emphasized the fact that the flesh is weak against temptation. Most of the sermon focused on identifying temptations Moody believed college students were facing in his day. While he occasionally quoted a verse of Scripture, the main emphasis was on the temptations themselves. Moody did not present the Gospel in this sermon. His entire focus was on Christians overcoming temptation. His typical emphasis on the Holy Spirit's work in aiding the Christian in overcoming was also missing in this message.

---

244. Delevan L. Pierson, ed., *Echoes* (1894), 115.
245. Ibid., 116.
246. Ibid., 117.
247. Ibid., 119–120.
248. Ibid., 120.
249. Ibid.

D.L. MOODY: TURNING POINTS TOWARD TEXT-DRIVEN PREACHING

Expository or Textual?

The sermon was not based on a text of Scripture. The text read at the beginning simply gave Moody a starting point to talk about temptation and human weakness. The sermon does not fit the descriptions or any of the criteria for either expositional or textual sermons.

Biographical?

While Moody did mention a few biblical characters in the message, they were used as illustrations. The sermon was not based on a person or his characteristics. The message does not fit the descriptions or criteria of the biographical sermon category.

Topical?

The concept of temptation served as the unifying theme of this sermon. Moody stayed on topic and did not speak about random, unrelated, topics. The sermon was based on a concept found in Mark 14:38. However, the opening verse was not explained, and its context was ignored. This verse and all others used in the sermon were chosen to support Moody's ideas concerning temptation. This message should be categorized as a topical sermon.

Summary of Findings from Moody's Northfield Sermons

D. L. Moody held his first Northfield Conference for Christian workers in September 1880. Every summer following this first event, Moody held conferences at Northfield. College students, professors, preachers, and lay leaders would gather for most of the summer. The *Northfield Echoes* was published annually from 1894–1902. This publication contained proceedings from the conferences, as well as other material. Sermons from the conference speakers were taken down verbatim and many of them included in the *Northfield Echoes*. Twenty-eight of the sermons published between the years 1894–1899 came from Moody.

These sermons provide a valuable source of material in understanding Moody's growth toward preaching text-driven sermons. It was at one of these summer conferences in 1892 that Moody confessed his need to change his preaching. As previously noted, Moody did on occasion call for expository preaching in these later years of his life. Examining the twenty-eight available sermons against our sermon rubric has demonstrated that Moody never reached a point where he was preaching only text-driven sermons, but he did appear to move toward a text-driven model.

The first four years of the *Northfield Echoes* demonstrate growth in the biblical content of Moody's sermons. In the 1894 edition of *Northfield Echoes,* we considered four sermons. Two of them were topical sermons, but he also preached two textual sermons. The 1895 edition included five Moody sermons. Three of these were topical, although they did include biblical content. Of the two remaining sermons, one was biographical and one was textual. The biographical sermon followed the narrative and relied heavily on Scriptural content from the book of Daniel. The 1896 edition contained three Moody sermons, all of which were topical but once again included significant Scripture readings, quotations, and allusions. The 1897 edition proved to be instructive. The three Moody sermons included that year all fit within the expository sermon category of the sermon rubric. The pattern observed during these years seems to indicate movement toward text-driven preaching.

Knowing of Moody's confession in 1892 and the growth in biblical content in his sermons at the summer conferences of 1894–1897, one would expect the final two years of Moody's life to demonstrate continued movement. However, the data does not support this conclusion. The 1898 *Northfield Echoes* provide eight sermons for evaluation. Seven of them were preached as a sermon series under the title, *Emblems of the Spirit*. Moody sought to preach a doctrinal series on the work of the Holy Spirit. By its very nature this type of series lends itself to a topical approach. However, it should be noted that all but two of these sermons contained significant Scriptural readings, quotations, and allusions. So, while the sermons were topical in nature, it may not indicate that Moody returned to his old method of preaching. He may have simply felt the need to address this topic as a systematic doctrinal study. The one sermon Moody preached that summer which was not a part of the series was a biographical sermon titled "Abraham's Four Surrenders." This sermon was biographical, but it followed the flow of the Genesis narrative and was heavily based on the biblical text. This may offer support for the idea that Moody continued to be concerned with preaching text-driven messages.

The 1899 edition of the *Northfield Echoes* included four sermons from Moody's last summer at the conferences. Three of the sermons were categorized as topical. The sermon titled "Fellowship with God" was filled with Scripture readings, quotations, and allusions but followed a topical pattern. All three topical sermons appear uncharacteristic of Moody during this later era of his life. They all began with Scripture, but Moody quickly left his text and followed a topical approach. The sermons titled "Fellowship with God" and "Temptation" were reminiscent of Moody's pre-Moorhouse days. Not only was there very little Scripture, the themes of grace, mercy, and the love of God were absent. The sermon titled "Revival," was more of an apologetic for conducting revival services than a regular Moody sermon. He did begin with Scripture, but he quickly moved to more practical and apologetic arguments, attempting to demonstrate the value of revivals.

One sermon from the 1899 *Northfield Echoes* did not fit the topical category. Moody's sermon titled, "Mary and Martha" was a biographical sermon, based primarily on the life of Mary of Bethany. Moody followed the biblical narrative and most of the content came from the Bible. Moody did provide some imagination along the way, but the sermon was guided by the Gospel accounts of Mary's life.

Conclusion

This chapter sought to demonstrate the content of Moody's sermons during the final years of his life. Sermons were sought from the years following Moody's 1892 confession of needing to change his preaching content. From 1894–1902, the Northfield Bookstore published proceedings from the conferences under the title *Northfield Echoes*. Nearly thirty Moody sermons were gathered and evaluated from the years 1894-1899.

This chapter demonstrated that Moody may have never arrived at the place where he was preaching only text-driven sermons. However, he did preach some text-driven sermons during the closing years of his life. These text-driven sermons included three expository sermons, three textual sermons, and three biographical sermons. Now that we have considered sermons from Moody's early years, his middle years, and his later years, Chapter Seven will attempt to summarize the findings from the entire study, consider implications from those findings, and offer modest suggestions for areas of further research.

Chapter Seven

Conclusion

The purpose of this monograph has been to answer the research question: How did Dwight Lyman Moody's preaching change over the course of his preaching tenure? This monograph has demonstrated that the content of Moody's sermons changed over time, moving toward a text-driven model. Chapter One sought to present the scope and direction of the monograph. Chapters Two and Three demonstrated the need to examine Moody's sermons and developed a sermon rubric to guide that examination. Chapters Four through Six analyzed seventy sermons from Moody's early, middle, and late years to demonstrate his growth toward text-driven preaching.

In Chapter Two, the monograph attempted to understand Moody's life as a life of learning and growth, accomplishing what it attempted by examining specific turning points in Moody's life. Among the many turning points, it was noted that two of these moments of growth related to Moody's preaching. The first shift came after being profoundly moved by the preaching of Henry Moorhouse. Moody wanted to learn how to preach like his new friend. Moorhouse told Moody, "You are sailing on the wrong track. You need to learn to study the Bible."[1] The second shift came in 1892 when Henry Weston preached a series of expository sermons at Moody's summer conferences held in Northfield, MA. Moody interrupted Weston's first sermon by saying, "There goes one of my

---
1. Charles R. Erdman, *D. L. Moody, His Message for Today* (Chicago: Fleming H. Revell, 1928), 42.

D.L. MOODY:
TURNING POINTS TOWARD TEXT-DRIVEN PREACHING

sermons."[2] Moody went on to say that he had been misusing the text Weston explained in his exposition. These two turning points in Moody's life led us to examine his sermons. The purpose of the examination was to understand the extent to which Moody moved toward a text-driven model.

Chapter Three sought to establish the criteria by which Moody's sermons would be analyzed. The chapter began by considering what others had said about Moody's preaching. Attention then turned to consider various ways conservative, evangelical homileticians have categorized sermons. From this survey of the literature, four specific categories were developed for consideration. A rubric was then developed that included a description of each sermon type, followed by three criteria that would be used to evaluate Moody's sermons. The analysis would begin on the left side of the rubric with the expository sermon, followed by the textual, biographical, and topical categories. Having established the sermon rubric, we analyzed Moody's sermons in chapters Four through Six.

Each of the sermon analysis chapters began with a description of the search and discovery of sermon material used for the evaluations. We then set the material in context by describing the setting in which the sermons were preached as well as how the sermons were reported. The analysis of each sermon included two sections. First, a description of the sermon was offered. Following the sermon description each message was analyzed, utilizing the sermon rubric established in Chapter Three. Chapters Four through Six concluded by offering a brief summary of the analysis conducted in each respective chapter. Summarizing the findings of each of these chapters demonstrates that Moody indeed grew toward a text-driven model, though he never reached a place of consistently preaching text-driven sermons.

---

2. Paul Moody, *My Father* (Boston: Little Brown and Company, 1936), 185.

Conclusion

Summary of Findings

Chapter Four

Chapter Four considered messages Moody gave at the Chicago noonday prayer meetings. The messages were characteristically short in length, fitting both the setting and Moody's general practice of that era of his ministry. The messages were reported in *The Advance*, a Congregational Church weekly newspaper. The newspaper reported twenty-two messages from Moody between November 1867–December 1869. Nine of the twenty-two messages made no mention of a Bible passage. Seven of the messages mentioned a Bible story or passage but provided no reference. These mentions were only short statements used to bolster Moody's point. Only five of the twenty-two messages are clearly connected in some way to a passage from the Bible. One message may have had a very slight allusion to 1 Kings 18:41–46, but it is not at all certain that Moody intended this allusion. Most likely then, ten of the twenty-two made no mention of Scripture at all.

The five messages where Moody did make a clear connection to a biblical passage further reveal a lack of concern for letting the text guide the message. Four of the messages only used a biblical reference in support of his topic. Only one message may have moved close to the textual sermon category. The message delivered on May 26, 1869 seems to be based on James 1:2. Moody read the text, offered a brief explanation of the verse. He then illustrated the verse briefly and applied it to his listeners. The difficulty of certainty comes from the fact that *The Advance* only reported this sermon as a summary. Therefore, certainty cannot be reached, though it does appear this sermon may possibly have fit into the textual category.

It is important to the thesis of this monograph to recognize the date of this sermon. This message was delivered on May 26, 1869. Moody's encounter with Moorhouse came during the week of February 8, 1868, more than a year prior to the delivery of this message.[3] Only one extant message from Moody's early

---

3. John Pollock, *Moody: The Biography* (Chicago: Moody Press, 1983), 90.

D.L. MOODY: TURNING POINTS TOWARD TEXT-DRIVEN PREACHING

preaching years sought to explain a verse of Scripture. This attempt came after Moorhouse's visit. These facts potentially demonstrate that growth toward a text-driven model began after the Moorhouse encounter. However, the scarcity of data negates forming any kind of firm conclusion.

The analysis of these sermons reveal that Moody's early sermons were lacking in biblical content. This fact clearly fits the testimony of W. H. Daniels.[4] Having confirmed the lack of Bible content, one understands why Moorhouse confronted Moody about his need to learn to study the Bible and include more biblical content in his sermons.[5] To demonstrate the effect Moorhouse had on Moody, we must now consider the findings from the middle years of his preaching ministry.

Chapter Five

Chapter Five examined Moody's sermons from the Boston campaign held from 1876–1877. In the early days of the campaign, Moody experienced much opposition and ridicule from the Boston newspapers. As time progressed the papers moved from ridicule to praise, and began publishing his sermons. Twenty-five sermons are preserved in the book *To All Peoples*. The consistency of his method during this era is strong. Twenty of the twenty-five sermons were examined in detail and provide a clear picture of the biblical content of Moody's preaching during the middle years of his ministry. The sermon rubric guided the evaluation helping to categorize each message as an expository, textual, biographical, or topical sermon.

Five of the Boston messages were classified as biographical sermons with at least some biblical content. The remaining fifteen messages were all topical sermons. Each of the topical messages contained Scriptural content. Indeed, the last Boston sermon was filled with numerous Scripture readings. Moody read a few passages, made a few brief comments, and then read more Scripture. Though the sermon was filled with Bible readings and quotations, the fact remains that Moody's topic drove the sermon content. The extensive Scripture

---

4. W. H. Daniels, *Moody and His Work* (Hartford, CT: American Publishing Company, 1875), 174–175.

5. Erdman, *Moody, His Message for Today*, 40–42.

Conclusion

quotations were used to support his topic. While Moody's sermons were not text-driven at this point, he certainly began to include more Bible readings, quotations, and references in the sermons he preached during his middle years.

Chapter Six

Chapter Six analyzed sermons Moody preached at the Northfield summer conferences between the years 1894–1999. It was during the summer conferences of 1892 that Moody encountered Weston's expositional preaching, and confessed his previous failures in preaching verses out of context. Two years later, in 1894, the Northfield Bookstore began recording the proceedings from the summer conferences and publishing them under the title, *Northfield Echoes*. These books contained information about the conferences, about Moody's schools, and verbatim records of the sermons preached at the meetings.

Twenty-eight of the sermons recorded between the years 1894–1899 were preached by Moody. These sermons provide valuable material for understanding Moody's growth toward preaching text-driven sermons. Evaluating these sermons against the sermon rubric demonstrated that while Moody never reached the place where he consistently preached text-driven sermons, he certainly grew toward a text-driven model. It is clearly documented that Moody called out the importance of text-driven preaching on occasion in the latter years of his life, including during his final preaching campaign.[6] Chapter Six demonstrated that Moody not only called for text-driven preaching but that the record indicates he preached several text-driven messages.

The first four years of the *Northfield Echoes* demonstrate a clear movement toward text-driven preaching. During the years 1894–1897 Moody preached seven messages including one biographical, three textual, and three expositional sermons, all of which must be seen as text-driven. During this same period Moody preached an additional eight sermons all of which failed to reach one of the text-driven categories. However, all eight of them included biblical content by reading, quoting, and alluding to Bible stories, events, and passages. All of Moody's recorded sermons from the summer conferences of these years con-

---

6. See chapter one, footnote 37.

tained significant biblical content. Seven of the sermons from these years fit a text-driven model. Three of the seven are in fact expository sermons. Thus, significant growth towards text-driven preaching has been demonstrated.

Recognizing Moody's growth toward a text-driven model during the 1894–1897 summer conferences, one would expect continued movement in that direction during his final two years of life. However, the data may not support this conclusion. The 1898 *Northfield Echoes* provide eight sermons for evaluation. Seven of them were preached as a sermon series under the title, *Emblems of the Spirit*. By its very nature, this type of doctrinal series lends itself to a topical approach. It should be noted, however, that all but two of these sermons contained significant Scripture readings, quotations, and allusions. Thus, while the sermons were topical in nature, it may not indicate that Moody returned to his old method of preaching. He may have simply wanted to address this topic as a systematic doctrinal study.

The one sermon Moody preached at the 1898 summer conferences which was not a part of the series on the Holy Spirit was a biographical sermon. The message was titled "Abraham's Four Surrenders." This biographical sermon followed the flow of the Genesis narrative closely. In addition, it was heavily based on the biblical text. This fact offers support for the idea that Moody continued to be concerned with a preaching text-driven approach to his preaching.

The 1899 edition of the *Northfield Echoes*, included four sermons from Moody's last summer at the conferences. Three of the sermons were categorized as topical. All three topical sermons appear uncharacteristic of Moody during this time of his life. They all began with Scripture, but Moody quickly left his text and followed a topical approach. The sermons titled, "Fellowship with God" and "Temptation" were reminiscent of Moody's pre-Moorhouse days. Not only was there very little Scripture; the grace, mercy, and love of God were absent. The sermon titled "Revival" was more of an apologetic for conducting revival services than a regular Moody sermon. He did begin with Scripture, but he quickly moved to more practical and apologetic arguments, attempting to demonstrate the value of conducting revival services.

One sermon from the 1899 Northfield Echoes did not fit the topical category. Moody's sermon titled, "Mary and Martha" was a biographical sermon, based primarily on the life of Mary. Moody followed the biblical narrative closely. Most of the sermon content came from the Bible. Moody did provide some imagination along the way, but the sermon was clearly guided by the Gospel accounts of Mary's life. This means that one can clearly verify that Moody preached at least nine text-driven sermons in his final years of preaching at the Northfield summer conferences. Moody's lifelong practice of preaching the same sermon repeatedly may indicate that he preached these text-driven sermons multiple times in the final years of his life.

Through the analysis of Moody's early, middle, and late sermons this monograph has demonstrated growth toward a text-driven model of preaching. Moody's early sermons were often missing any Scripture reference at all. When they did contain a Bible verse or a biblical allusion, it was not explained, but simply used to support a point Moody desired to make in his message. After Henry Moorhouse told Moody that he needed to learn to study the Bible and make it the source of his preaching, the biblical content of Moody's sermons grew. Despite the growth in the use of the Bible in his sermons during the middle years, the messages continued to be guided more by topics than by texts. In the final six years of Moody's life, he called for text-driven preaching. There is no question that he indeed preached at least nine text-driven messages himself, three of which were expository sermons. Considering the sermons that did not reach one of the text-driven categories, one must recognize that most of them contained biblical content. This content came from reading, quoting, and alluding to Bible passages. Moody never reached a point where he consistently preached text-driven sermons, but he certainly demonstrated growth toward a text-driven model.

Implications of Findings

This study has demonstrated that Moody grew toward a text-driven model of preaching. The implications of this monograph reach into at least four areas of theological study. Those who engage in Moody studies will also discover at least four relevant concerns highlighted in this monograph including: his high view of Scripture, his teachable spirit, his humility, and his movement toward

D.L. MOODY: TURNING POINTS TOWARD TEXT-DRIVEN PREACHING

text-driven preaching. Additional implications from this study will impact the disciplines of Church History, Applied Theology, and Homiletics. Below, we will offer a few implications for each of these theological disciplines.

Moody Studies

At least four implications from the findings of this monograph impact Moody studies. First, one should recognize that Moody maintained a high view of Scripture throughout his preaching career. In Chapter Five the monograph noted the controversy that arose in the 1930's between Moody's son Paul, the Northfield conferences, and the Moody Bible Institute in Chicago.[7] In Paul's defense, Elmer Powell wrote an unpublished manuscript focused on re-evaluating Dwight L. Moody. In the book Powell sought to defend Paul.

He also argued that after Moody's encounter with Moorhouse, he abandoned such doctrines as the verbal, plenary, inspiration of Scripture and the substitutionary atonement. However, both middle and late sermons examined in this work demonstrate that Moody continued to hold his high view of inspiration throughout his entire ministry.

A second implication of this monograph on the area of Moody studies can be found in Moody's teachable spirit. Chapter Two of the monograph presented a biographical sketch that demonstrated Moody was a person who was constantly learning. Due to growing up in poverty and his dad's sudden death, Moody was not afforded much of a formal education. However, his teachable spirit propelled him to personal study, which allowed him to grow in business, in Sunday School work, in leadership, in organization, in Bible study, in theology, and in preaching. Moody scholars have noted these and many other areas of evangelical Christianity that Moody influenced. Yet, one cannot fully understand Moody's work in any realm without interacting with his teachable spirit.

A third implication on Moody studies relates to Moody's humility. It was R. A. Torrey who first argued that Moody's humble attitude proved to be one of the reasons for his effectiveness.[8] This monograph confirmed Torrey's argu-

---

7. See chapter five, footnote 118.

8. R. A. Torrey, *Why God Used D. L. Moody* (Murfreesboro, TN: Sword of the Lord Publishers, no date), 16–19. This publication is a pamphlet containing a speech by

ment, particularly when it came to Moody's preaching. When Moorhouse confronted Moody, he responded in humility.[9] When Moody heard Weston preach an expository message, he humbly confessed his own preaching failures in front of the entire summer conference crowd.[10] At the time of the Moorhouse encounter, Moody was growing in popularity, yet he humbly listened and learned from someone he considered too young to preach. When Weston came to Northfield, Moody was recognized throughout the western world as a key figure in Christianity. Yet, his popularity did not lead to pride. He humbly acknowledged his failures in front of a large crowd. Humility played a significant role in Moody's life and ministry.

A fourth implication this monograph offers to Moody studies is found directly in the growth of his preaching. Moody's high view of Scripture, his teachable spirit, and his humility compelled him to adjust his preaching methods at least twice. As noted in Chapter One, most Moody biographers say very little about Moody's preaching. It is often assumed that his preaching had very little Bible content.[11] However, this monograph has demonstrated that while this assumption may have been the case in Moody's early sermons, he grew in the biblical content of his sermons. After the Moorhouse encounter it was noted that Moody included more Scripture readings, quotations, and biblical allusions in his messages. After his encounter with Weston in 1892, Moody not only called for text-driven preaching, he preached some text-driven sermons himself.

Church History

Church historians have long noted the importance of D. L. Moody in understanding western Christianity. As early as 1900, William Moody noted the testimony of various scholars concerning the impact of his dad's life. William reports that "Dr. Cuyler of Brooklyn" says, "Of one thing I feel sure, and that is, if another book of the Acts of Christ's faithful Apostles were to be written,

---

R. A. Torrey given on the occasion of Moody's birthday anniversary, February 5, 1937.

9. Lyle W. Dorsett, *A Passion for Souls: The Life of D. L. Moody* (Chicago: Moody Press, 1997), 140.

10. Paul Moody, *Father*, 185.

11. See chapter one, footnotes 3 and 4.

probably the largest space in the record of the nineteenth century would be given to the soul-saving work of Charles H. Spurgeon and Dwight L. Moody."[12] Despite this recognition of Moody's importance to western church history, chapter one noted that most church historians and biographers say very little about his preaching. When church historians do write about his preaching, they tend to emphasis his conservative nature, his masterful use of illustrations, and his passion.

This monograph expands the knowledge base of Moody in a way that will help church historians better understand his preaching. The study has demonstrated a distinct difference in the Bible usage from his earliest years to his later years. In the early days, Moody's preaching attracted interest, but contained very little biblical content. After the Moorhouse encounter, he began to include more Scripture in his messages. As Moody included Scripture readings, quotations, and allusions, his effectiveness grew. After the Weston encounter of 1892, Moody occasionally called for text-driven preaching. This monograph demonstrated that he grew in that direction in his own preaching to the point of preaching several text-driven sermons in the final years of his life. When one considers the fact that Moody often preached three times a day Monday–Friday and up to five times a day on Sundays for almost thirty-five years, the importance of understanding Moody's growth toward a text-driven model becomes clear. Historians seeking to understand Moody's role in late nineteenth century Christianity, will thus benefit from this study.

Applied Theology

The discipline of Applied Theology seeks to relate one's theological belief to one's practice. Moody demonstrated his high view of Scripture in several of the sermons examined in this monograph. In addition, this monograph has noted the testimony of several Moody contemporaries. The testimony is nearly unanimous that Moody believed in the verbal, plenary inspiration of Scripture. One of Moody's contemporaries, Elias Nason wrote of Moody's view of the Bible. Speaking of Moody, Nason wrote, "He received its teachings, not as question-

---

12 William R. Moody, *The Life of Dwight L. Moody* (New York: Fleming H. Revell Company, 1900), 258.

able or mythical, but as real, practical, and obligatory. It was the voice of God speaking into the innermost chambers of his soul. It meant precisely what it said; and this he felt must be translated by him, just as far as he had power, into immediate practice."[13] Moody's doctrine influenced his practice. His view of Scripture demanded that the more he learned about hermeneutics, the more Bible content showed up in his sermons.

When Moorhouse challenged Moody telling him he really did not know the Bible, Moody immediately changed his study habits. He asked Moorhouse to teach him how to study the Bible and more Scripture began showing up in Moody's sermons.[14] Moody's view of Scripture could not allow for any other response to Moorhouse's challenge. The same could be said of Moody's encounter with Weston in 1892. When Moody was confronted with the understanding that he had been preaching a passage incorrectly, he immediately acknowledged this fact and indicated he must change his preaching.[15] The testimony of others concerning Moody's view of Scripture and noting the two major shifts he made in his preaching are helpful. Yet, this monograph has demonstrated that Moody's change was not only something he claimed verbally, but his preaching itself further demonstrates his growing concern to include biblical content in his sermons. After Moorhouse, we have seen that almost every sermon contained Scripture. After Weston, we saw Moody preach at least some text-driven sermons. Therefore, his theology of Scripture did indeed impact his practice over time.

Homiletics

The implications for the discipline of Applied Theology above, certainly impact the area of homiletics. Beyond this general implication, homileticians may discover a few more helpful suggestions, specific to their discipline. C. I. Scofield

---

13. Elias Nason, *The American Evangelists: Dwight Lyman Moody and Ira David Sankey, with an Account of their Work in England and America* (Brasted, Kent, UK: B. B. Russell, 1877), 56.

14. Pollock, *Moody,* 91.

15. Paul Moody, *Father,* 185.

noted the struggle homileticians face in looking at Moody's sermons, but he also indicated the importance of considering Moody's preaching. Scofield says,

> As a preacher D. L. Moody was much criticized from the standpoint of academic homiletics. Nor would any think of defending his preaching method on that ground. But the fact that for thirty-five continuous years, in centers of culture and active practical thought in the English-speaking world, this self-taught preacher drew the greatest audiences which have faced any modern speaker on any theme—this fact, one would say, should suggest to teachers of homiletics that possibly they might learn something from him.[16]

The findings of this monograph demonstrate at least three lessons homileticians can learn from Moody.

First, Moody's humility serves as an example for preachers. Despite his growing popularity, he humbly listened to Moorhouse's instruction. Even late in life, Moody's humility proves instructive. In front of many who viewed him as the chief preacher of the day, Moody was willing to humble himself and admit his own failures in preaching. This humility serves as an example for homileticians of any age.

Second, Moody's teachable spirit serves as an example to preachers in all ages. While closely related to humility, a teachable spirit demonstrates a willingness to grow. Moody not only listened humbly to the instructions of Moorhouse and Weston, he wanted to learn from them. He then practiced what he was taught. This teachable spirit allowed him to grow toward a text-driven model. Throughout his life, Moody exhibited a desire to learn and grow in his preaching. His desire to grow sets a strong example for everyone engaged in homiletics.

---

16. Harry J. Albus, *A Treasury of Dwight L. Moody* (Grand Rapids: William B. Eerdmans, 1949), 39. While this sentiment is attributed to Scofield in several places, including in William R. Moody's biography of his father, this researcher has yet to find the original source that definitively demonstrates whether this was written or spoken by Scofield.

Third, Moody's growth toward a text-driven model is also instructive. In the early days, Moody simply wanted to motivate lost people to be saved and saved people to get busy working for God. His messages were often short and filled with illustrations and passion. As he learned from Moorhouse, he began spending hours studying the Bible. His son Paul writes, "Father rose early and retreated to his upstairs study, where he worked."[17] In the study, he applied Moorhouse's topical study method and his sermons demonstrated more biblical content in the middle years. Late in life, he continued to grow in his preaching. Hearing Weston, Moody began calling for text-driven preaching. Writing the year after Moody's death, Wilbur Chapman quotes Moody as saying, "It is not the man now that makes a fine oration in the pulpit so much as it is a man that expounds the Word of God that we need."[18] This monograph has demonstrated that Moody grew from using very little Scripture in his sermons, to using more biblical content, and he ultimately moved toward a text-driven model in his preaching. Moody provides an example of concern for being as true to the Word of God as possible, utilizing the tools and skills one possesses.

Need for Further Research

Inevitably, in a study like this, one discovers research trails that appear interesting and that may yield fruit in academic studies. This proved to be true in the present monograph. The present researcher would like to offer a few modest suggestions for further research. In Chapter Five, footnote eighteen speaks of Moody's approach to sharing the gospel and offering an invitation. There is wide discussion today about Christ-centered and gospel-centered preaching. Knowing Moody as an evangelist one would expect that his sermons were filled with the gospel. However, the majority of the sermons examined did not actually proclaim a clear gospel message. Moody would make general appeals in his sermons, but he often saved his gospel presentation and his invitation for his "inquiry meeting." Moody's "inquiry meeting" technique may provide

---

17. Paul Moody, *Father*, 38.

18. J. Wilbur Chapman, *The Life and Work of Dwight Lyman Moody* (New York: International Publishing Co, 1900), 1.

fruitful research with implications for the current discussion on gospel-centered preaching. Another avenue of research concerning Moody's invitation method could be to study the relationship between his method and the methods of Charles Finney, Billy Sunday, and Billy Graham.

A second area of concern for further research can be found in the relationship between Moody and his children. While it appears that William and Emma continued in the basic theology of their dad, Paul moved in a different direction. This researcher noted that all three children exhibited a deep respect for their dad. However, they saw him differently. This reality bears further research.

A third area of possible Moody research could focus on Moody and his schools. Following Moody's death, the three Massachusetts schools followed a theological path differing from that of the Moody Bible Institute in Chicago. As a side interest, prior to writing this monograph, the present writer spent a little time researching this area, but more work is needed. It would prove a fruitful study to thoroughly examine the differences in the schools and to consider the causes of their differing theological paths.

A fourth area of possible Moody research would be to examine Moody's associations. Moody considered many preachers and Christian leaders friends. Often these leaders represented a diverse background. This group included men who founded the fundamentalist movement, those who were far more liberal in their understanding of the Bible, and numerous leaders from diverse denominational and methodological backgrounds. Furthermore, Moody worked with many different colleges and schools that exhibited a wide diversity of thought. This area of research could provide a fruitful study. One could seek to understand where Moody drew his boundaries and how he maintained his own theology while working among such diversity.

Conclusion

On December 26, 1899, people from all over the United States gathered in Northfield, MA for Moody's memorial service. C. I. Scofield spoke at the Congregational church, noting, "No one will ever question that we are laying today in the kindly bosom of earth the mortal body of a great man. Whether we measure greatness by quality of character or by qualities of intellect or by things accomplished, Dwight L. Moody must be accounted great."[19] Moody's legacy lives on. Among his many accomplishments memorialized in biographies, history books, and academic works, this study has offered an understanding of his growth toward text-driven preaching.

---

19. William R. Moody, *Life of D. L. Moody*, 561.

Bibliography

Abbott, Lyman. *The Power of Moody's Ministry, North American Review, CLXX* (February, 1900), 263–271.

———. *Silhouettes of My Contemporaries.* New York: Garden City, 1921.

———. "Snapshots of My Contemporaries. Dwight Lyman Moody—Evangelist," *Outlook*, 127 (June 22, 1921): 324.

Abbot, Waldo. *Handbook of Broadcasting.* New York: McGraw-Hill Book Co., 1941.

Abell, Aaron Ignatius. *The Urban Impact on American Protestantism, 1865–1900.* Cambridge: Harvard University Press, 1943.

Adams, Henry W. "First Days in Chicago." *Moody Monthly* Vol. 15 (February, 1915): 232–252.

Adam, Peter. *Speaking God's Words: A Practical Theology of Preaching.* The 1993 Moore College Lectures. Vancouver: Regent, 1996.

Akin, Daniel L., Bill Curtis, and Stephen Rummage. *Engaging Exposition.* Nashville: B&H, 2011.

Akin, Daniel L., David Allen, and Ned L. Mathews Ed. *Text-Driven Preaching: God's Word at the Heart of Every Sermon.* Nashville: B&H, 2010.

D.L. MOODY:
TURNING POINTS TOWARD TEXT-DRIVEN PREACHING

Albus, Harry J. *A Treasury of Dwight L. Moody.* Grand Rapids: William B. Eerdmans Publishing Co., 1949.

Alderman, Max W. *The Strategy of Preaching: A Handy Guide for Sermon Preparation.* Ontario: Bethel, 1988.

Allan, Arthur. *The Act of Preaching.* New York: Philosophical Library, 1943.

Allen, Alexander. *The Life and Letters of Phillips Brooks.* Vol. II. London, 1900.

Andreas, A. T. *History of Chicago from the Earliest Period to the Present Time.* Chicago: A. T. Andreas Co., 1885.

Ann Arbor. *Register*, January, 1890.

Armitage, Frank Guy. "The Influence of Dwight L. Moody on the City of New York and Vice Versa." *Christian Work 98* (February, 1915): 174.

Atkins, Gaius Glenn. *Religion in Our Times.* New York: Round Table Press, 1932.

Atlanta. Journal. November 16, 1895.

Bailey, Faith Coxe. *D. L. Moody: The Greatest Evangelist of the Nineteenth Century.* Chicago: Moody Publishers, 1937

Baird, A. Craig. *Argumentation, Discussion and Debate.* New York: McGraw Hill, 1950.

Baker, Daniel. *Addresses to Young Men.* New York: Revell, 1874.

Baker, Ray Stannard. *The Spiritual Unrest.* New York: Stokes, 1910.

Baltimore. *Sun,* October, 1878–June, 1879.

Baumann, J. Daniel. *An Introduction to Contemporary Preaching.* Grand Rapids: Baker, 1972.

Beadenkopf, Thomas M. and Raymond W. Stricklen. *Moody in Baltimore.* Baltimore: Sun, 1879.

Bibliography

Beardsley, Frank Grenville. *A History of American Revivals*. New York: American Tract Society, 1904.

Begg, Alistair. *Preaching for God's Glory*. Wheaton: Crossway, 2010.

Behrends, A. J. F. *The Philosophy of Preaching*. New York: Harper & Brothers, 1935.

Bell, James S. Jr. *The D. L. Moody Collection: the Highlights of His Writings, Sermons, Anecdotes, and Life Story*. Edited by James S. Bell Jr. Chicago: Moody, 1977.

Belmonte, Kevin. *D. L. Moody: A Life*. Chicago: Moody Press, 2014.

Benson, Clarence H. "How Moody Reached the Masses." *Moody Monthly* 38 (February, 1938): 318.

Berkley, James D. "Preaching to Convince." *Word/Christianity Today* (1986).

Blackwood, Andrew W. *Preaching From the Bible*. New York: Abington, 1941.

———. *Expository Preaching for Today: Case Studies of Bible Passages*. New York: Abington, 1953.

Bordon, Richard C. *Public Speaking as Listeners Like It!* New York: Charles Scribner's Sons, 1890.

Boston Globe. January 9, 1900.

———. November 27, 1875.

Boston Herald. September 14, 1874.

———. September 14, 1877.

———. December 27, 1899.

Boston News. January 20, 1897.

Boreham, F. W. "So This Is Moody." *Watchman-Examiner* (March 8, 1945): 230–231.

D.L. MOODY:
TURNING POINTS TOWARD TEXT-DRIVEN PREACHING

Boyd, Robert. *The Lives and Labors of Moody and Sankey.* Toronto: A. H. Honey, 1877.

Bradford, Gamaliel. *D. L. Moody: A Worker in Souls.* New York: Doran, 1927.

Brigance, William N. *A History and Criticism of American Public Address.* New York: McGraw-Hill Book Co., 1943.

———. *Speech Composition.* New York: Appleton-Century-Crofts, 1937.

———. *Speech Communication.* New York: Appleton-Century-Crofts, 1947.

Briggs, Charles Augustus. *The Authority of the Holy Scripture.* Second Edition. New York: Charles Scribner's Sons, 1891.

Broadus, John A. *On the Preparation and Delivery of Sermons.* Fourth Edition, Revised by Stanfield, Vernon L. San Francisco: Harper, 1979.

Brown, Charles Reynolds. *The Art of Preaching.* New York: Macmillan Co., 1922.

Brown, Marianna C. *Sunday School Movements in America.* New York: Revell, 1901.

Brown, William Adams. *A Teacher and His Times.* New York: Charles Scribner's Sons, 1936.

Bryant, Donald C. and Karl R. Wallace. *Fundamentals of Public Speaking.* New York: Appleton-Century-Crofts, 1946.

Burke, Kenneth. *Rhetoric of Motives.* New York: Prentice-Hall, 1950.

Campbell, George. *Philosophy of Rhetoric.* New York: Harper & Brothers, Publishers, 1855.

Candler, Warren A. *The Great Revivals and the Great Republic.* Nashville: Broadman, 1904.

Carter, Burnham. *So Much to Learn.* Northfield, MA: Northfield Mount Hermon School, 1976.

Chapell, Bryan. *Christ-Centered Preaching: Redeeming the Expository Sermon.* Second Edition. Grand Rapids: Baker Academic, 2005.

———. *Christ-Centered Sermons: Models of Redemptive Preaching.* Second Edition. Grand Rapids: Baker Academic, 2013.

Chapman, J. Wilbur. *The Life and Work of Dwight L. Moody.* New York: Noble, 1900.

———. *The Personal Touch.* New York: Fleming H. Revell, (no date).

———. *The Problem of the Work.* New York: George H. Doran Co., 1911.

Chartier, Myron R. "The Social Views of Dwight L. Moody And Their Relationship To The Workingman Of 1860–1900." MA thesis University of Colorado, 1969.

Chicago Advance. 1867–1869.

Chicago Daily News. December 23, 1899.

Chicago Daily Tribune. October 1, 1876.

Chicago Evening Post. April 5, 1897.

———. December 22, 1899.

Chicago Times-Herald. December 23, 1899.

"Christian Century." February 3, 1937," *The Evangelical Record* (October 1883).

Cooper, Lane. *The Rhetoric of Aristotle.* New York: D. Appleton, 1932.

Cram, D. W. "Moody at the Fair." *Moody Monthly* 49 (December, 1949): 244–246, 279.

Crocker, Lionel. *Public Speaking for College Students.* Second Edition. New York: American Book Co., 1950.

Cuckson, John. *Religious Excitement: a sermon on the Moody and Sankey Revival.* London: 1875.

D.L. MOODY:
TURNING POINTS TOWARD TEXT-DRIVEN PREACHING

Curtis, Richard K. *They Called Him Mister Moody*. Grand Rapids: Eerdmans, 1962.

———. *The Pulpit Speaking of Dwight L. Moody Part 1*. Michigan: University Microfilms, 1954.

———. *The Pulpit Speaking of Dwight L. Moody Part 2*. Michigan: University Microfilms, 1954.

Cuyler, Theodore L. *Recollections of a Long Life*. New York: 1902.

Dale, R. W. *Nine Lectures on Preaching*. New York: Hodder and Stoughton, (no date).

Daniels, W. H. *D. L. Moody and His Work*. London: Hodder and Stoughton, 1875.

———. *Moody, His Words, Works, and Workers*. New York: Nelson and Phillips, 1877.

Davenport, Frederick Morgan. *Primitive Traits in Religious Revivals*. New York: Macmillan Co., 1905.

Davis, George T. B. *Dwight L. Moody; the Man and His Mission*. Chicago: Monarch, 1900.

Davidson, Randall Thomas, and William Benham. *Life of Archibald Campbell Tait, Archbishop of Canterbury*. Vol. II. London: Macmillan Co., 1891.

Day, Richard Ellsworth. *Bush Aglow: The Life Story of Dwight Lyman Moody Commoner of Northfield*. Philadelphia: Judson, 1936.

"Death and Burial of Moody." *Missionary Review of the World 28* (February, 1900): 137.

"D. L. Moody." *The Outlook* (December 30, 1899).

"D. L. Moody and Britain." *Christian* (December 16, 1949).

"D. L. Moody Centenary." *Publisher's Weekly* (January 30, 1937): 530.

Dwight Lyman Moody, the Great Evangelist of the Nineteenth Century. Chicago: Donohue, Henneberry & Co., 1935.

Bibliography

Dombrowski, James. *The Early Days of Christian Socialism in America.* New York: Columbia University Press, 1936.

Dorsett, Lyle W. *A Passion for Souls: The Life of D. L. Moody.* Chicago: Moody, 1997.

Douglass, H. Paul. *100 City Churches: Phases of Adaption to Urban Environment.* New York: George H. Doran Co., 1926.

Driver, G. H. "Moody: The Man of the Nineteenth Century." *Bibliotheca Sacra* XCIV (July, 1937): 343.

Drummond, Henry. "Mr. Moody: Some Impressions and Facts." *McClure's Magazine* 4 (December, 1894-January, 1895): 54, 188.

Drummond, Henry and George A. Smith. *Dwight L. Moody: Impressions and Facts (1900).* New York: McClure Phillips, (Kissinger Reprint – year unknown).

Drummond, Lewis A. *Spurgeon: Prince of Preachers.* Grand Rapids: Kregel Publications, 1992.

Duduit, Michael, ed. *Handbook of Contemporary Preaching: A Wealth of Counsel for Creative and Effective Proclamation.* Nashville: Broadman Press, 1992.

Dunn, James B. *Moody's Talks on Temperance.* New York: National Temperance Society & Publishing House, 1877.

Erdman, Charles R. *D. L. Moody: His Message for Today.* New York: Revell, 1928.

———. *Great Pulpit Masters.* Chicago: 1905.

Ewbank, Henry. "Objective Studies in Speech Style with Special Reference to One Hundred English Sermons." PhD. Thesis, University of Wisconsin, 1913.

Farwell, John V. *Early Recollections of Dwight L. Moody.* Chicago: Bible Institute Colportage Association, (no date).

———. *Early Work in the Chicago Association.* New York: Revell, 1890.

Fauntleroy, T. S. "Original Testimony in Moodyana." Exhibit of the Moody Bible Institute.

Fifty Evenings at the Great Revival Meetings Conducted by Moody and Sankey. Philadelphia: Yost, 1876.

Fifty-Five Years: The Young Men's Christian Association of Chicago, 1858–1913. Chicago, 1913.

Findlay Jr., James F. *Dwight L. Moody: American Evangelist, 1837–1899*. Chicago: The University of Chicago Press, 1969.

Finney, Charles G. *Lectures on Revivals of Religion*. Oberlin, OH: E. J. Goodrich, 1868.

———. *Memoirs of Charles G. Finney*. New York: A. S. Barnes & Co., 1876.

Fisk, Franklin W. *Manual of Preaching: Lectures on Homiletics*. New York: Ac. C. Armstrong & Son, 1904.

Fitt, Arthur Percy. *All about Northfield: A Brief History and Guide*. Northfield, MA: Northfield Press, 1910.

———. *Moody Still Lives*. New York: Revell, 1936.

Flesch, Robert. *The Art of Plain Talk*. New York: Harper & Brothers, 1946.

Garvie, Alfred Ernest. *A Guide to Preaching*. London: Hodder and Stoughton, 1911.

George, Timothy ED. *Mr. Moody and the Evangelical Tradition*. Edited by Timothy George. Reprinted. London: T & T Clark, 2005.

Gericke, Paul. *Crucial Experiences in the Life of D. L. Moody*. Covington, LA: Insight Press, 1978.

Gibbons, Herbert Adams. *John Wanamaker*. Vol. I. New York, 1926.

Gilbert, Simeon. *The Lesson System: The Story of Its Origin and Inauguration*. New York, 1879.

Godkin, E. L. "D. L. Moody in Brooklyn." *Nation* 21 (no date): 321.

Goldsworthy, Graeme. *Preaching the Whole Bible as Christian Scripture: An Application of Biblical Theology to Expository Preaching*. Grand Rapids: Eerdmans, 2000.

Goodspeed, E. J. *A Full History of the Wonderful Career of Moody and Sankey in Great Britain and America*. New York: Henry S. Goodspeed & Co., 1876.

———. *History of the Great Fires in Chicago and the West*. New York: H. S. Goodspeed & Co., 1871.

Goss, Charles F. *Echoes from the Pulpit and Platform*. Hartford: A. D. Worthington & Co., 1900.

Gray, Giles W. and Waldo W. Braden. *Public Speaking: Principles and Practice*. New York: Harper, 1951.

Gray, Giles W. and Clause M. Wise. *The Bases of Speech*. Revised Edition. New York: Harper, 1946.

"Great American Evangelist." *Literary Digest 123* (January, 1937): 34.

Gundry, Stanley N. *Love Them In: The Proclamation Theology of D. L. Moody*. Chicago: Moody, 1976.

———. *Love Them In: The Life and Theology of D. L. Moody*. Chicago: Moody, 1976.

Hall, Thomas Cuming. *The Religious Background of American Culture*. Boston: Little, Brown & Co., 1930.
Hamlin, T. S. "Northfield—Without Mr. Moody." *Independent 52* (August 23, 1900): 2021.

Harper's Weekly. (March, 1876).

Hastings, James. *Encyclopedia of Religion and Ethics*. Edinburgh: T&T Clark, 1908–1926.

D.L. MOODY:
TURNING POINTS TOWARD TEXT-DRIVEN PREACHING

Heindel, Richard Heathcote. *The American Impact on Great Britain; A Study of the United States in World History Between 1898 and 1914.* Philadelphia: University of Pennsylvania Press, 1940.

Hervey, G. W. *Manual of Revivals, Practical Hints and Suggestions.* New York: Funk & Wagnalls, 1884.

Holding the Fort: Comprising Sermons and Addresses at the Great Revival Meeting Conducted by Moody and Sankey. Philadelphia: Quaker City, 1877.

Holt, Arthur E. *Christian Roots of Democracy in America.* New York: Friendship Press, 1940.

Hopkins, Charles Howard. *The Rise of the Social Gospel in American Protestantism, 1865–1915.* New Haven: Yale University Press, 1940.

Howard, Grant J. *Creativity in Preaching: The Craft of Preaching.* Special Edition for Western Conservative Baptist Theological Seminary. Grand Rapids: Zondervan, 1987.

Huber, Robert B. "Dwight L. Moody: Salesman of Salvation—A Case Study on Audience Psychology." Unpublished PhD. Diss., University of Wisconsin, 1942.

"In Moody's Steps." *Newsweek* (May 24, 1948).

Johnson, Dennis E. *Him We Proclaim: Preaching Christ From All The Scriptures.* Edited by John J. Hughes. New Jersey: P&R, 2007.

Johnston, Graham. *Preaching to a Postmodern World.* Grand Rapids, Michigan: Baker Books, 2001.

Johnston, R. D. *The Man Who Moved Multitudes and the Secrets to His Success.* Pickering & Ingalls, 1937.

Kemper, Deane A. *Effective Preaching: A Manual for Students and Pastors.* Philadelphia: Westminster Press, 1985.

Kirk, Edward Norris. *Lectures on Revivals.* Edited By David O. Mears. Boston: Congregational Publishing Society, 1875.

Bibliography

Koessler, John. *The Moody Handbook of Preaching*. Chicago: Moody Publishers, 2008.

Koller, Charles W. *Expository Preaching Without Notes Plus Sermons Preached Without Notes*. Grand Rapids: Baker, 1962.

Kooienga, William H. *Elements of Style for Preaching: The Craft of Preaching*. Grand Rapids: Zondervan, 1989.

Larson, David L. *The Anatomy of Preaching: Identifying the Issues in Preaching Today*. Grand Rapids: Baker, 1989.

Lawson, Stephen J. *The Kind of Preaching God Blesses*. Eugene: Harvest, 2013.

Lewis, Lloyd, and Henry J. Smith. *Chicago: The History of Its Reputation*. New York: Harcourt, Brace & Co., 1929.

Lischer, Richard. *A Theology of Preaching: The Dynamics of the Gospel*. Eugene: Revised Edition. WIPF and Stock, 2001.

Lloyd-Jones, Martyn D. *Preaching & Preachers 40th Anniversary Edition*. Edited by Kevin DeYoung. Grand Rapids: Zondervan, 2011.

Loud, Grover C. *Evangelical America*. New York: Longmans, Green & Co., 1928.

Lovett, Robert M. "Moody and Sankey." *New Republic* 53 (December 14, 1927): 94.

Lynch, Frederick, "D. L. Moody as an Inspirer of Youth." *The Christian Work* 102 (1917): 235–236.

MacArthur, John Jr. and The Master's Seminary Faculty. *Rediscovering Expository Preaching: Balancing the Science and Art of Biblical Exposition*. Edited by Richard L. Mayhue and Associate Editor, Robert L. Thomas. Dallas: Word, 1992.

Marvin, A. P. "Three Eras of Revivals in the United States." *Bibliotheca Sacra and Biblical Repository 26*.

Masters, Edgar Lee. *The Tale of Chicago*. New York: G. P. Putnam's Sons, 1933.

D.L. MOODY:
TURNING POINTS TOWARD TEXT-DRIVEN PREACHING

Matheson, Rev. W. S. "Reminiscences of Moody and Sankey." *Presbyterian Messenger.* (July, 1937).

Matthews, Brander. *Notes on Speech-Making.* London: Longmans, Green, & Co., 1942.

Mathews, Shailer. *The Church and the Changing Order.* New York: Macmillan Co., 1907.

———. *The Social Gospel.* Philadelphia: Griffith and Rowland Press, 1910.

Mawhinney, Bruce. *Preaching with Freshness.* Grand Rapids: Kregel, 1997.

McClure, J. B. *Anecdotes and Illustrations of D. L. Moody.* Boston: Rhodes & McClure, 1881.

———. *D. L. Moody's Child Stories.* Chicago: Rhodes & McClure, 1877.

McConnell, Francis J. "The Old-Time Religion." *Christian Century* 66 (March 2, 1949): 267.

McDowell, John. "D. L. Moody: Ambassador of Christ." *Missionary Review of the World* 59 (May, 1936): 235.

McDill, Wayne V. *The Moment of Truth: A Guide to Effective Sermon Delivery.* Nashville: Broadman, 1999.

———. *12 Essential Skills for Great Preaching.* Nashville: B&H Academics, 2006.

McFarland, John T and Benjamin S. Winchester. *The Encyclopedia of Sunday Schools and Religious Education II.* New York: Revell, 1915 (s.v. "*Moody, Dwight Lyman*" contributed by P. E. Zartman).

McKinnon, Mrs. Jesse M. *Recollections of D. L. Moody and His Work in Britain, 1874–1892.* Printed for Private Circulation, 1905.

McNeill, Rev. John. "D. L. Moody's Influence on Scotland." *Record of Christian Work* 43 (February, 1924): 104–107.

Bibliography

Merida, Tony. *Faithful Preaching: Declaring Scripture with Responsibility, Passion, and Authenticity*. Nashville: B&H, 2009.

"Messages from D. L. Moody." *Missionary Review* (December, 1937).

Meyer, Jason C. *Preaching: A Biblical Theology*. Wheaton: Crossway, 2013.

"Messages from D. L. Moody." *Missionary Review* (December, 1937).

Michigan Chronical. January, 1890.

"Mighty Work." *TIME* (August 11, 1936): 30.

Miller, Calvin. *Marketplace Preaching*. Grand Rapids: Baker Books, 1995.

———. *Spirit, Word, and Story A Philosophy of Preaching*. Dallas: Word, 1989.

Mohler, Albert R. Jr. *He Is Not Silent: Preaching in a Postmodern World*. Chicago: Moody, 2008.

Monroe, Alan H. *Principles and Types of Speech*. Third Edition. New York: Scott Foresman, 1949.

"Moody and Modernism." (Editorial). *Literary Digest 88* (January 16, 1926): 32.

Moody, D. L. *A College of Colleges*. New York: Revell, 1889.

———. "Mr. Moody's Institute." *Christian Union 41* (April 3, 1890): 484.

———. *Notes from My Bible: From Genesis to Revelation*. Reprinted. Grand Rapids: Baker, 1975.

———. *One Thousand and One Thoughts from My Library*. New York: Revell, 1898.

———. *Pleasure and Profit in Bible Study*. New York: Revell, 1899.

———. *Secret Power or the Secret of Success in Christian Life and Work*. Chicago: Moody, (no date).

Moody, Paul. *My Father*. Boston: Little and Brown Co., 1938.

Moody, Paul Dwight and Arthur P. Fitt. *Shorter Life of D. L. Moody, 2 Vols*. Chicago: Bible Institute Colportage Association, 1900.

Moody, William R. *D. L. Moody*. New York: Macmillan, 1930.

———. *The Life of Dwight L. Moody*. The Official Authorized Edition. New York: Revell, 1900.

———. *The Story of Northfield Schools*. Northfield: Northfield School, 1930.

———. Review of *Saturday Review of Literature D. L. Moody*, by William R. Moody. September 9, 1930.

Moody Bible Institute of Chicago. *The Best of D. L. Moody*. Edited by Wilbur M. Smith. Chicago: Moody, 1971.

Moody, D. L. *Glad Tidings, Comprising Sermons and Prayer-Meeting Talks*. New York: E. B. Treat, 1876.

———. *Great Joy, Comprising Sermons and Prayer-Meeting Talks*. New York: E. B. Treat, 1877.

———. *New Sermons, Addresses, and Prayers*. Chicago: J. W. Goodspeed. Publisher, 1877.

———. *To All People*. New York: E. B. Treat. 1877.

Moody's Latest Sermons. Chicago: The Bible Institute Colportage Association, 1900.

"Moody – The Consecrated Commoner." *Christian Century* 54 (February 3, 1937): 136.

Morgan, G. Campbell. "Dwight L. Moody." *The Presbyterian* (June 24, 1937): 6–7.

Morgan, George E. *A Veteran in Revival, R. C. Morgan, His Life and Time*. London, 1909.

Morris, George Perry. "Character Sketch." *Review of Reviews* 21 (February, 1900): 163.

———. "Dwight L. Moody: A Character Sketch." *Review of Reviews* 21, 163–176.

Morse, Richard C. "D. L. Moody Among Students." *North American Student* (October, 1913): 65.

———. *History of the North American Young Men's Christian Associations*. New York: Association Press, 1913.

———. *My Life with Young Men*. New York: Association Press, 1900.

Moses and Kirkland. *History of Chicago*. Vol. II. Chicago, 1895.

Moss, Lemuel. *Annals of the United States Christian Commission*. Philadelphia, 1868.

Nason, Elias. *The American Evangelists: Dwight Lyman Moody and Ira David Sankey, with an Account of their Work in England and America*. Brasted, Kent, UK: B. B. Russell, 1877.

Nation. (1875–1876, 1893, 1899–1900).

Neal, Joel K. "The Concept Of The Mystery Of God In The Theology Of D. L. Moody." MA thesis. Trinity Evangelical Divinity School, 1988.

Nevins, Allen. *The Emergence of Modern America, 1865–1878. Vol. III of History of American Life*. Edited by Arthur M. Schlesinger and Dixon Ryan Fox. 12 vols. New York: Macmillan Co., 1927–1944.

New Sermons, Addresses and Prayers. St. Louis: Mound City, 1877.

New York *Daily Tribune*, January-March, 1876.

Newell, William W. *Revivals: How and When?* New York: A. C. Armstrong & Son, 1882.

Newton, Derek Dr. *And The Word Became ... A Sermon: A Guide to Biblical Expository Preaching*. IV20 ITW, Scotland and TN15 8BG, England: Mentor/OMF, 2003.

Noble, William P. F. *A Century of Gospel Work*. Philadelphia, 1876.

D.L. MOODY:
TURNING POINTS TOWARD TEXT-DRIVEN PREACHING

———. *God's Doings in Our Vineyard, Being a History of the Growth of Evangelical Religion in the United States.* Philadelphia: H. C. Watts Co., 1882.

Noll, Mark A. *A History of Christianity in the United States and Canada.* Grand Rapids: William B. Eerdmans, 1992.

Northrop, Henry D. *Life and Labors of Dwight L. Moody, the Great Evangelist.* Cincinnati: Ferguson, 1899.

Olford, David L. *A Passion for Preaching: Reflections on the Art of Preaching, Essays in Honor of Stephen F. Olford.* Compiled by David L. Olford. Nashville: Thomas, 1989.

Olford, Stephen F. with David L. Olford. *Anointed Expository Preaching.* Nashville: B & H Academic, 1998.

Pasquarello, Michael III. *Christian Preaching: A Trinitarian Theology of Proclamation.* Grand Rapids: Baker Academic, 2006.

Patrick, Johnstone G. "D. L. Moody Jubilee." *Christian* (December 28, 1949).

Pell, Edward L. *Dwight L. Moody. His Life, His Life, His Work, His Words.* Richmond: Johnson, 1900.

Perry, Lloyd M. *Biblical Preaching for Today's World.* Revised. Chicago: Moody, 1973.

Philadelphia *Bulletin.* November 22, 1875.

———. November 24, 1875.

———. November 25, 1875.

———. November 27, 1875.

———. December 2, 1875.

———. December 11, 1875.

———. February 1, 1876.

Bibliography

Philadelphia *Inquirer*. November 20, 1875.

———. November 22, 1875.

———. November 30, 1875.

———. December 1, 1875.

———. December 13, 1875.

———. December 20, 1875.

———. December 27, 1875.

———. January 10, 1876.

———. January 14, 1876.

———. January 17, 1876.

———. January 20, 1876.

———. February 1, 1876.

Philadelphia *National Baptist*. November 25, 1875.

———. November 29, 1875.

———. December 2, 1875.

———. December 8, 1875.

———. December 9, 1875.

———. December 16, 1875.

———. December 30, 1875.

———. January 13, 1876.

———. January 20, 1876.

———. January 27, 1876.

———. February 1, 1876.

———. February 3, 1876.

———. February 10, 1876.

———. February 17, 1876.

———. March 2, 1876.

Philadelphia Press. November 20, 1875.

Philadelphia *Times*. November 22, 1875.

Philadelphia *Public Ledger*. November 22, 1875.

———. November 23, 1875.

———. November, 1875–February, 1876.

Pierson, Arthur T. "D. L. Moody and His Life Lessons." *Record of Christian Work* (1905).

———. *Evangelistic Work in Principle and Practice.* New York: Baker & Taylor Co., 1887.

———. "Moody as an Educator." *Missionary Review of the World 23* (March, 1900): 168.

———. "Moody the Evangelist." *Missionary Review of the World 23* (February, 1900): 80.

———. "Tribute to the Work of D. L. Moody." *Missionary Review of the World 23* (April, 1910): 276.

Pierson, Delevan L., ed. *Northfield Echoes*. East Northfield, MA: The Northfield Bookstore, 1894 (Issues referenced by year of publication after *Echoes*).

———. *Northfield Echoes*. The Northfield Bookstore: (1895).

———. *Northfield Echoes*. The Northfield Bookstore: (1896).

———. *Northfield Echoes*. The Northfield Bookstore: (1897).

———. *Northfield Echoes*. The Northfield Bookstore: (1898).

———. *Northfield Echoes*. The Northfield Bookstore: (1899).

———. *The Northfield Yearbook*. New York: Revell, 1896.

Piper, John. *The Supremacy of God in Preaching*. Grand Rapids: Baker, 1990.

Pittenger, Norman W. *Preaching the Gospel*. Wilton: Morehouse-Barlow, 1984.

Pollock, John, *Moody*. Chicago: Moody, 1963.

———. "Moody at Cambridge." *Moody Monthly* 53 (February, 1953): 498–499, 546.

Popham, J.K. *Moody and Sankey's Errors Versus the Scriptures of Truth*. Richmond: Johnson, 1900.

Powell, Elmer William. "Moody of Northfield. A Revaluation in the Light of Research." Not published.

Powell, Emma Moody. *Heavenly Destiny. The Life Story of Mrs. D. L. Moody.* Chicago: Moody, 1943.

Proceedings of the Twenty-Third Convention of the Young Men's Christian Convention of the United States and British Provinces. New York: International Committee, 1879.

Providence *Daily Journal*. January 3, 1894.

Providence *News*. January 24, 1894.

D.L. MOODY:
TURNING POINTS TOWARD TEXT-DRIVEN PREACHING

Quiggle, Gregg William. "An Analysis of Dwight Moody's Urban Social Vision." PhD Diss., Open University, England, 2009.

Quimby, Rollin Walker. "Dwight L. Moody: An Examination of the Historical Conditions and Rhetorical Factors which Contributed to His Effectiveness as a Speaker." PhD Diss., University of Michigan, Ann Arbor, MI: University Press, 1951.

Rankin, Henry M. *Handbook of the Northfield Seminary and the Mount Hermon School.* Mr. Hermon, 1889.

Rawson, J. A. Jr. "Dwight L. Moody as a Social Service Leader." *Survey* 33 (November 21, 1914): 196.

Recent Ridiculous Religious (?) Revivals Rationally Reprobated. By a Protestant Dissenter. London: 1875.

Regarding Revivals. Including article by D. L. Moody, "How to Awaken Fresh Interest in Our Churches." (Compiler, publisher, and date unknown, due to condition of book.

"Revell: Seventy-Five Years of Religious Book Publishing." *Publisher's Weekly* 146 (December 9, 1944): 2232–2236.

Review of Reviews (Editorial), September, 1895, 264.

Robinson, Haddon W. *Biblical Preaching: The Development and Delivery of Expository Messages*. Grand Rapids: Baker, 1980.

Rosell, Garth, ed. *Commending the Faith: The Preaching of D. L. Moody*. Peabody, MA: Hendrickson Publishers, 1999.

Ryder, W. H. *An Open Letter from Chicago to D. L. Moody, Esq., the Evangelist*. Boston: Universalist, 1877.

Sanford, William P. and Willard H. Yeager. *Principles of Effective Speaking*. New York: Nelson, 1928.

Bibliography

Sankey, Ira D. *My Life and the Story of the Gospel Hymns.* Philadelphia: P. W. Ziegler Co., 1906.

Sarett, Lew, and William T. Foster. *Basic Principles of Speech.* Revised Edition. Boston: Houghton Mifflin Co., 1946.

Schaff-Herzog Encyclopedia of Religious Knowledge. New York: Funk and Wagnalls Co., 1908–1912.

Schlesinger, Arthur Meier. *A Critical Period in American Religion, 1875–1900.* Massachusetts Historical Society LXIV, 1932

———. *The Rise of the City, 1878–1898.* Vol. 10 of *History of American Life.* Edited by Arthur M. Schlesinger and Dixon Ryan Fox. 12 vols. New York: Macmillan Co., 1927–1944.

Shedd, Clarence P. *Two Centuries of Christian Movement.* New York: Association Press, 1934.

Shindler, Robert. *From the Usher's Desk to the Tabernacle Pulpit--The Life and Labors of Charles Haddon Spurgeon.* New York: A. C. Armstrong, 1892 (Available at URL: https://archive.org/details/fromushersdeskto00shin/page/n13/mode/2up)

Schultze, Quentin J. *Communicating for Life.* Grand Rapids: Baker Academic, 2000.

Schwalm, Vernon Franklin. "Moody and the Revival of the Seventies." Master's Thesis, University of Chicago, 1916.

Sedgwick, A. G. "D. L. Moody in New York." *Nation.* Vol. 22 (no date): 156.

Shaddix, Jim. *The Passion Driven Sermon: Changing the Way Pastors Preach and Congregations Listen.* Nashville: B&H, 2003.

Shanks, T. J. *D. L. Moody at Home.* Chicago: Fleming H. Revell, 1886.

Sharp, John K. *Our Preaching.* Philadelphia: Dolphin Press, 1936.

Shillito, Edward. "Moody in England." *Christian Century* 54 (February 17, 1937): 217.

D.L. MOODY:
TURNING POINTS TOWARD TEXT-DRIVEN PREACHING

———. "What Moody Stood For." *Spectator* 157 (February 5, 1937): 215.

Simons, M. Laird, ed. *Holding the Fort*. Cincinnati: United States Book and Bible Company, 1879.

Smith, George A. "Dwight L. Moody: Personal Tribute." *Outlook* 64 (January 20, 1900): 163.

Smith, H. Shelton, Robert T. Handy, and Lefferts A. Loetscher. L.A. Loetscher, "Variant Orthodoxies" in *American Christianity: An Historical Interpretation with Representative Documents*. New York: Charles Scribner's Sons, 1963, 2 vols.

Smith, Robert Jr. *Doctrine That Dances: Bringing Doctrinal Preaching and Teaching to Life*. Nashville: B&H, 2008.

Smith, Wilbur M. *An Annotated Bibliography of D. L. Moody*. Chicago: Moody Press, 1948.

———. "Bush Aglow, Revelation." book review of R. E. Day, October, 1936, 439–440.

———. "In the Study." *Moody Monthly* 52 (May, 1952): 623.

———. "Estimate." *Outlook* 63 (December 30, 1899): 1003.

Soper, Paul D. *Basic Public Speaking*. New York: Oxford University Press, 1949.

Speer, Robert E. "D. L. Moody." Address delivered to the Northfield Schools on Founder's Day. Northfield, MA. 5 February 1931.

———. "Mr. Moody and Young People." *Northfield Echoes* 7, (1900): 37–42.

Spencer, M. A. "Glasgow Remembers D. L. Moody." *Christian Century* 54 (March 24, 1937): 395.

Spurgeon, Charles Haddon. *Sermons* 4. London, (no date).

———. *Spurgeon's Lectures to My Students*. Edited by David R. Shepherd. Nashville:

———. *The Preacher's Portrait: Some New Testament Word Studies.* Grand Rapids: Eerdmans, 1961.

Stackhouse, Harry J. *Chicago and Its Baptists.* Chicago: University of Chicago, 1933.

Stalker, James. *The Preacher and His Models.* New York: Anson D. F. Randolph, 1876.

———. "Mr. D. L. Moody." *Living Age 224* (May 17 1900): 690.

Stetzle, Charles. "Meeting Some of America's Big Men." *Outlook 143* (June 23, 1926): 283.

Stevenson, George A. *Pastor C. H. Spurgeon, His Life and Work to His Fiftieth Birthday.* London: Passmore & Alabaster, 1885.

Storrs, Richard S. *Preaching Without Notes.* New York: George H. Doran, Co., 1875.

Stott, John R. W. *The Art of Preaching in the Twentieth Century: Between Two Worlds.* Grand Rapids: Eerdmans, 1982.

———. *The Preacher's Portrait: Some New Testament Word Studies.* Grand Rapids: Eerdmans, 1961.

Stowe, Harriet Beecher. *Men of Our Times.* New York: J. D. Denison, 1868.

Strong, Josiah. *Our Country.* Revised. New York: Baker & Taylor Co. for American Home Missionary Society, 1891.

Stuart, C. M. "Inner Life of D. L. Moody." *Chautauquan 30* (February, 1900): 527.

Sunderland, J. T. "Orthodoxy, the Worst Enemy of Christianity." A sermon preached in the Unitarian Church at Northfield, MA. 19 September 1875.

———. "The Good and the Evil in the Teachings of Mr. Moody." Sermon preached in the Unitarian Church, Ann Arbor, MI, 19 January 1890. The Courier Press, 1890.

Sweet, William Warren. *The American Churches, an Interpretation.* New York: Abington-Cokesbury Press, 1947.

———. *Revivalism in America, its Origin, Growth, and Decline.* New York: Charles Scribner's Sons, 1944.

———. *The Story of Religions in America.* Second Edition. New York: Harper, 1950.

———. *Makers of Christianity.* New York: Scribner, 1937.

Sweeting, George and Donald Sweeting. *Lessons from the Life of Moody.* Chicago: Moody, 1989.

Taylor, William. *The Ministry of the Word.* New York: Anson D. F. Randolph, 1876.

Thompson, James W. *Preaching Like Paul: Homiletical Wisdom for Today.* Louisville: Knox, 2001.

Thonssen, Lester. *Selected Readings in Rhetoric and Public Speaking.* New York: McGraw-Hill, 1948.

Thonssen, Lester, and Craig Baird. *Speech Criticism: The Development of Standards for Rhetorical Appraisal.* New York: Ronald Press Co., 1948.

Thonssen, Lester, Howard Gilkinson and Ordway Teal. *Basic Training in Speech.* Boston: D. C. Heath, 1947.

Torrey, R.A. *Why God Used D. L. Moody.* Chicago: Revell, 1923.

Townsend, L. T. *The Supernatural Factor in Religious Revivals.* Boston: Lee and Shepard, 1877.

Vaughan, Rev. John. *Life Stories of Remarkable Preachers.* 1892.

Vines, Jerry and Jim Shaddix. *Power in The Pulpit: How to Prepare and Deliver Expository Sermons.* Chicago: Moody Press, 1999.

———————————————. *Power in the Pulpit: How to Prepare and Deliver Expository Sermons* (rev. ed.). Chicago: Moody Press, 2017.

Wagenknecht, Edward. *Ambassadors for Christ: Seven American Preachers.* New York: Oxford, 1972.

Bibliography

Walsh, John T. *Moody Versus Christ and His Apostles.* St. Louis: Burns, 1880.

Weighed and Wanting. New York: Revell, 1898.

Wells, C. Richard and A. Boyd Luter. *Inspired Preaching: A Survey of Preaching Found in the New Testament.* Nashville: Broadman, 2002.

Whipple, Leon. Review of *Portrait D. L. Moody, A Worker in Souls,* by G. Bradford. March 1928.

Wilkerson, William C. "Dwight L. Moody as a Man of Affairs." *Homiletic Review 36* (August, 1898): 110.

Wilkinson, William C. *Modern Masters of Pulpit Discourse.* New York: Funk & Wagnalls, 1905.

Williams, Alfred. *Weak Points in Mr. Moody's Preaching.* Kingston on Thames, 1875.

Wilson, P. Whitwell. *The Meaning of Moody.* New York: Revell, 1938.

Winans, James. *Speech Making.* New York: Appleton-Century-Crofts, 1938.

Woolbert, Charles. *Fundamentals of Speech.* Revised Edition. New York: Harper, 1927.

Yeager, W. Hayes. *Effective Speaking for Every Occasion.* Prentice-Hall, Inc., 1941.

Young, B. "Moody Recalled at Mass Meeting." *Christian Century 54* (November 10, 1937): 1403.

Zumbrunnen, Albert Clay. *The Community Church: A Probable Approach to and Bases for Denominational Unity.* Chicago: University of Chicago Press, 1922.

www.ingramcontent.com/pod-product-compliance
Lightning Source LLC
Chambersburg PA
CBHW070722240426
43673CB00003B/107